Garfield by the pound

BY: JIM DAVIS

BALLANTINE BOOKS · NEW YORK

Copyright © 1992 United Feature Syndicate, Inc.
GARFIELD Comic Strips: © 1990, 1991 United Feature
Syndicate, Inc.

All rights reserved under International and Pan-American
Copyright Conventions. Published in the United States
by Ballantine Books, a division of Random House, Inc.,
New York, and simultaneously in Canada by Random
House of Canada Limited, Toronto.

Library of Congress Catalog Card Number: 91-92161

ISBN: 0-345-37579-3

Manufactured in the United States of America

First Edition: March 1991

10 9 8 7 6 5 4 3 2 1

KNOW YOUR CAT MOODS

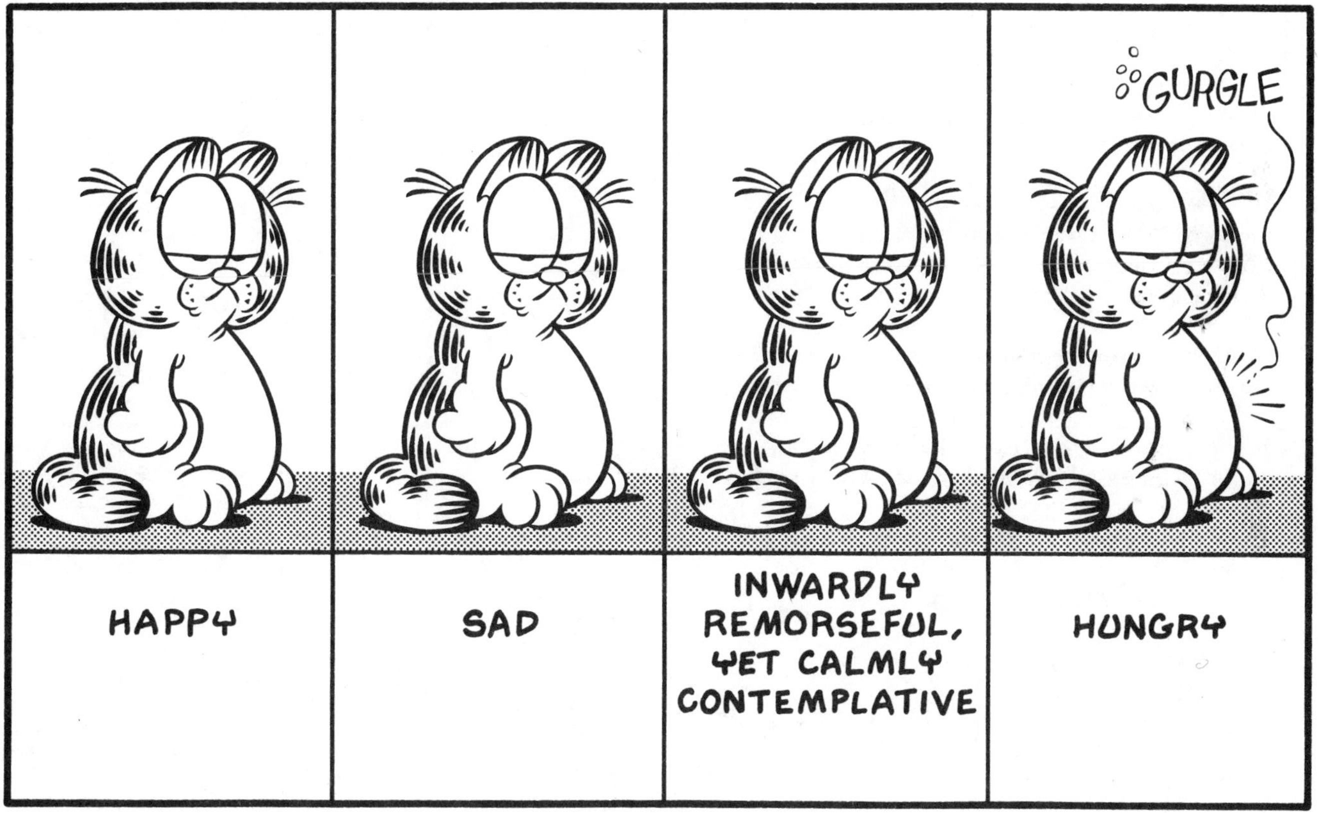
GURGLE
HAPPY
SAD
INWARDLY REMORSEFUL, YET CALMLY CONTEMPLATIVE
HUNGRY

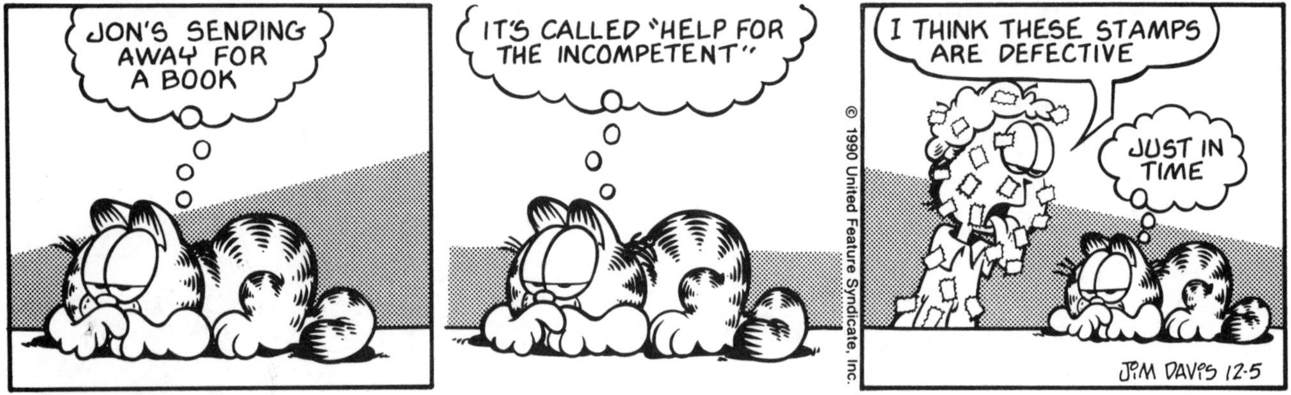
JON'S SENDING AWAY FOR A BOOK
IT'S CALLED "HELP FOR THE INCOMPETENT"
I THINK THESE STAMPS ARE DEFECTIVE
JUST IN TIME
© 1990 United Feature Syndicate, Inc.
JIM DAVIS 12-5

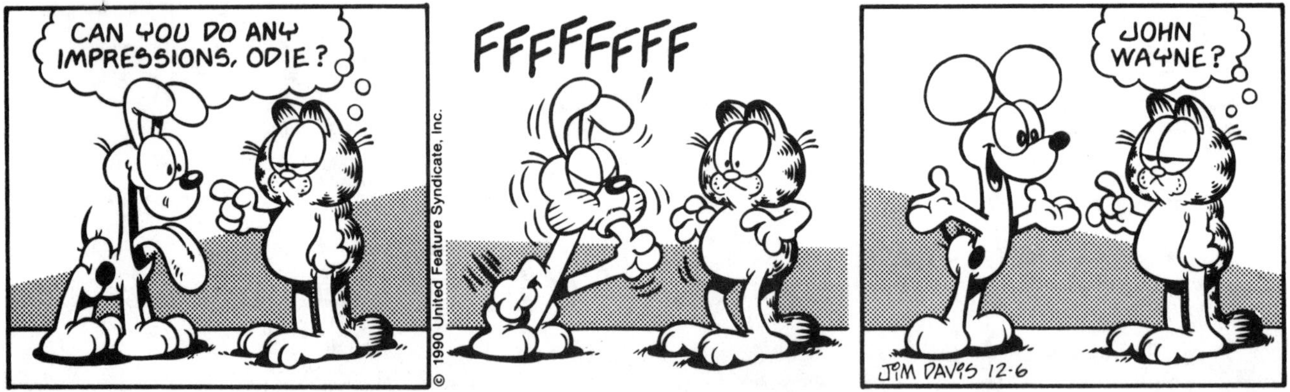
CAN YOU DO ANY IMPRESSIONS, ODIE?
FFFFFFFF
JOHN WAYNE?
© 1990 United Feature Syndicate, Inc.
JIM DAVIS 12-6

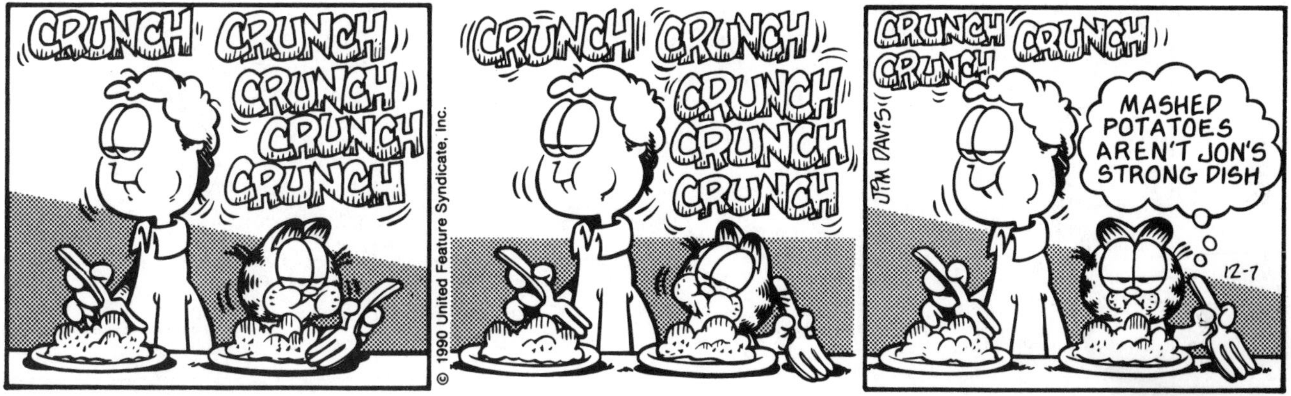
CRUNCH CRUNCH CRUNCH CRUNCH CRUNCH
© 1990 United Feature Syndicate, Inc.
CRUNCH CRUNCH CRUNCH CRUNCH CRUNCH
CRUNCH CRUNCH CRUNCH
JIM DAVIS
MASHED POTATOES AREN'T JON'S STRONG DISH
12-7

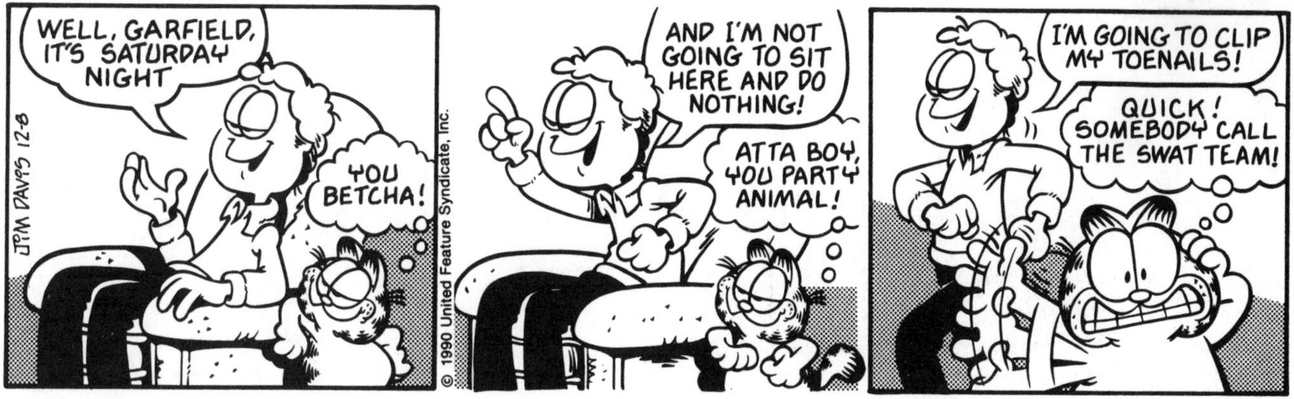
WELL, GARFIELD, IT'S SATURDAY NIGHT
JIM DAVIS 12-8
YOU BETCHA!
© 1990 United Feature Syndicate, Inc.
AND I'M NOT GOING TO SIT HERE AND DO NOTHING!
ATTA BOY, YOU PARTY ANIMAL!
I'M GOING TO CLIP MY TOENAILS!
QUICK! SOMEBODY CALL THE SWAT TEAM!

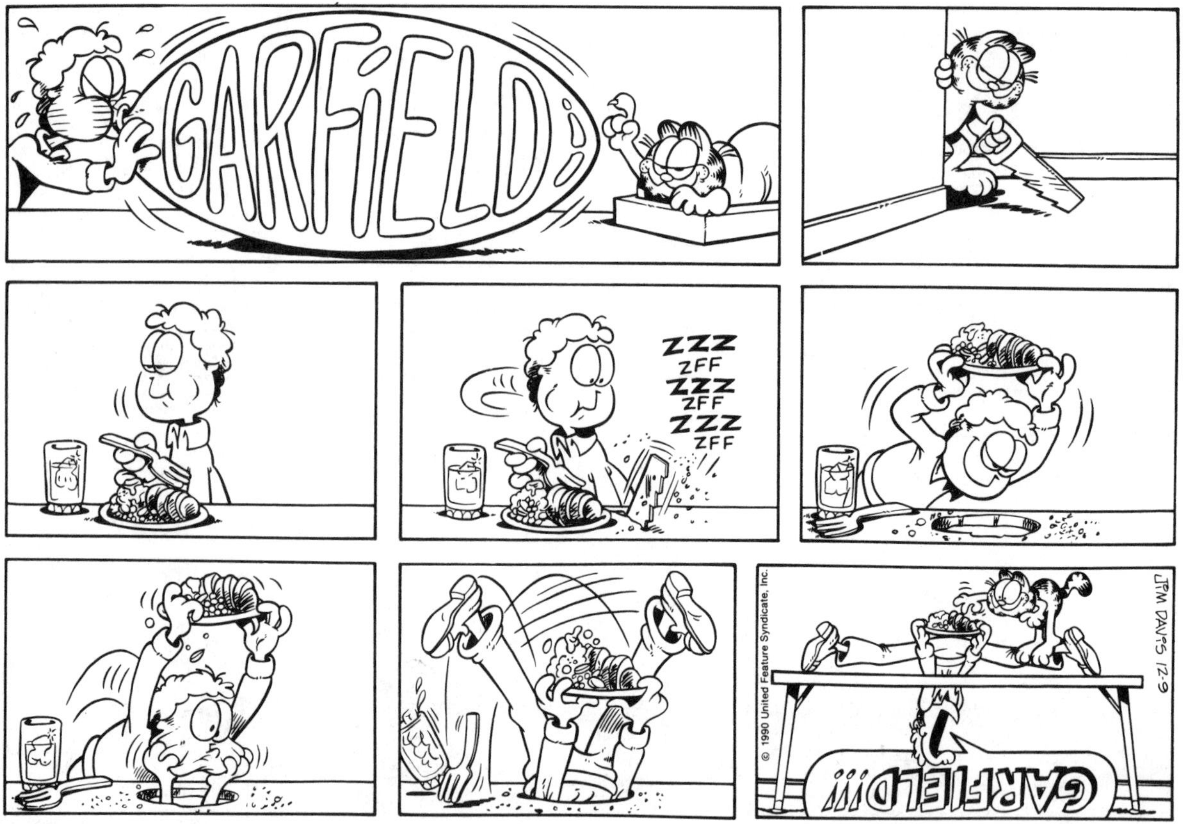
GARFIELD
ZZZ
ZFF
ZZZ
ZFF
ZZZ
ZFF
JIM DAVIS 12-9
© 1990 United Feature Syndicate, Inc.
GARFIELD!!!

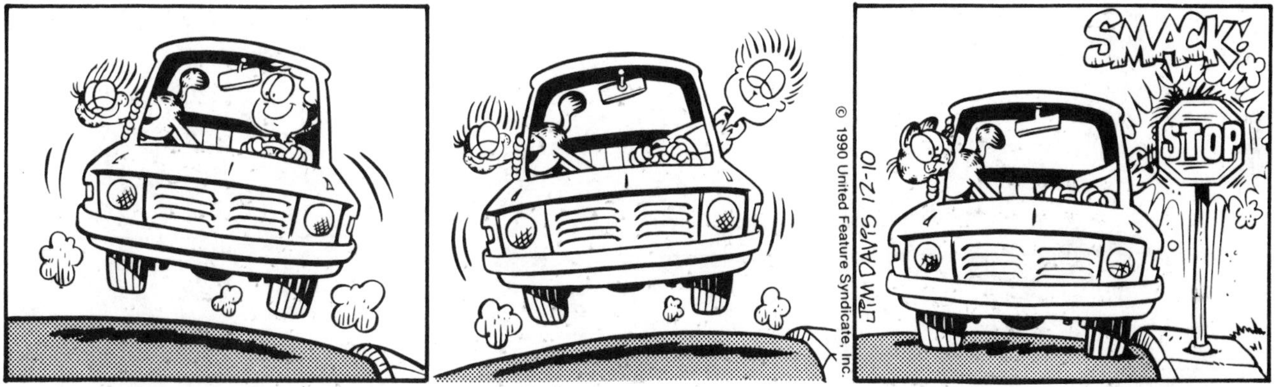
SMACK!
STOP
JIM DAVIS 12-10

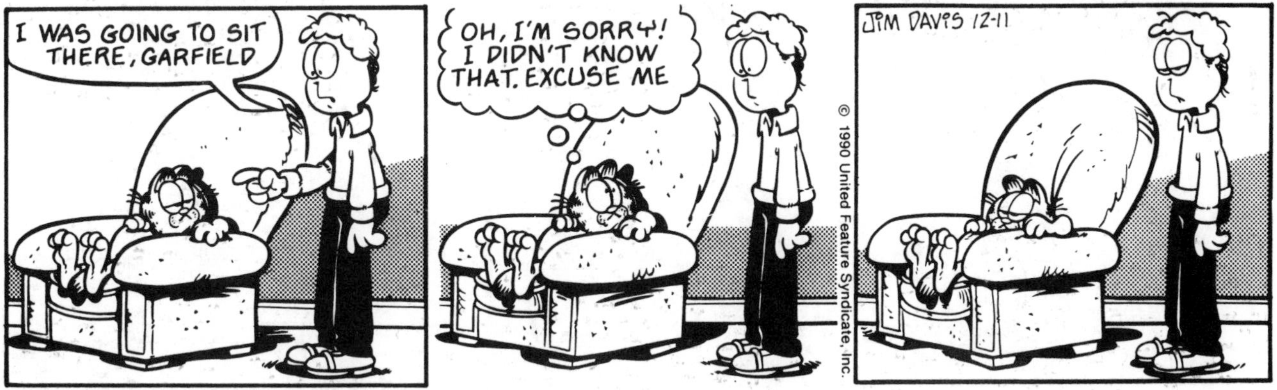
I WAS GOING TO SIT THERE, GARFIELD
OH, I'M SORRY! I DIDN'T KNOW THAT. EXCUSE ME
JIM DAVIS 12-11

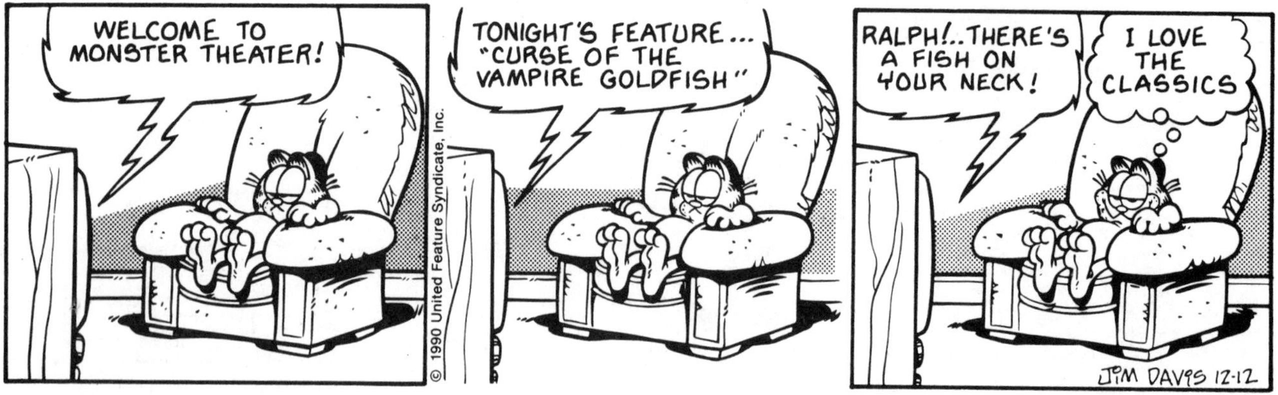
WELCOME TO MONSTER THEATER!
TONIGHT'S FEATURE... "CURSE OF THE VAMPIRE GOLDFISH"
RALPH!..THERE'S A FISH ON YOUR NECK!
I LOVE THE CLASSICS
© 1990 United Feature Syndicate, Inc.
JIM DAVIS 12-12

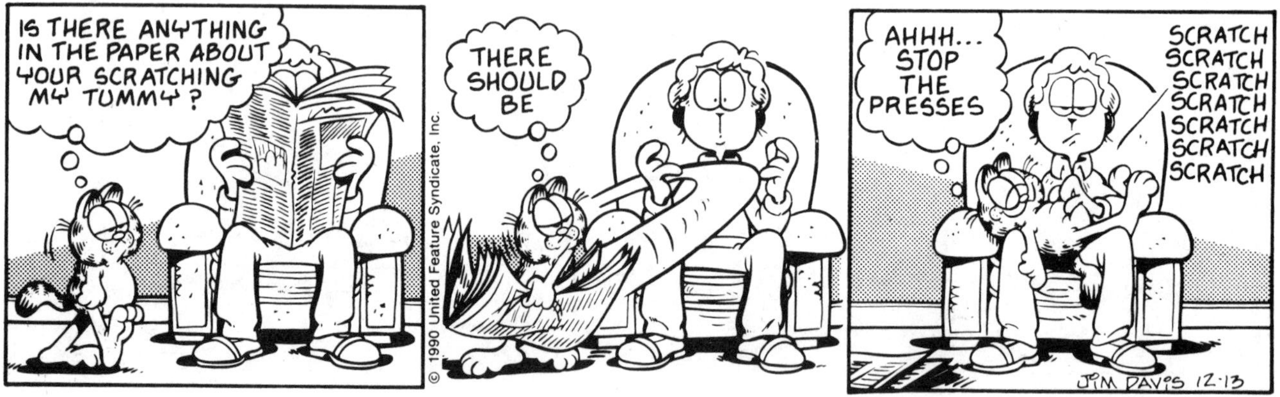
IS THERE ANYTHING IN THE PAPER ABOUT YOUR SCRATCHING MY TUMMY?
THERE SHOULD BE
AHHH... STOP THE PRESSES
SCRATCH SCRATCH SCRATCH SCRATCH SCRATCH SCRATCH SCRATCH
© 1990 United Feature Syndicate, Inc.
JIM DAVIS 12-13

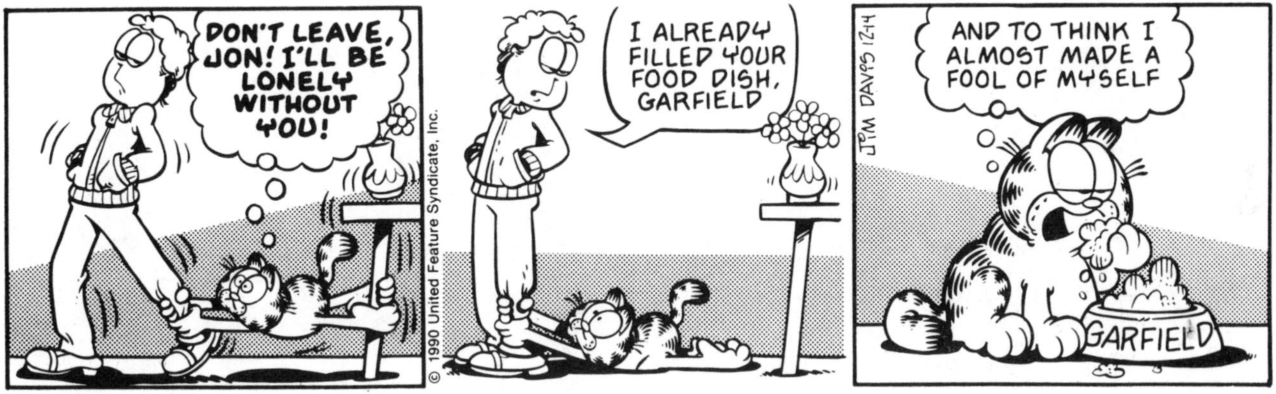
DON'T LEAVE, JON! I'LL BE LONELY WITHOUT YOU!
© 1990 United Feature Syndicate, Inc.
I ALREADY FILLED YOUR FOOD DISH, GARFIELD
JIM DAVIS 12-14
AND TO THINK I ALMOST MADE A FOOL OF MYSELF
GARFIELD

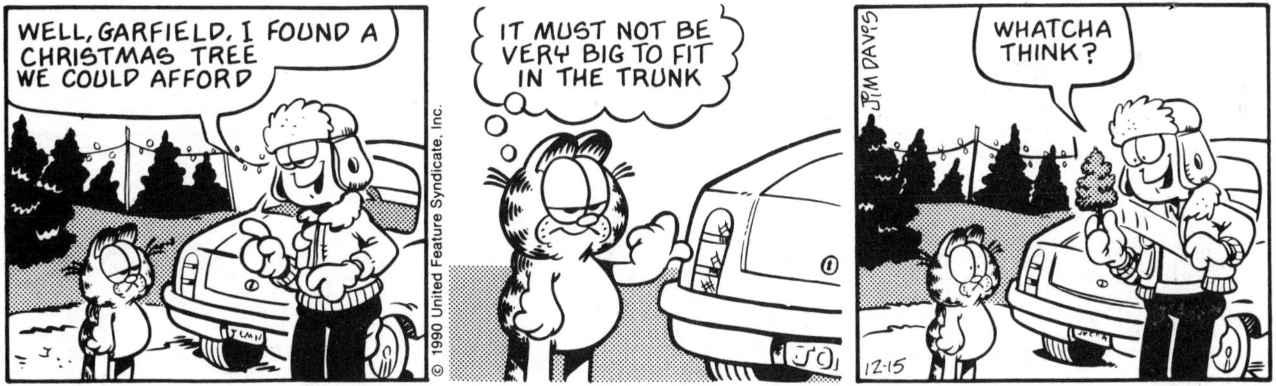
WELL, GARFIELD, I FOUND A CHRISTMAS TREE WE COULD AFFORD
© 1990 United Feature Syndicate, Inc.
IT MUST NOT BE VERY BIG TO FIT IN THE TRUNK
JIM DAVIS
WHATCHA THINK?
12-15

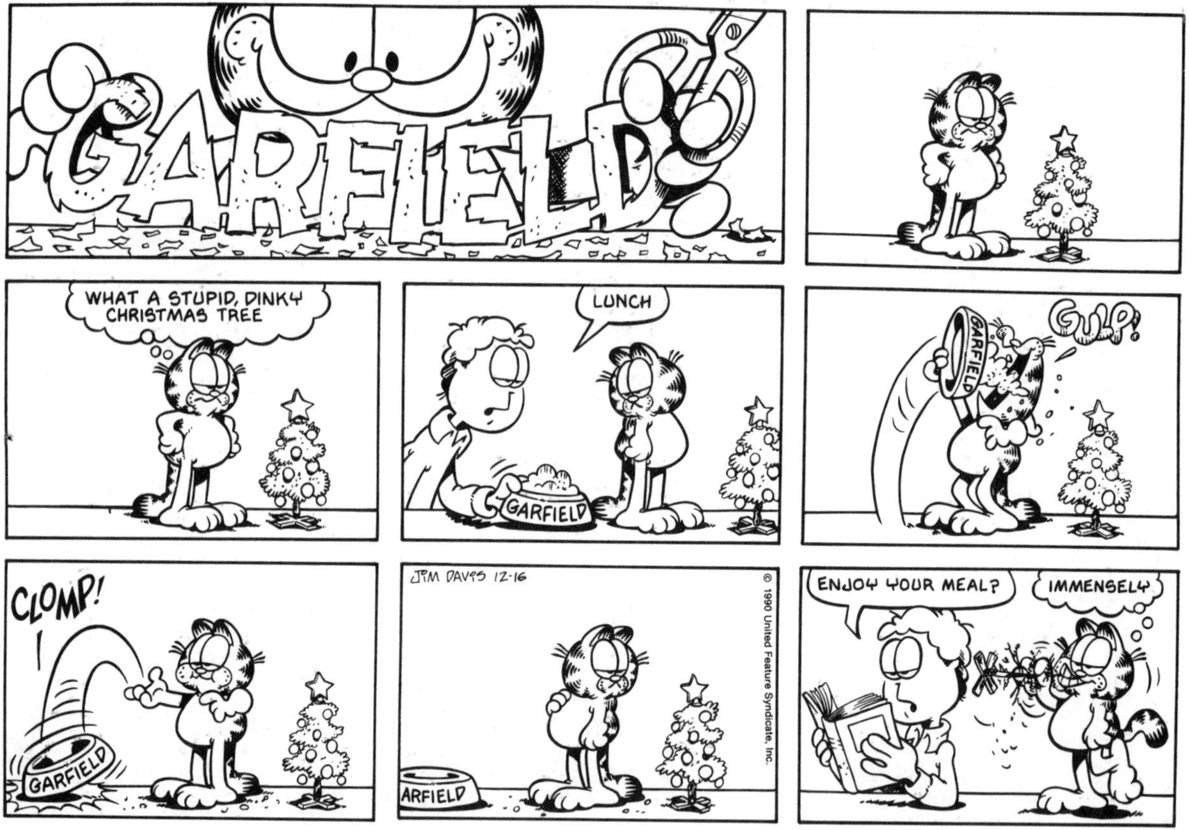
GARFIELD
WHAT A STUPID, DINKY CHRISTMAS TREE
LUNCH
GARFIELD
GARFIELD
GULP!
CLOMP!
GARFIELD
JIM DAVIS 12-16
© 1990 United Feature Syndicate, Inc.
ARFIELD
ENJOY YOUR MEAL?
IMMENSELY

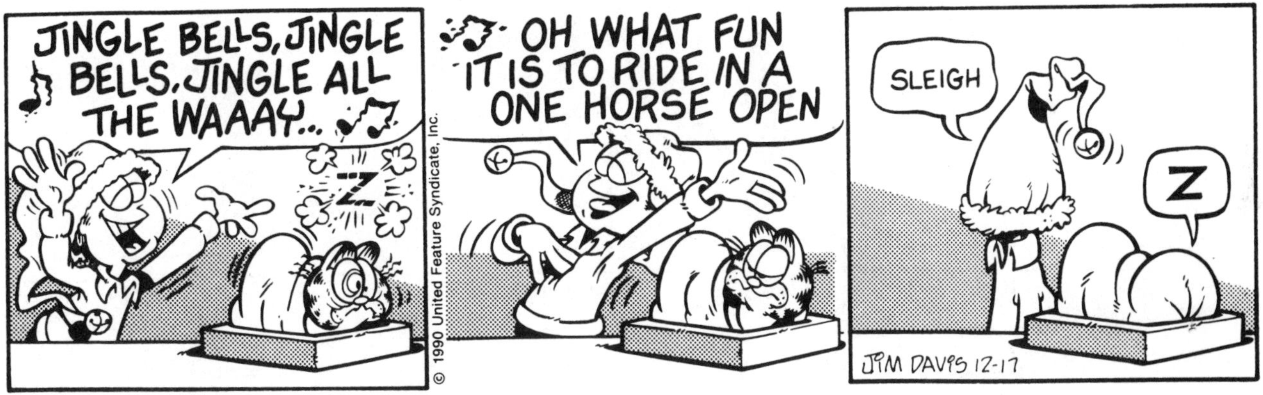
JINGLE BELLS, JINGLE BELLS, JINGLE ALL THE WAAAY...
Z
OH WHAT FUN IT IS TO RIDE IN A ONE HORSE OPEN
SLEIGH
Z
JIM DAVIS 12-17
© 1990 United Feature Syndicate, Inc.

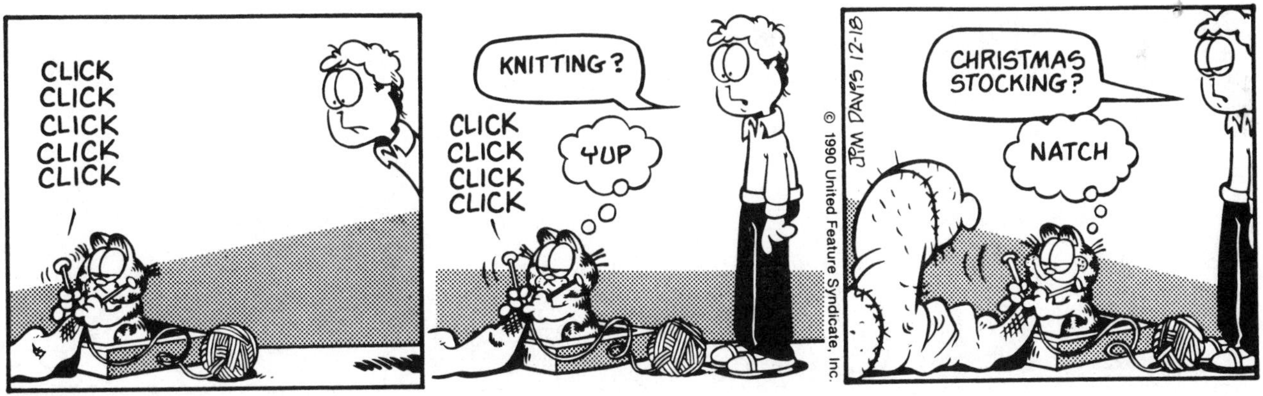
CLICK CLICK CLICK CLICK CLICK
KNITTING?
CLICK CLICK CLICK CLICK
YUP
CHRISTMAS STOCKING?
NATCH
JIM DAVIS 12-18
© 1990 United Feature Syndicate, Inc.

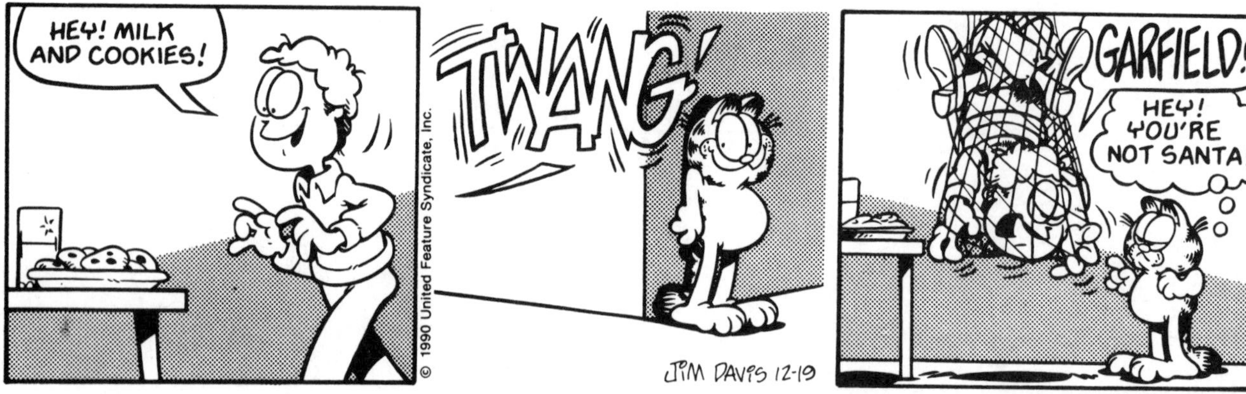
HEY! MILK AND COOKIES!
TWANG!
GARFIELD!
HEY! YOU'RE NOT SANTA!
© 1990 United Feature Syndicate, Inc.
JIM DAVIS 12-19

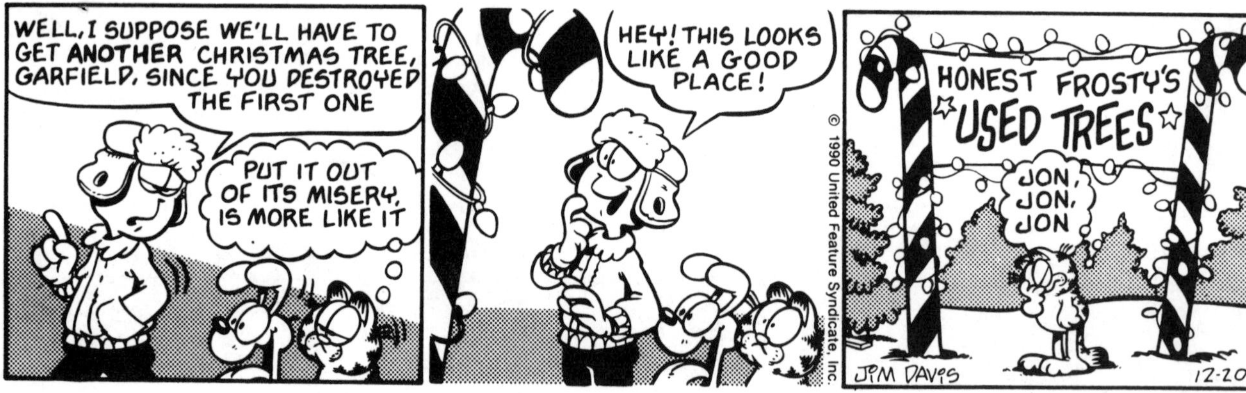
WELL, I SUPPOSE WE'LL HAVE TO GET **ANOTHER** CHRISTMAS TREE, GARFIELD, SINCE YOU DESTROYED THE FIRST ONE
PUT IT OUT OF ITS MISERY, IS MORE LIKE IT
HEY! THIS LOOKS LIKE A GOOD PLACE!
HONEST FROSTY'S USED TREES
JON, JON, JON
© 1990 United Feature Syndicate, Inc.
JIM DAVIS 12-20

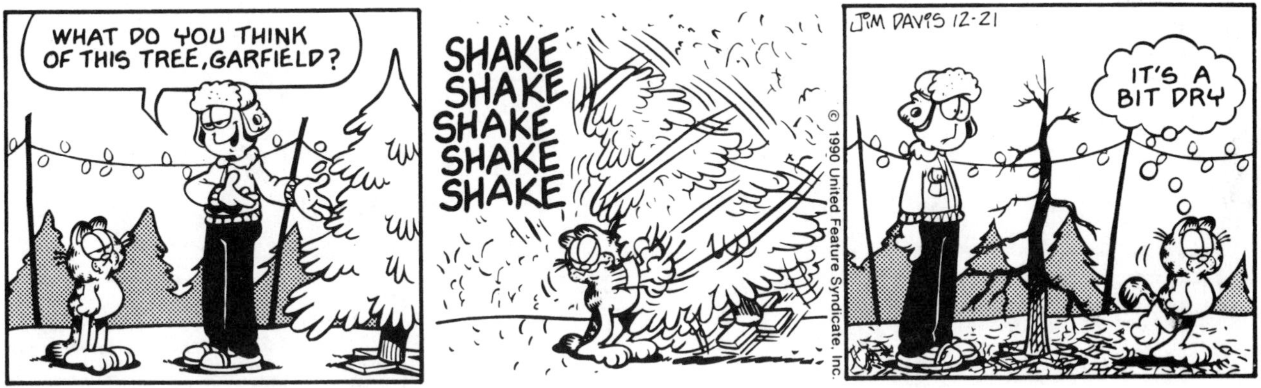
WHAT DO YOU THINK OF THIS TREE, GARFIELD?
SHAKE SHAKE SHAKE SHAKE SHAKE
© 1990 United Feature Syndicate, Inc.
JIM DAVIS 12-21
IT'S A BIT DRY

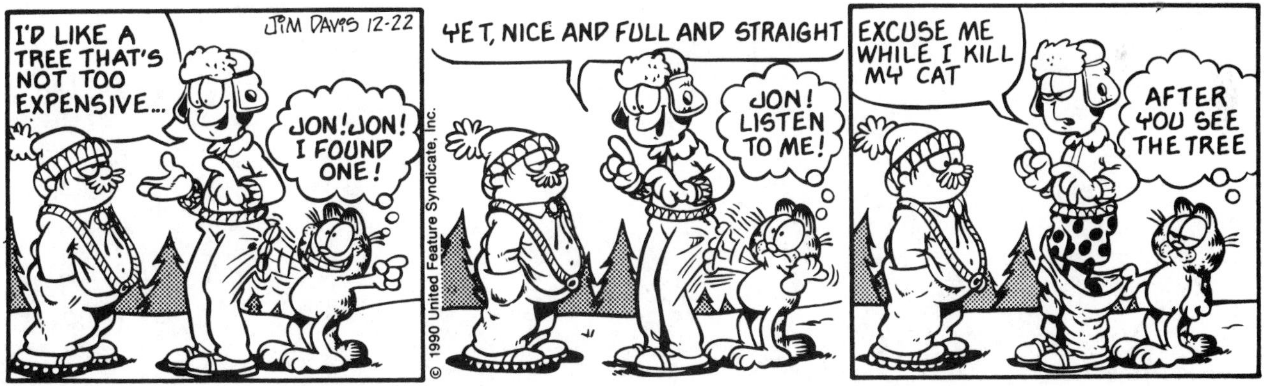
JIM DAVIS 12-22
I'D LIKE A TREE THAT'S NOT TOO EXPENSIVE...
JON! JON! I FOUND ONE!
© 1990 United Feature Syndicate, Inc.
YET, NICE AND FULL AND STRAIGHT
JON! LISTEN TO ME!
EXCUSE ME WHILE I KILL MY CAT
AFTER YOU SEE THE TREE

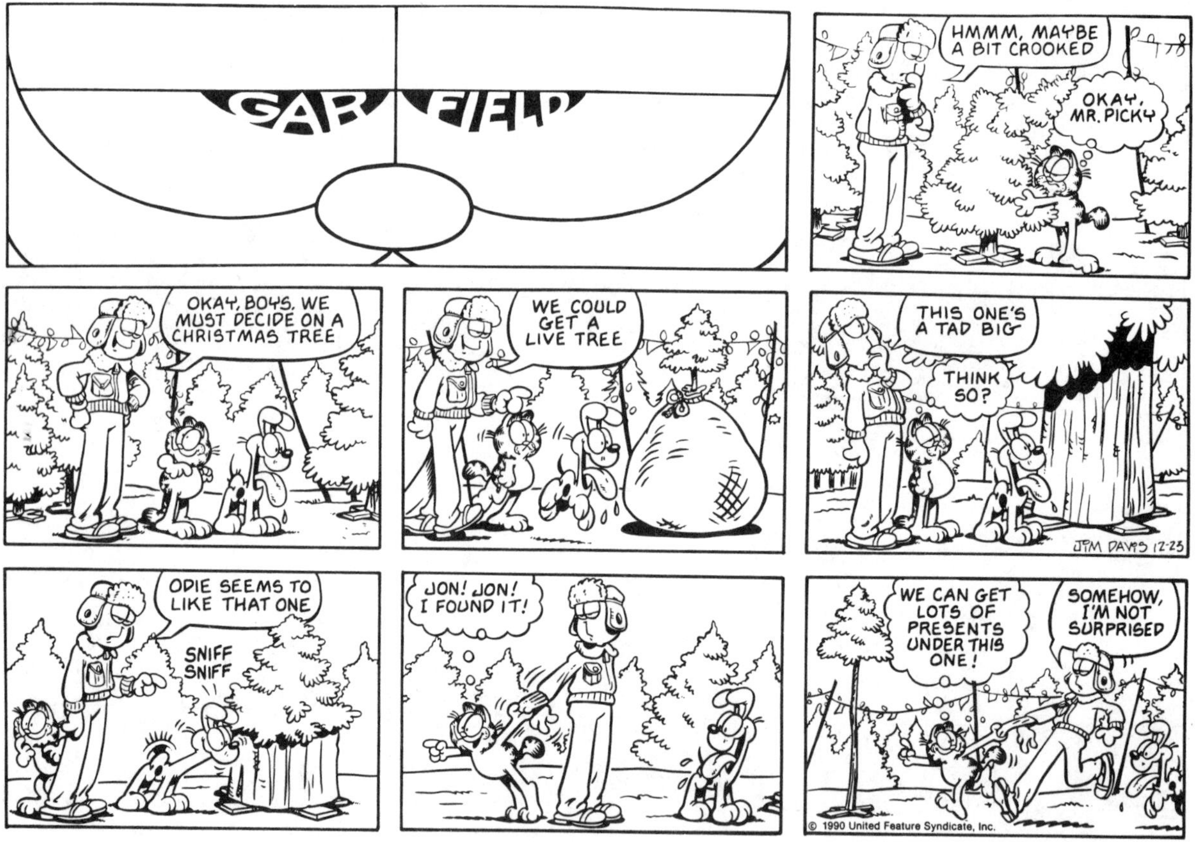
GARFIELD
HMMM, MAYBE A BIT CROOKED
OKAY, MR. PICKY
OKAY, BOYS, WE MUST DECIDE ON A CHRISTMAS TREE
WE COULD GET A LIVE TREE
THIS ONE'S A TAD BIG
THINK SO?
JIM DAVIS 12-23
ODIE SEEMS TO LIKE THAT ONE
SNIFF SNIFF
JON! JON! I FOUND IT!
WE CAN GET LOTS OF PRESENTS UNDER THIS ONE!
SOMEHOW, I'M NOT SURPRISED
© 1990 United Feature Syndicate, Inc.

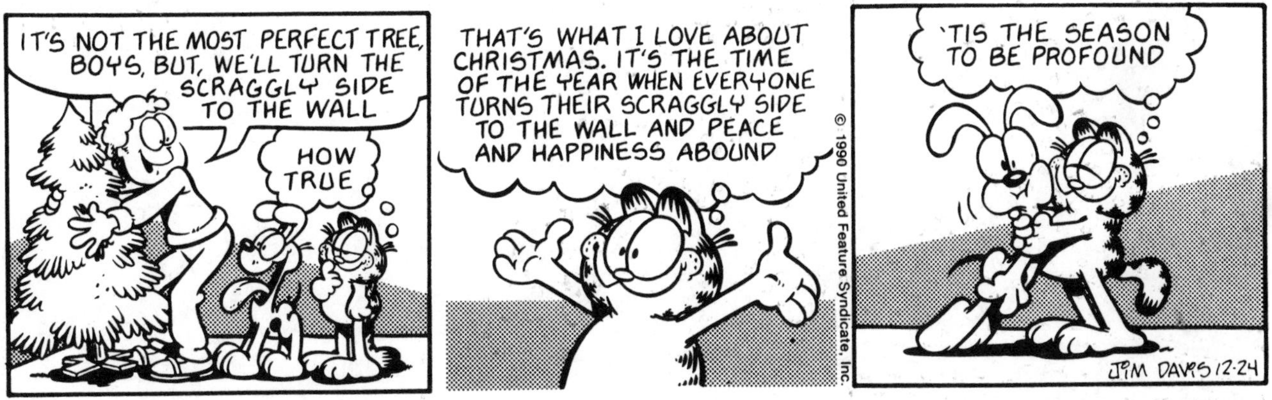
IT'S NOT THE MOST PERFECT TREE, BOYS, BUT, WE'LL TURN THE SCRAGGLY SIDE TO THE WALL
HOW TRUE
THAT'S WHAT I LOVE ABOUT CHRISTMAS. IT'S THE TIME OF THE YEAR WHEN EVERYONE TURNS THEIR SCRAGGLY SIDE TO THE WALL AND PEACE AND HAPPINESS ABOUND
© 1990 United Feature Syndicate, Inc.
'TIS THE SEASON TO BE PROFOUND
JIM DAVIS 12-24

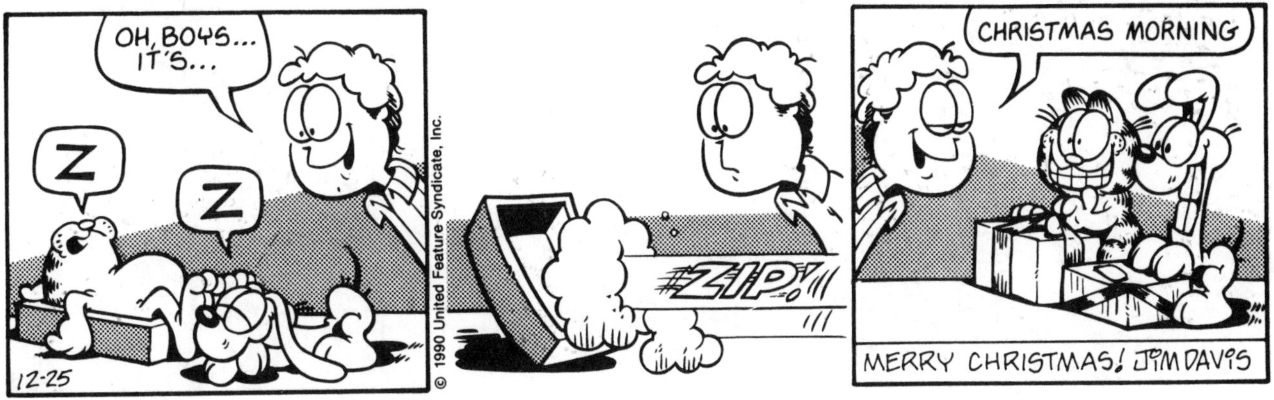
OH, BOYS... IT'S...
Z
Z
12-25
© 1990 United Feature Syndicate, Inc.
ZIP!
CHRISTMAS MORNING
MERRY CHRISTMAS! JIM DAVIS

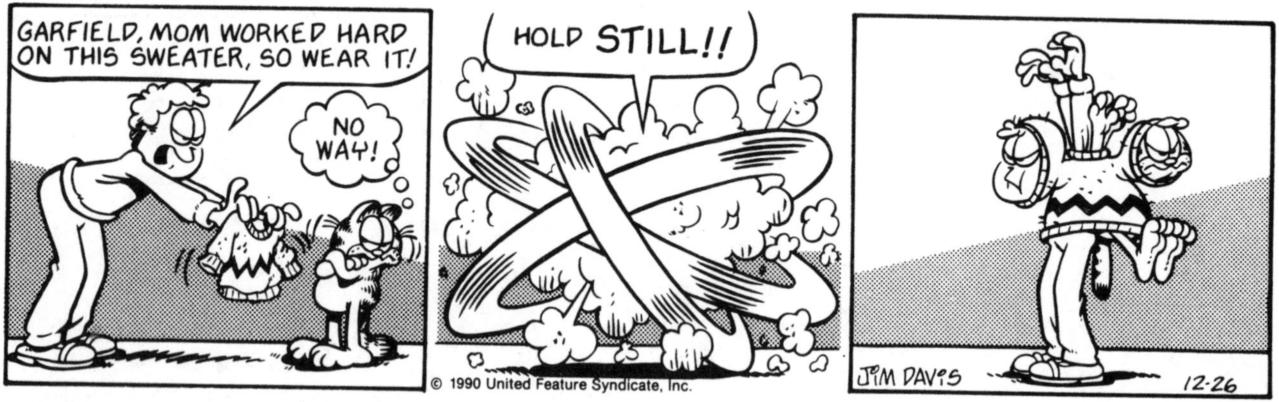
GARFIELD, MOM WORKED HARD ON THIS SWEATER, SO WEAR IT!
NO WAY!
HOLD STILL!!
JIM DAVIS
12-26

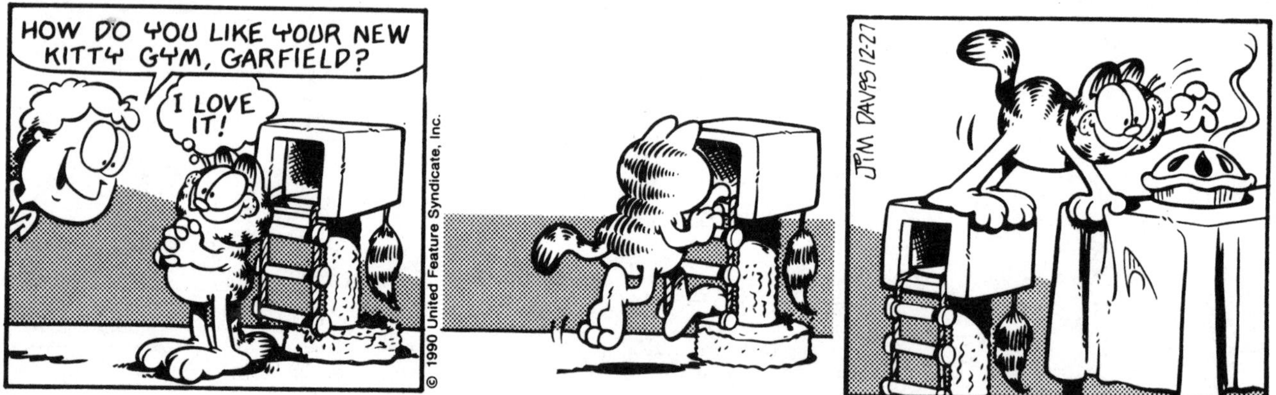
HOW DO YOU LIKE YOUR NEW KITTY GYM, GARFIELD?
I LOVE IT!
JIM DAVIS 12-27

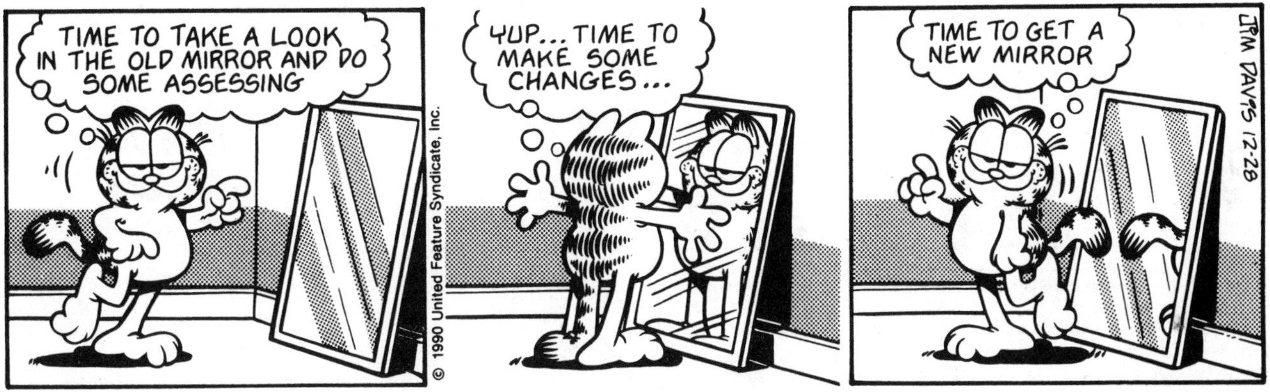
TIME TO TAKE A LOOK IN THE OLD MIRROR AND DO SOME ASSESSING
YUP... TIME TO MAKE SOME CHANGES...
TIME TO GET A NEW MIRROR
JIM DAVIS 12-28
© 1990 United Feature Syndicate, Inc.

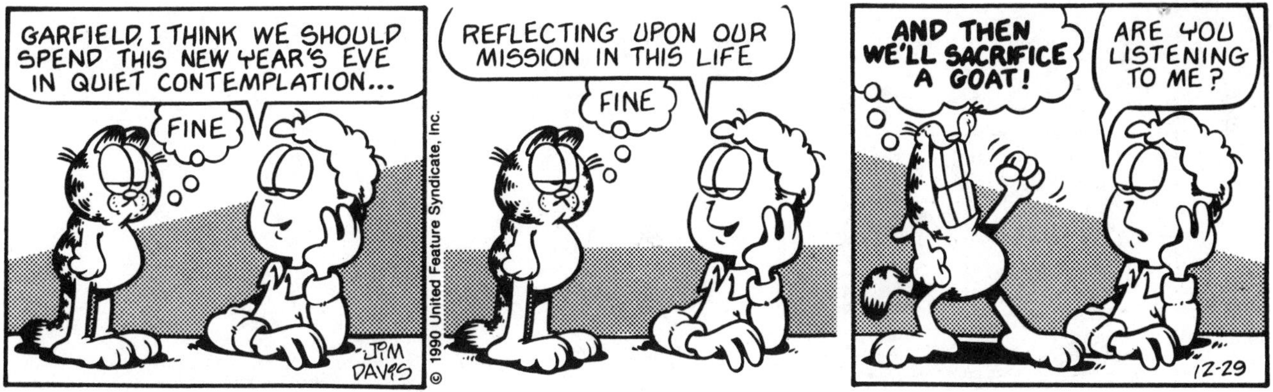
GARFIELD, I THINK WE SHOULD SPEND THIS NEW YEAR'S EVE IN QUIET CONTEMPLATION...
FINE
JIM DAVIS
REFLECTING UPON OUR MISSION IN THIS LIFE
FINE
AND THEN WE'LL SACRIFICE A GOAT!
ARE YOU LISTENING TO ME?
12-29
© 1990 United Feature Syndicate, Inc.

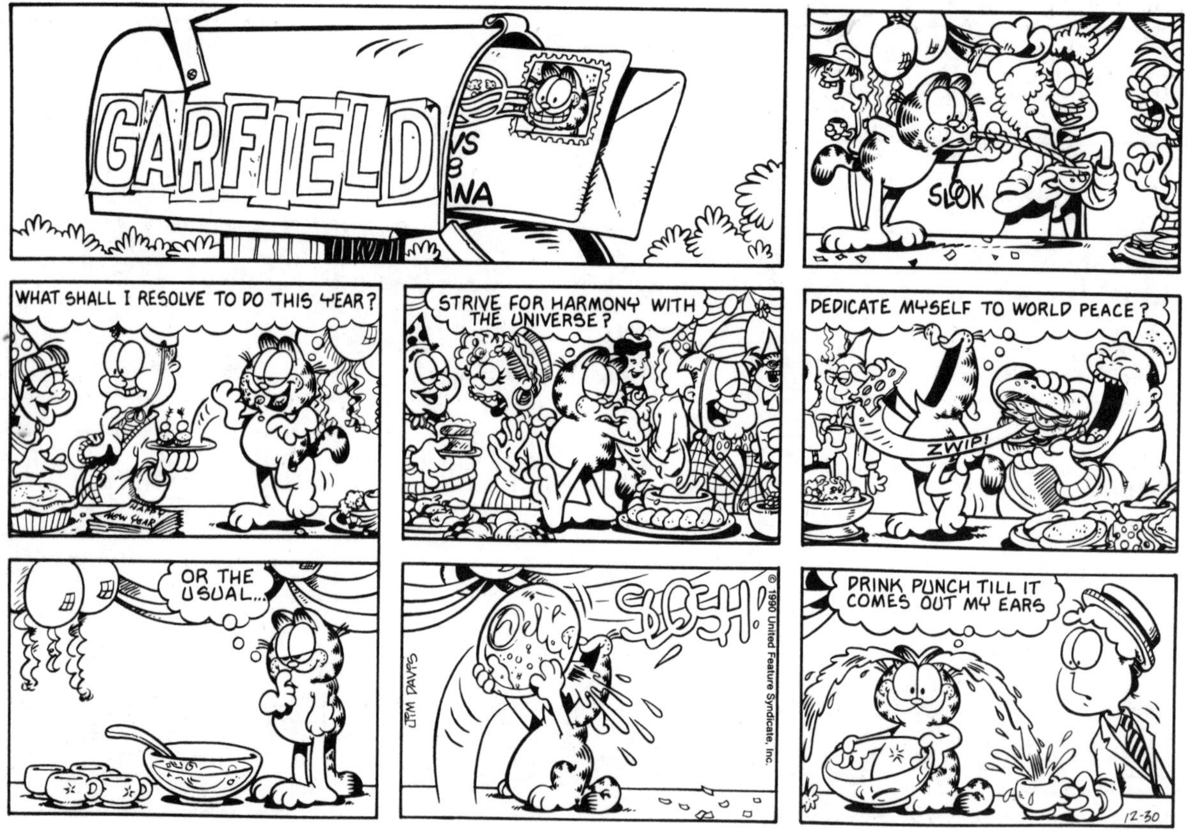
GARFIELD
SLOK
WHAT SHALL I RESOLVE TO DO THIS YEAR?
HAPPY NEW YEAR
STRIVE FOR HARMONY WITH THE UNIVERSE?
DEDICATE MYSELF TO WORLD PEACE?
ZWIP!
OR THE USUAL...
JIM DAVIS
SLOSH!
© 1990 United Feature Syndicate, Inc.
DRINK PUNCH TILL IT COMES OUT MY EARS
12-30

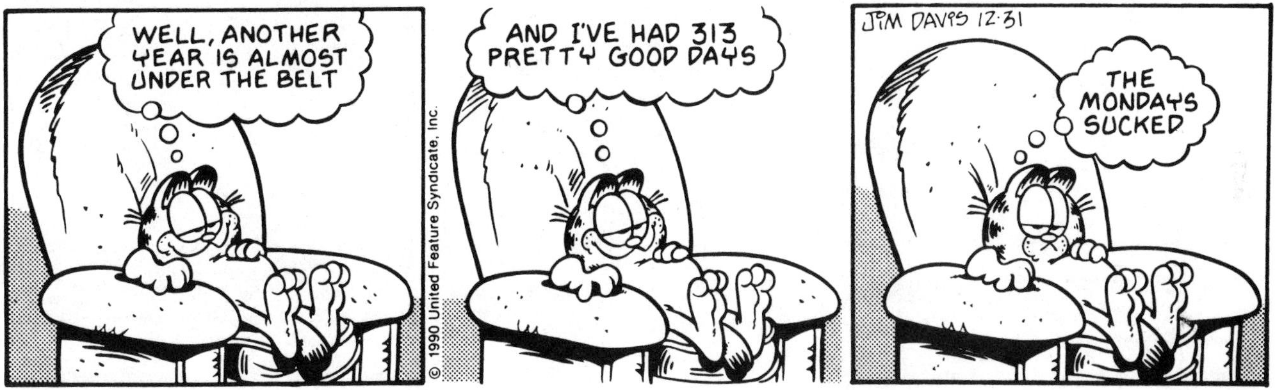
WELL, ANOTHER YEAR IS ALMOST UNDER THE BELT
© 1990 United Feature Syndicate, Inc.
AND I'VE HAD 313 PRETTY GOOD DAYS
JIM DAVIS 12·31
THE MONDAYS SUCKED

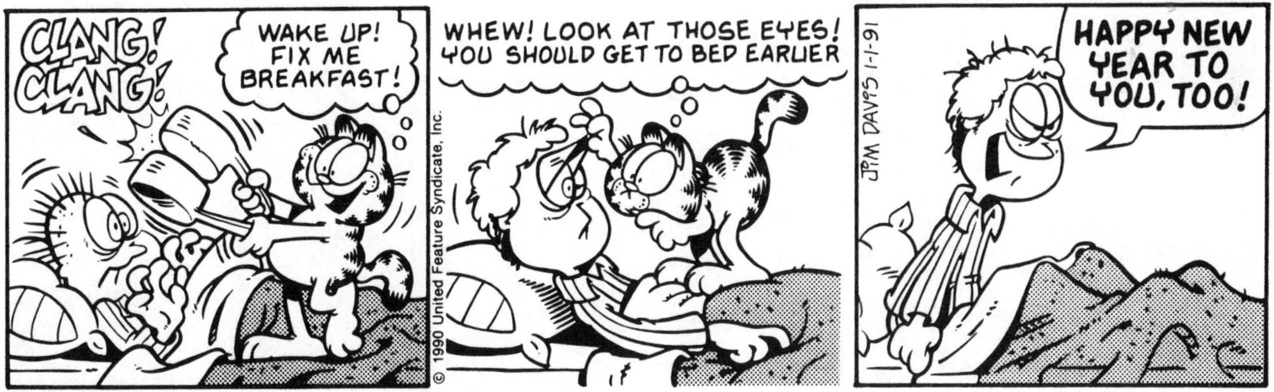
CLANG! CLANG!
WAKE UP! FIX ME BREAKFAST!
© 1990 United Feature Syndicate, Inc.
WHEW! LOOK AT THOSE EYES! YOU SHOULD GET TO BED EARLIER
JIM DAVIS 1-1-91
HAPPY NEW YEAR TO YOU, TOO!

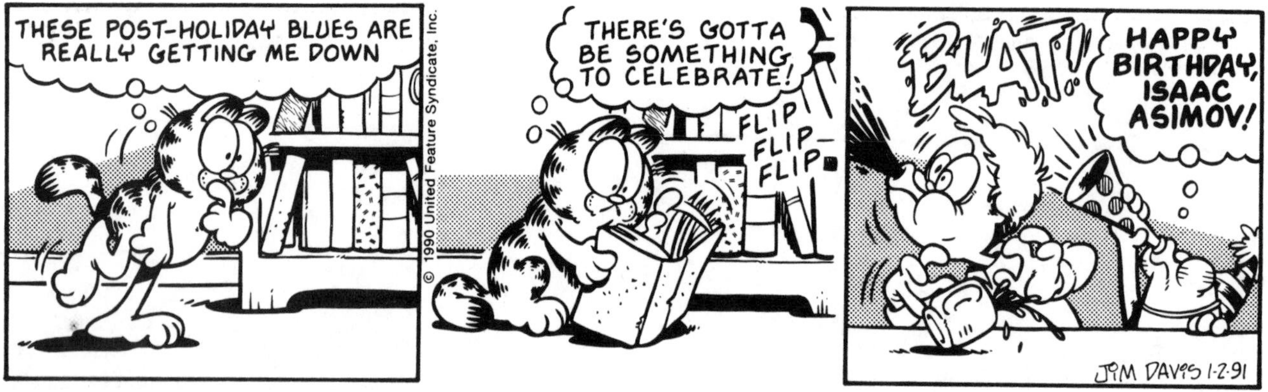

THESE POST-HOLIDAY BLUES ARE REALLY GETTING ME DOWN
© 1990 United Feature Syndicate, Inc.
THERE'S GOTTA BE SOMETHING TO CELEBRATE!
FLIP FLIP FLIP FLIP
BLAT!!
HAPPY BIRTHDAY, ISAAC ASIMOV!
JIM DAVIS 1-2-91

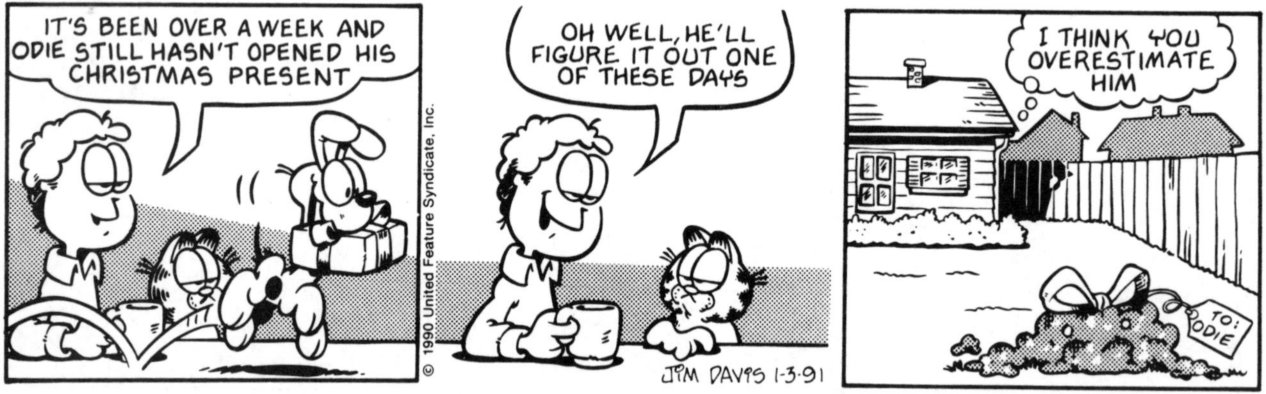

IT'S BEEN OVER A WEEK AND ODIE STILL HASN'T OPENED HIS CHRISTMAS PRESENT
© 1990 United Feature Syndicate, Inc.
OH WELL, HE'LL FIGURE IT OUT ONE OF THESE DAYS
JIM DAVIS 1-3-91
I THINK YOU OVERESTIMATE HIM
TO: ODIE

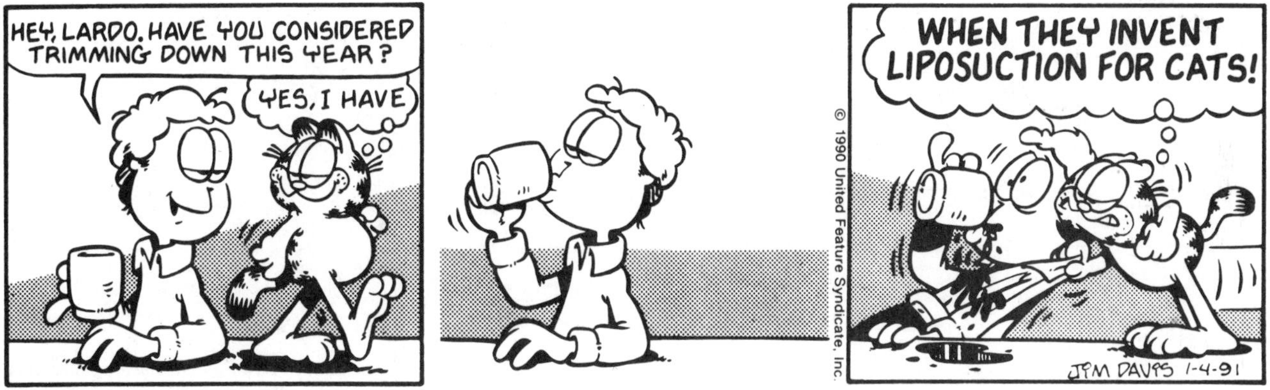
HEY, LARDO. HAVE YOU CONSIDERED TRIMMING DOWN THIS YEAR?
YES, I HAVE
WHEN THEY INVENT LIPOSUCTION FOR CATS!
© 1990 United Feature Syndicate, Inc.
JIM DAVIS 1-4-91

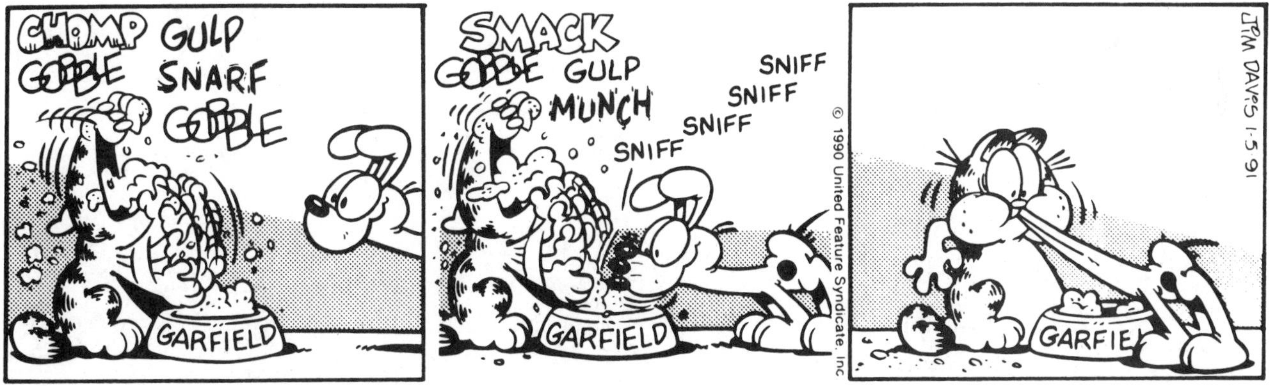
CHOMP GULP
GOBBLE SNARF
GOBBLE
GARFIELD
SMACK
GOBBLE GULP
MUNCH
SNIFF
SNIFF
SNIFF
SNIFF
GARFIELD
© 1990 United Feature Syndicate, Inc.
JIM DAVIS 1-5-91
GARFIE

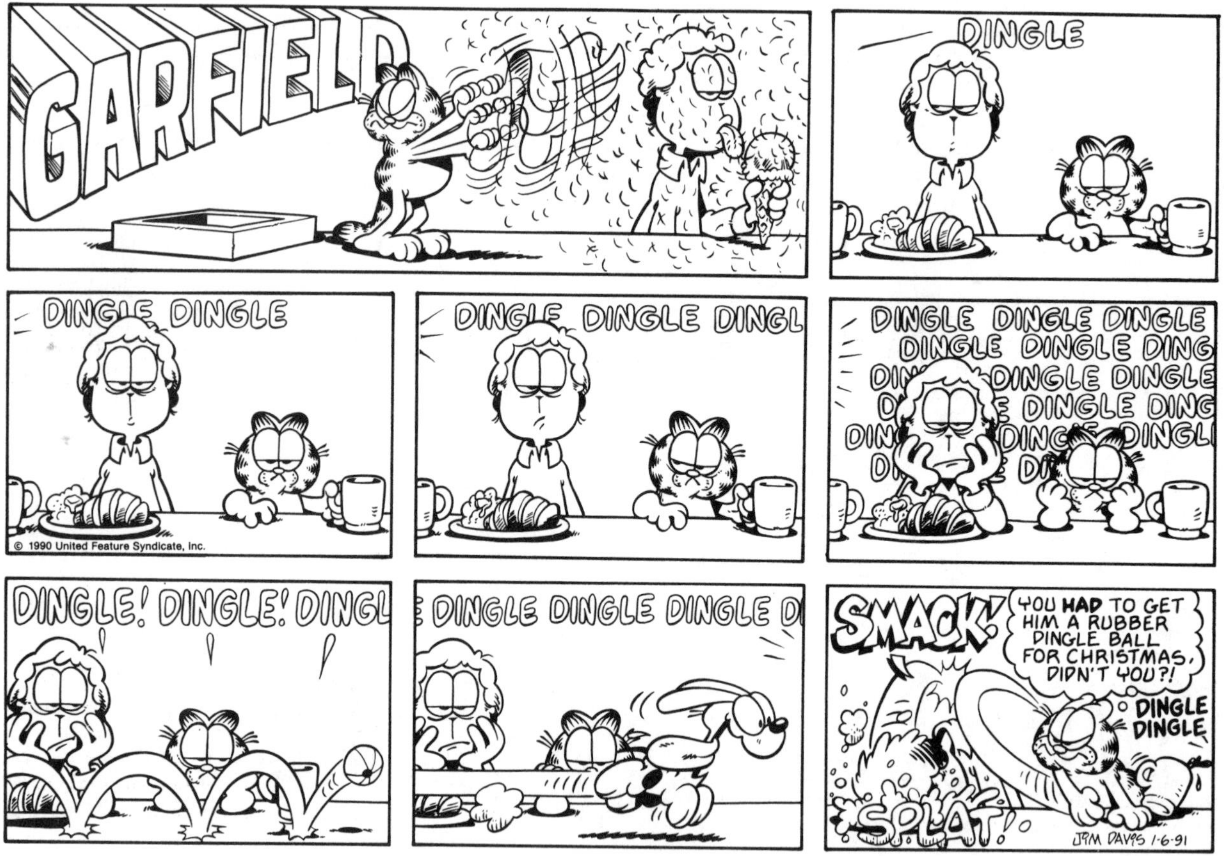
GARFIELD
DINGLE
DINGLE DINGLE
DINGLE DINGLE DINGL
DINGLE DINGLE DINGLE DINGLE DINGLE DING DINGLE DINGLE DINGLE DINGLE DING DINGLI
DINGLE! DINGLE! DINGL
DINGLE DINGLE DINGLE
SMACK!
YOU HAD TO GET HIM A RUBBER DINGLE BALL FOR CHRISTMAS, DIDN'T YOU?!
DINGLE DINGLE
SPLAT!
JIM DAVIS 1-6-91
© 1990 United Feature Syndicate, Inc.

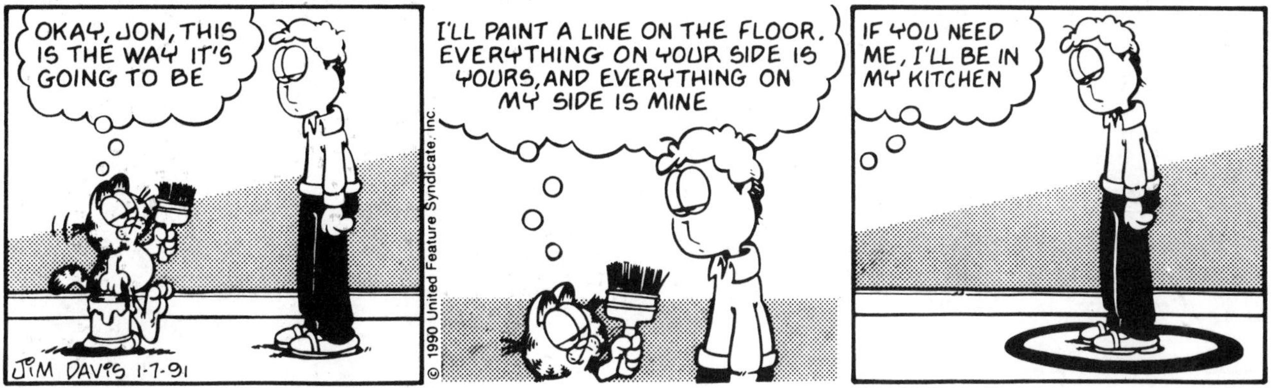
OKAY, JON, THIS IS THE WAY IT'S GOING TO BE
JIM DAVIS 1-7-91
© 1990 United Feature Syndicate, Inc.
I'LL PAINT A LINE ON THE FLOOR. EVERYTHING ON YOUR SIDE IS YOURS, AND EVERYTHING ON MY SIDE IS MINE
IF YOU NEED ME, I'LL BE IN MY KITCHEN

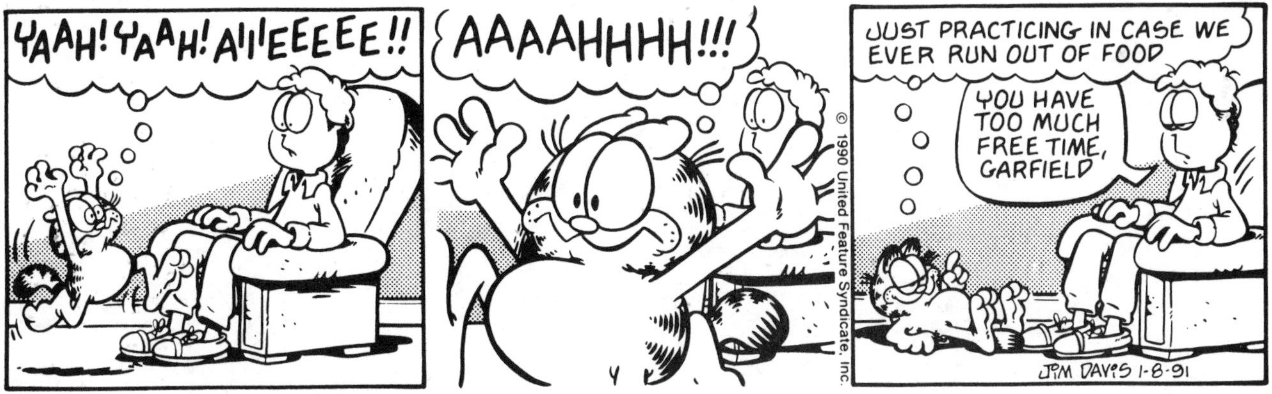
YAAH! YAAH! AIIEEEEEE!!
AAAAHHHH!!!
© 1990 United Feature Syndicate, Inc.
JUST PRACTICING IN CASE WE EVER RUN OUT OF FOOD
YOU HAVE TOO MUCH FREE TIME, GARFIELD
JIM DAVIS 1-8-91

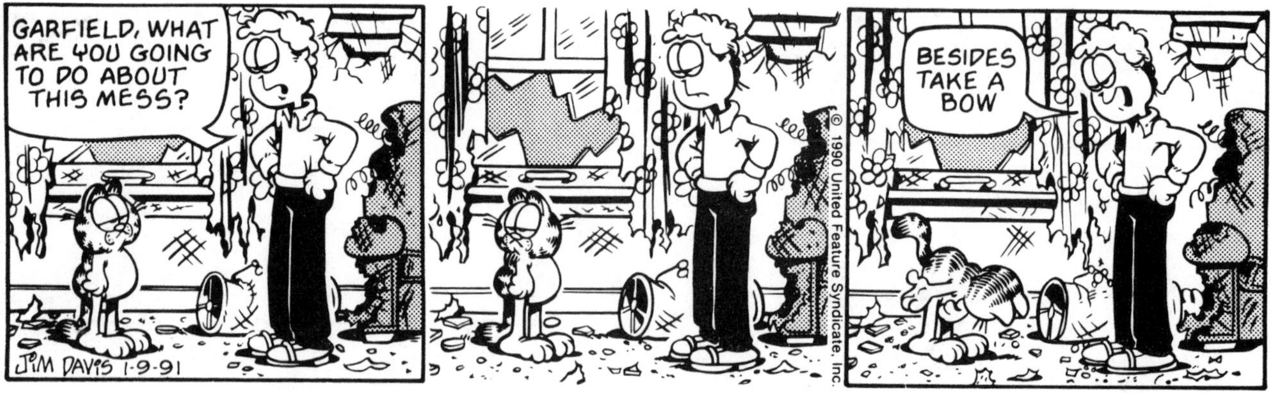
GARFIELD, WHAT ARE YOU GOING TO DO ABOUT THIS MESS?
JIM DAVIS 1-9-91
© 1990 United Feature Syndicate, Inc.
BESIDES TAKE A BOW

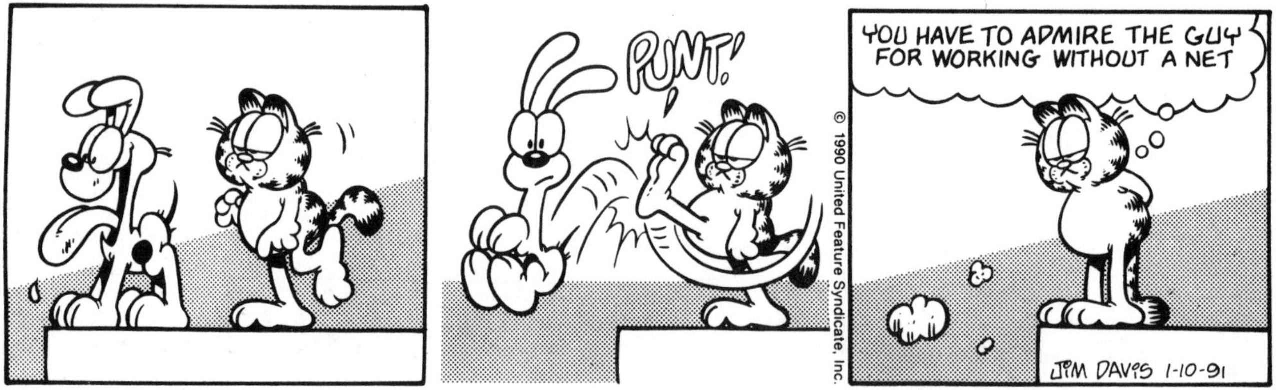
PUNT!
© 1990 United Feature Syndicate, Inc.
YOU HAVE TO ADMIRE THE GUY FOR WORKING WITHOUT A NET
JIM DAVIS 1-10-91

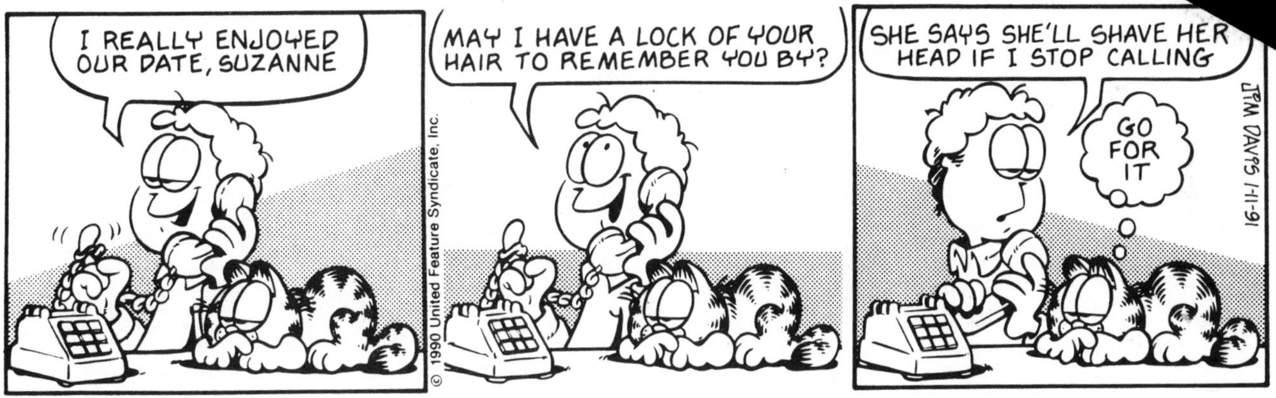
I REALLY ENJOYED OUR DATE, SUZANNE
MAY I HAVE A LOCK OF YOUR HAIR TO REMEMBER YOU BY?
SHE SAYS SHE'LL SHAVE HER HEAD IF I STOP CALLING
GO FOR IT
© 1990 United Feature Syndicate, Inc.
JIM DAVIS 1-11-91

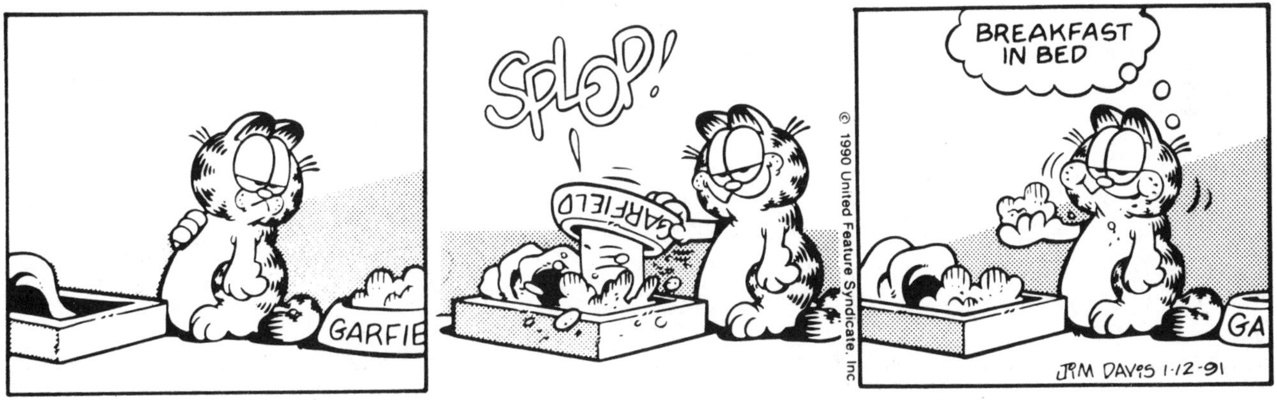
GARFIE
SPLOP!
GARFIELD
BREAKFAST IN BED
GA
© 1990 United Feature Syndicate, Inc.
JIM DAVIS 1-12-91

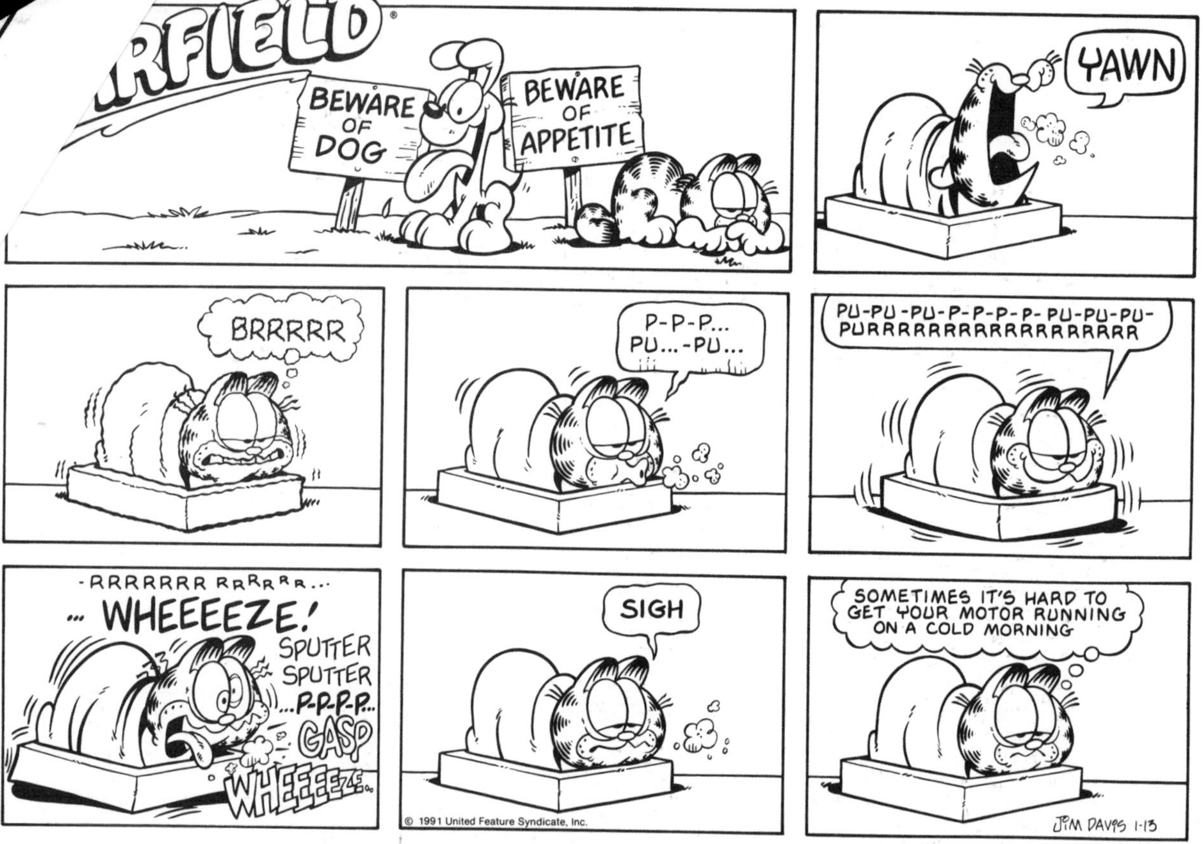
BEWARE OF DOG
BEWARE OF APPETITE
YAWN
BRRRRR
P-P-P... PU...-PU...
PU-PU-PU-P-P-P-P-PU-PU-PU-PURRRRRRRRRRRRRRRRRR
-RRRRRRR RRRRRR...
... WHEEEEZE!
SPUTTER SPUTTER ...P-P-P-P...
GASP
WHEEEEZE
SIGH
SOMETIMES IT'S HARD TO GET YOUR MOTOR RUNNING ON A COLD MORNING
© 1991 United Feature Syndicate, Inc.
JIM DAVIS 1-13

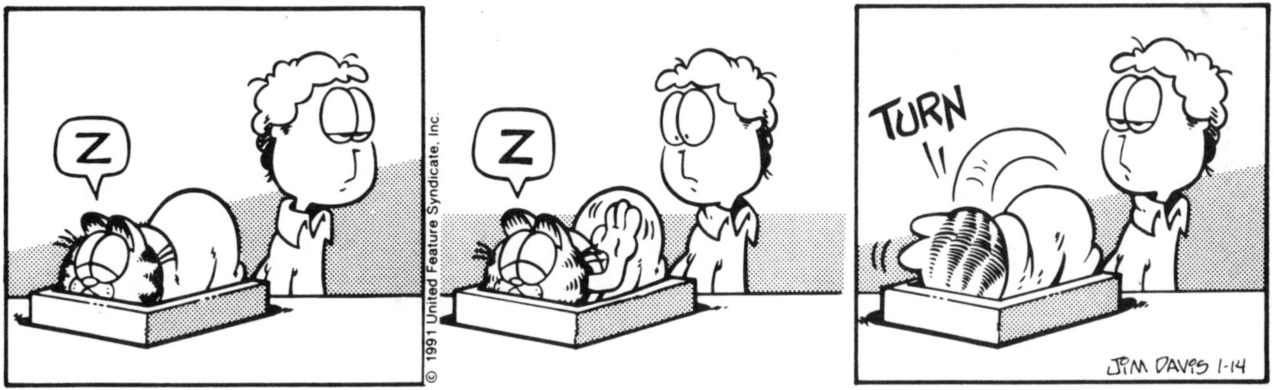
Z
Z
TURN
JIM DAVIS 1-14

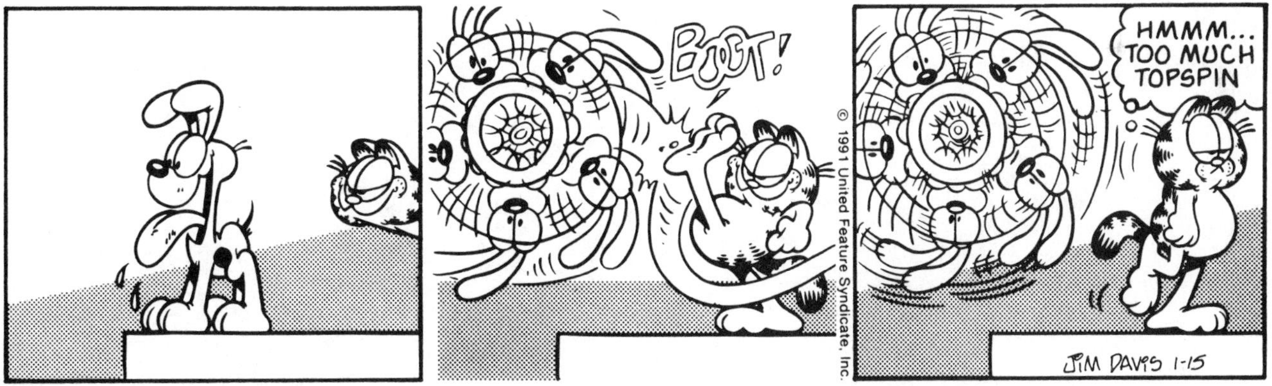
BOOT!
HMMM... TOO MUCH TOPSPIN
JIM DAVIS 1-15

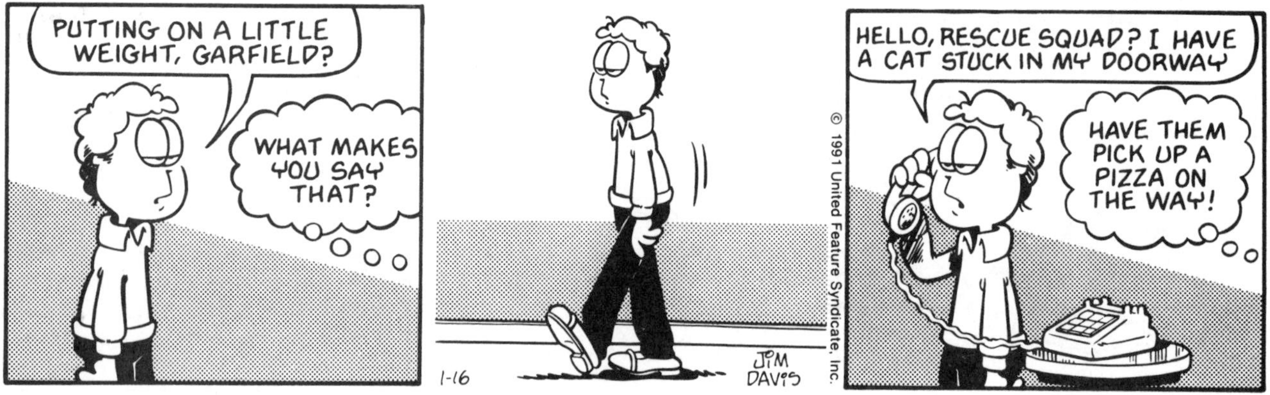
PUTTING ON A LITTLE WEIGHT, GARFIELD?
WHAT MAKES YOU SAY THAT?
1-16
JIM DAVIS
HELLO, RESCUE SQUAD? I HAVE A CAT STUCK IN MY DOORWAY
HAVE THEM PICK UP A PIZZA ON THE WAY!
© 1991 United Feature Syndicate, Inc.

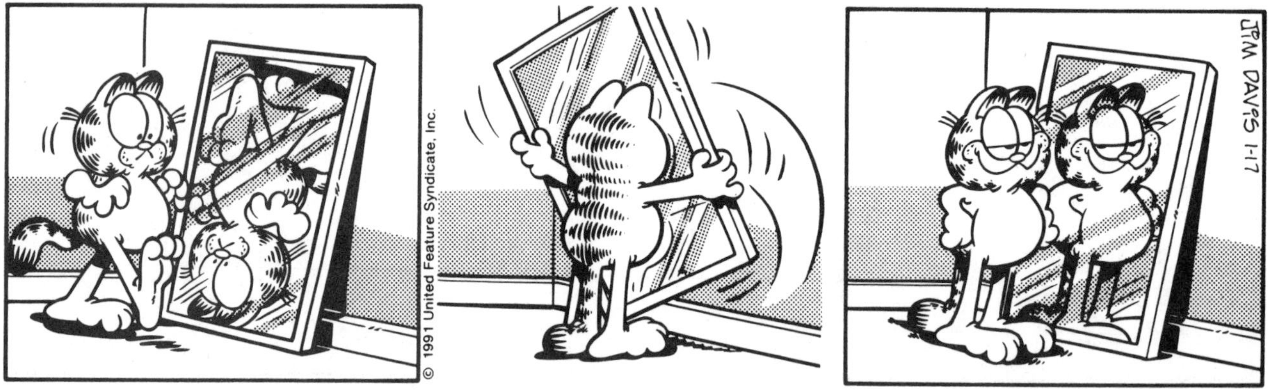
© 1991 United Feature Syndicate, Inc.
JIM DAVIS 1-17

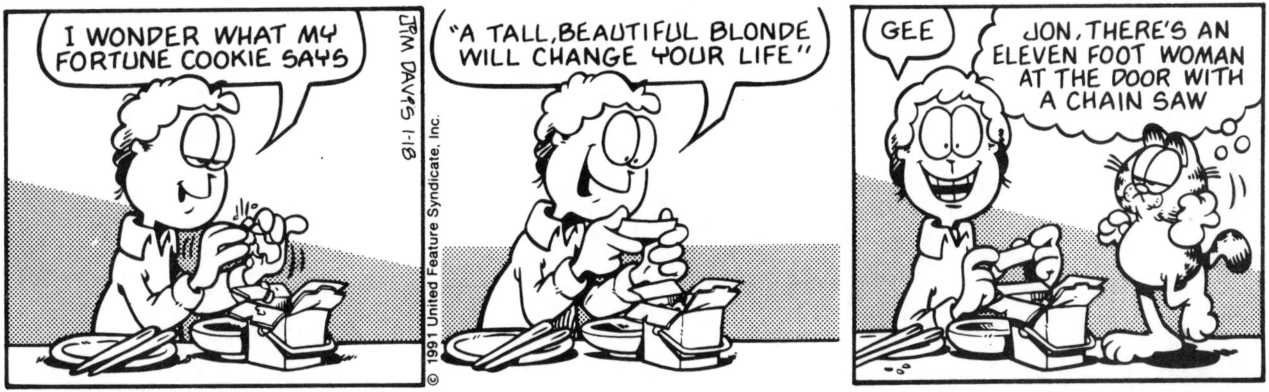
I WONDER WHAT MY FORTUNE COOKIE SAYS
JIM DAVIS 1-18
© 1991 United Feature Syndicate, Inc.
"A TALL, BEAUTIFUL BLONDE WILL CHANGE YOUR LIFE"
GEE
JON, THERE'S AN ELEVEN FOOT WOMAN AT THE DOOR WITH A CHAIN SAW

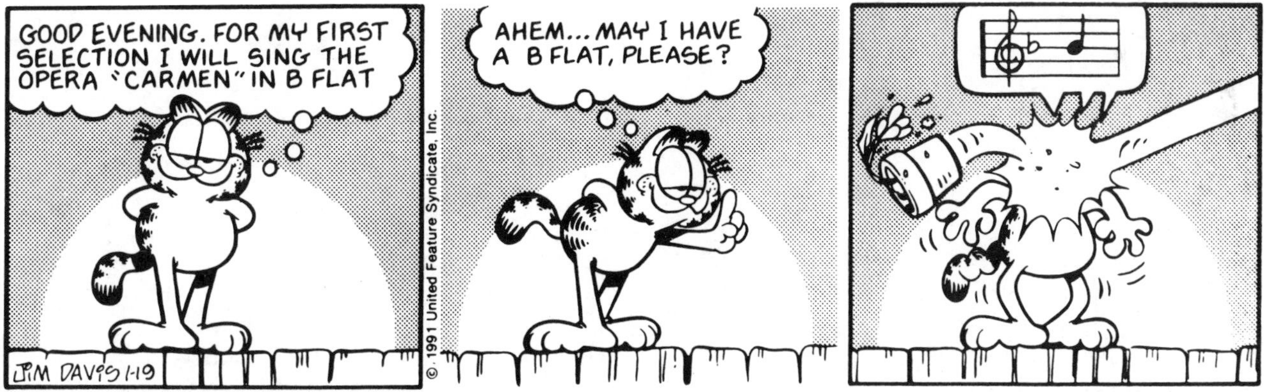
GOOD EVENING. FOR MY FIRST SELECTION I WILL SING THE OPERA "CARMEN" IN B FLAT
JIM DAVIS 1-19
© 1991 United Feature Syndicate, Inc.
AHEM... MAY I HAVE A B FLAT, PLEASE?

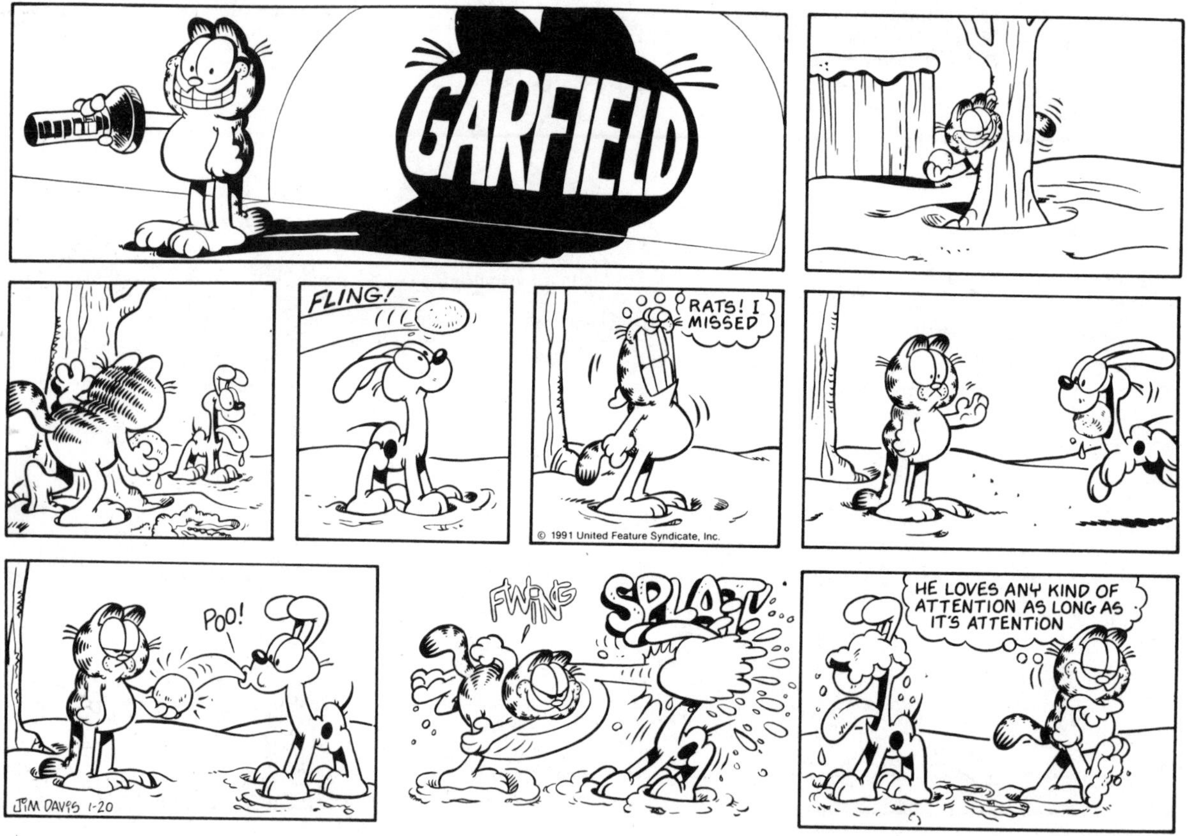

GARFIELD
FLING!
RATS! I MISSED
© 1991 United Feature Syndicate, Inc.
POO!
JIM DAVIS 1-20
FWING
SPLAT!
HE LOVES ANY KIND OF ATTENTION AS LONG AS IT'S ATTENTION

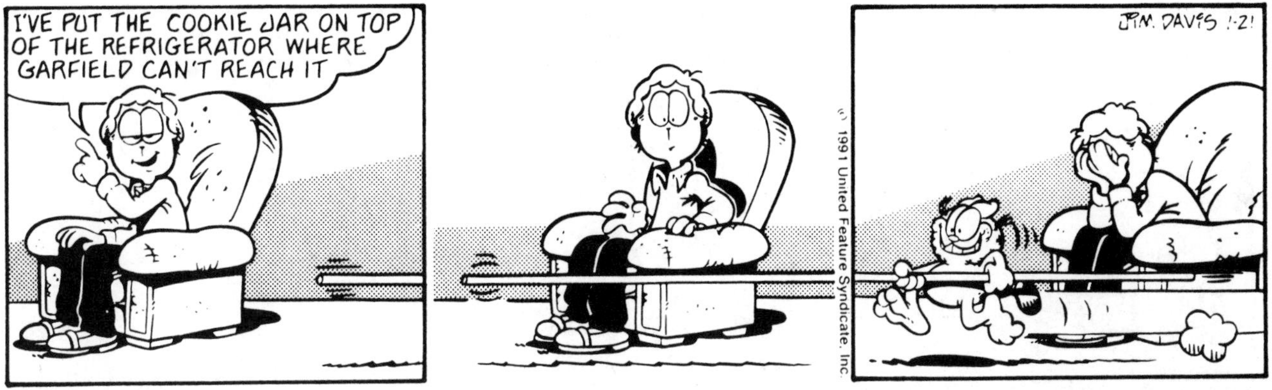
I'VE PUT THE COOKIE JAR ON TOP OF THE REFRIGERATOR WHERE GARFIELD CAN'T REACH IT
JIM DAVIS 1-21
© 1991 United Feature Syndicate, Inc.

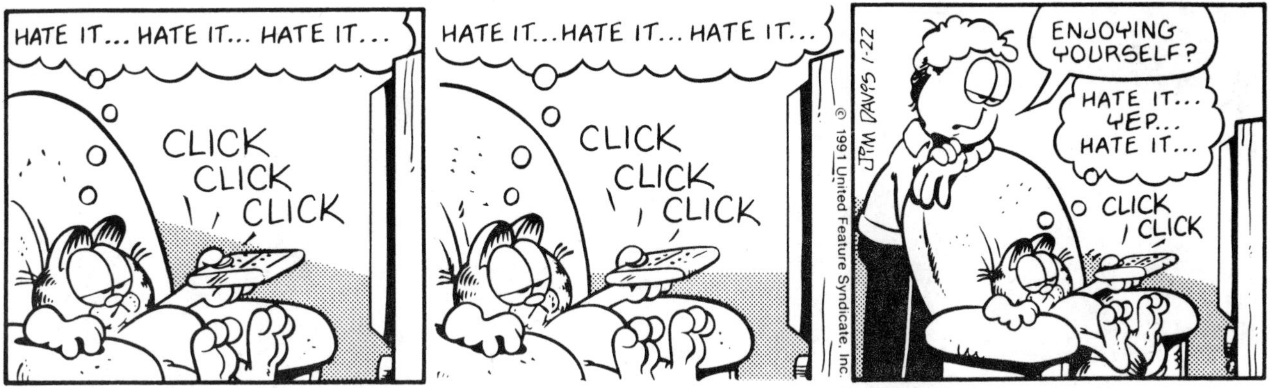
HATE IT... HATE IT... HATE IT...
CLICK
CLICK
CLICK
HATE IT...HATE IT... HATE IT...
CLICK
CLICK
CLICK
JIM DAVIS 1-22
© 1991 United Feature Syndicate, Inc.
ENJOYING YOURSELF?
HATE IT... YEP... HATE IT...
CLICK
CLICK

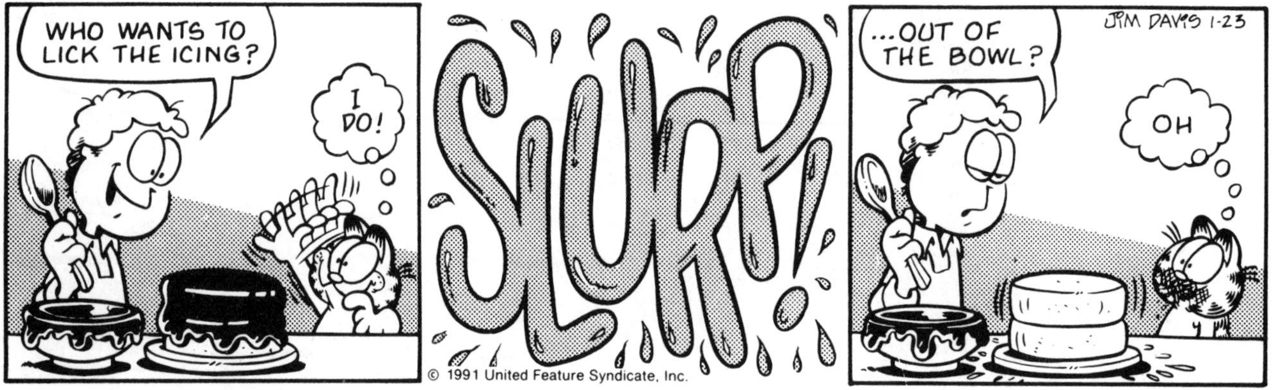
WHO WANTS TO LICK THE ICING?
I DO!
SLURP!
© 1991 United Feature Syndicate, Inc.
...OUT OF THE BOWL?
JIM DAVIS 1-23
OH

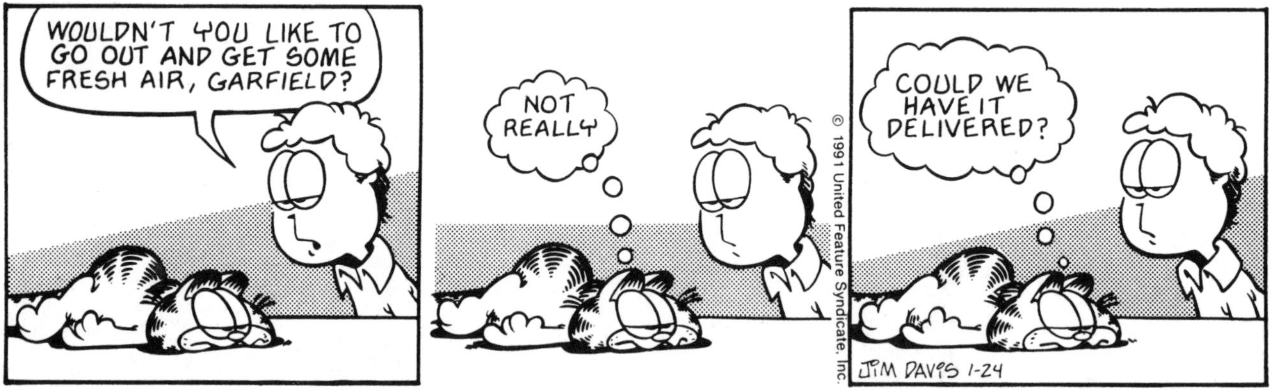
WOULDN'T YOU LIKE TO GO OUT AND GET SOME FRESH AIR, GARFIELD?
NOT REALLY
© 1991 United Feature Syndicate, Inc.
COULD WE HAVE IT DELIVERED?
JIM DAVIS 1-24

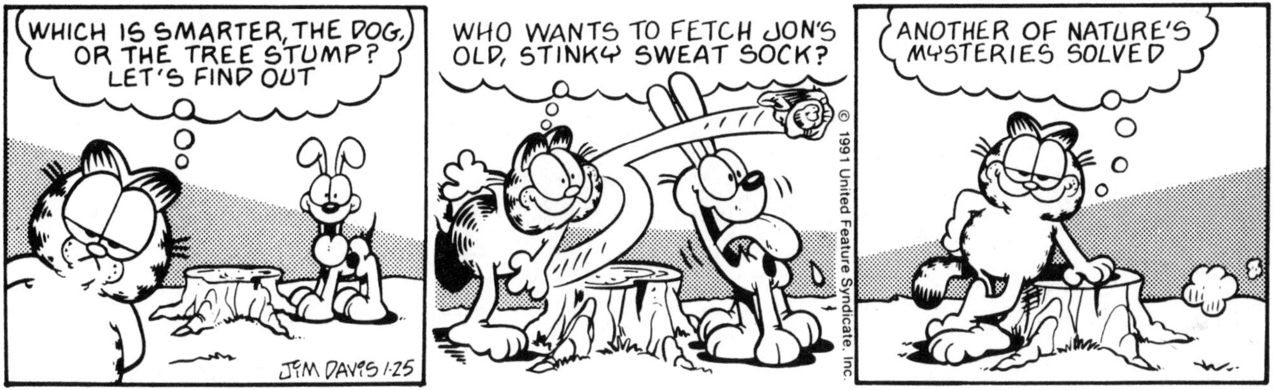
WHICH IS SMARTER, THE DOG, OR THE TREE STUMP? LET'S FIND OUT
JIM DAVIS 1-25
WHO WANTS TO FETCH JON'S OLD, STINKY SWEAT SOCK?
© 1991 United Feature Syndicate, Inc.
ANOTHER OF NATURE'S MYSTERIES SOLVED

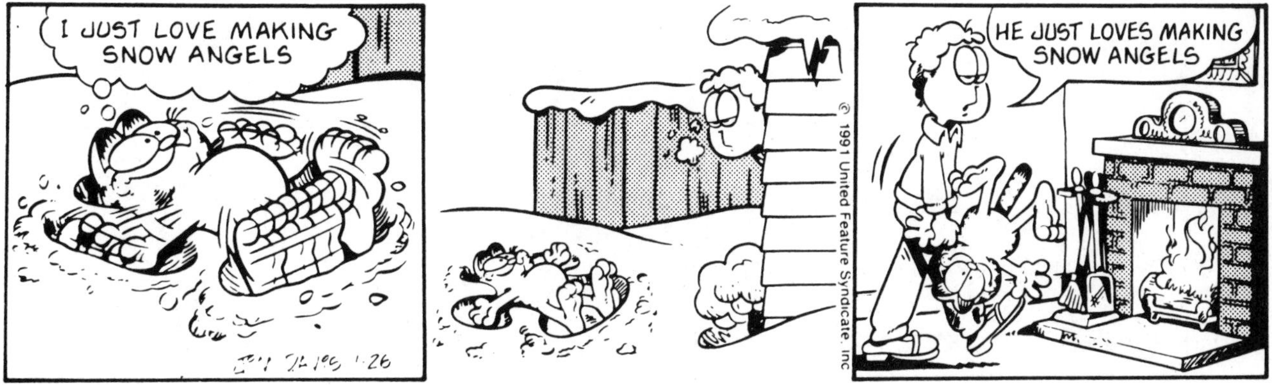
I JUST LOVE MAKING SNOW ANGELS
© 1991 United Feature Syndicate, Inc.
HE JUST LOVES MAKING SNOW ANGELS

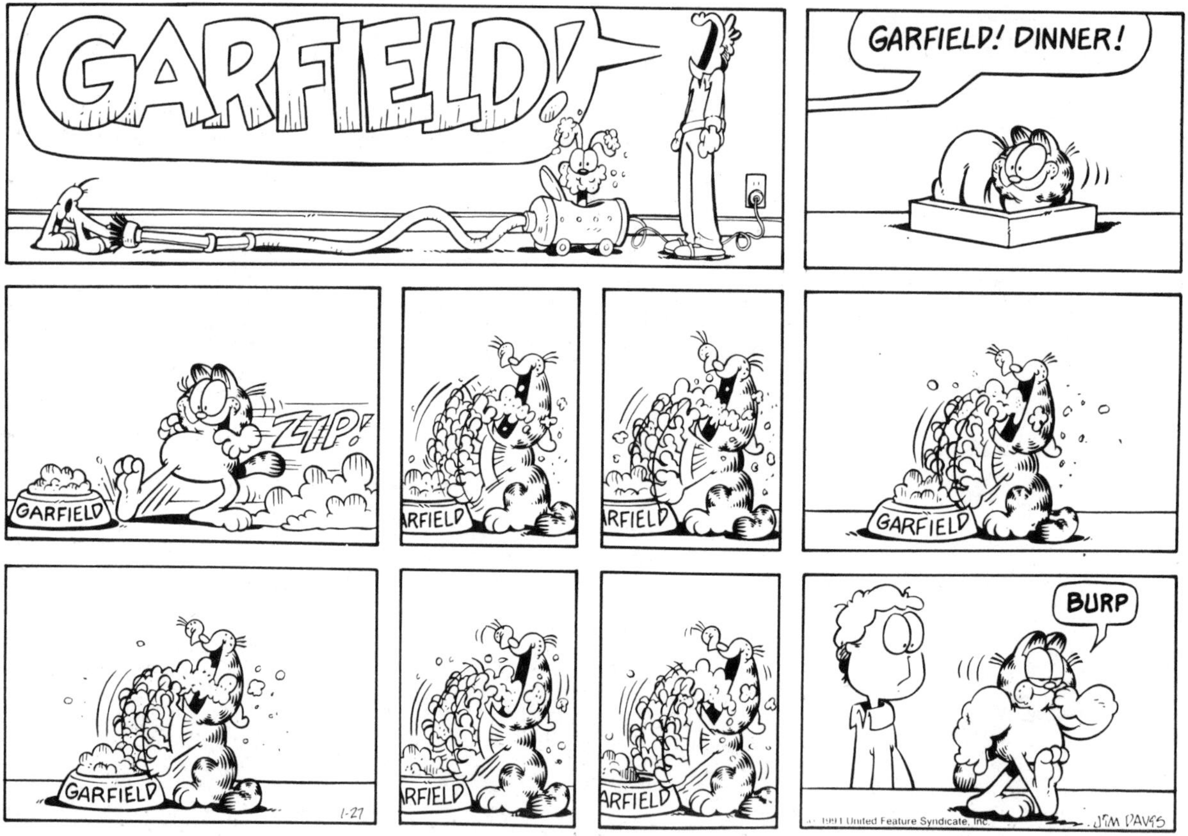
GARFIELD!
GARFIELD! DINNER!
ZIP!
GARFIELD
BURP
1-27
© 1991 United Feature Syndicate, Inc.
JIM DAVIS

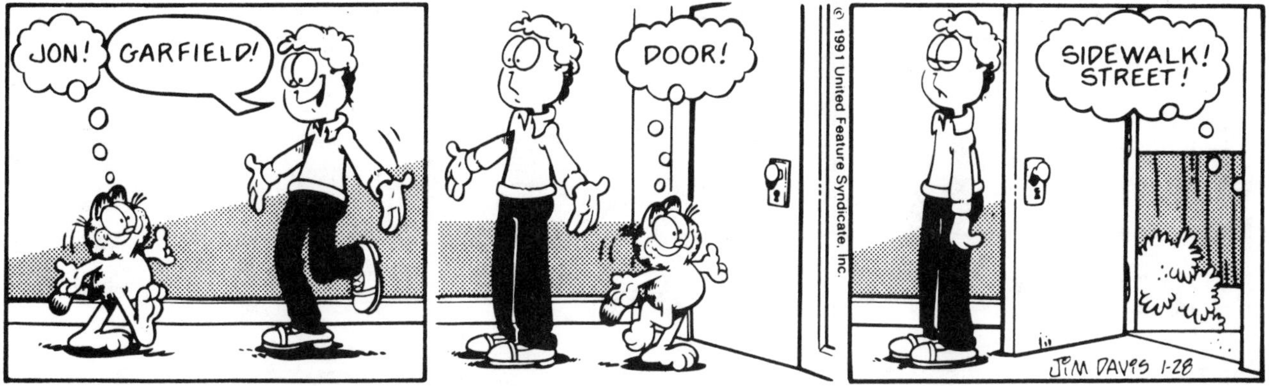
JON!
GARFIELD!
DOOR!
SIDEWALK! STREET!
© 1991 United Feature Syndicate, Inc.
JIM DAVIS 1-28

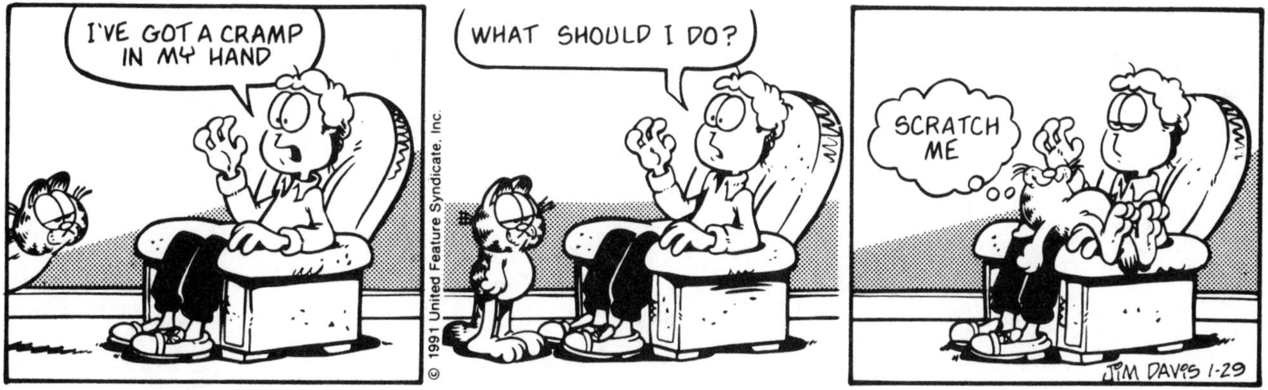
I'VE GOT A CRAMP IN MY HAND
WHAT SHOULD I DO?
SCRATCH ME
© 1991 United Feature Syndicate, Inc.
JIM DAVIS 1-29

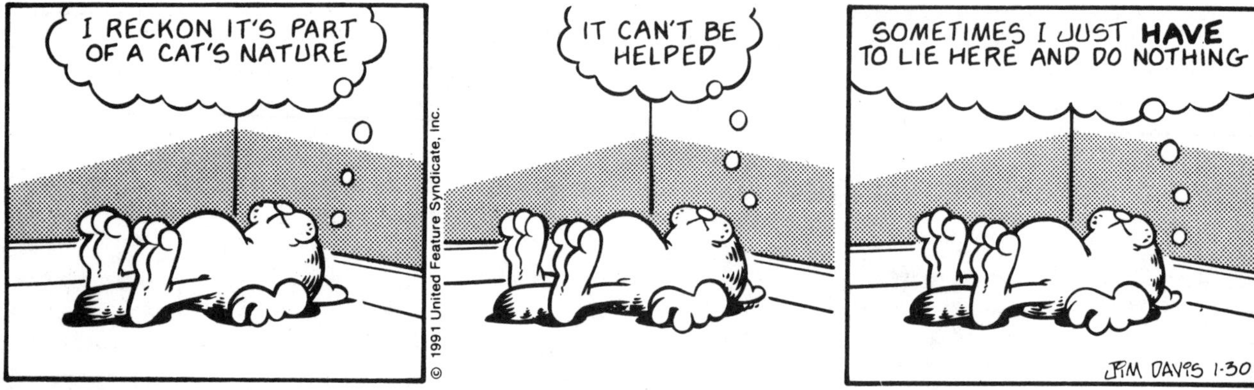
I RECKON IT'S PART OF A CAT'S NATURE
© 1991 United Feature Syndicate, Inc.
IT CAN'T BE HELPED
SOMETIMES I JUST **HAVE** TO LIE HERE AND DO NOTHING
JIM DAVIS 1-30

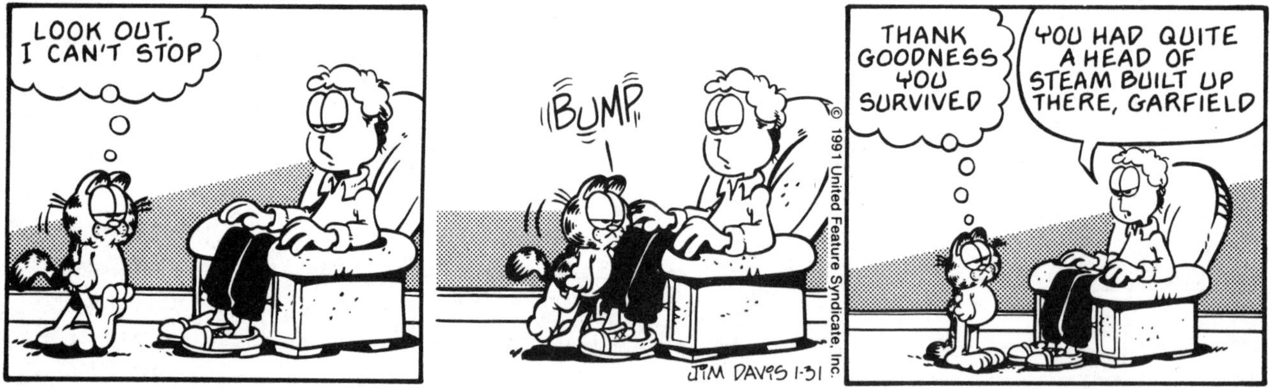
LOOK OUT. I CAN'T STOP
BUMP
© 1991 United Feature Syndicate, Inc.
JIM DAVIS 1-31
THANK GOODNESS YOU SURVIVED
YOU HAD QUITE A HEAD OF STEAM BUILT UP THERE, GARFIELD

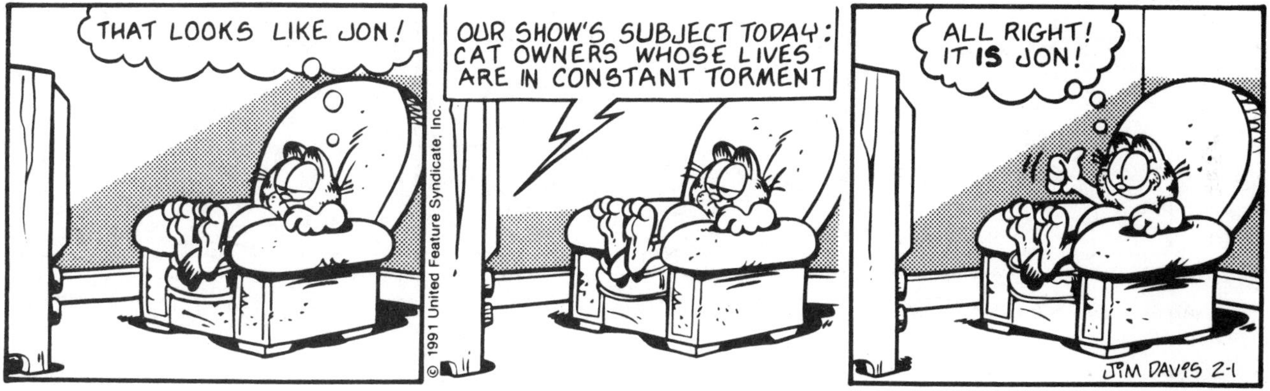
THAT LOOKS LIKE JON!
OUR SHOW'S SUBJECT TODAY: CAT OWNERS WHOSE LIVES ARE IN CONSTANT TORMENT
ALL RIGHT! IT **IS** JON!
© 1991 United Feature Syndicate, Inc.
JIM DAVIS 2-1

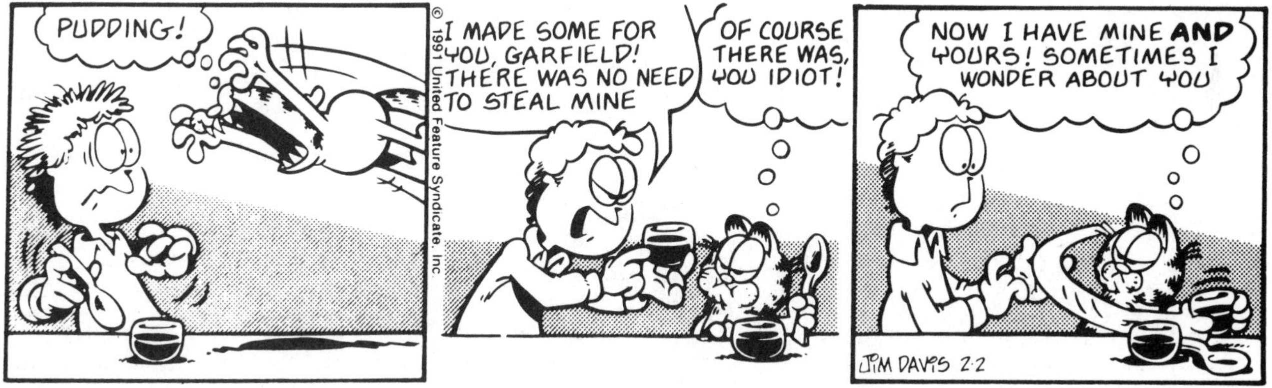
PUDDING!
I MADE SOME FOR YOU, GARFIELD! THERE WAS NO NEED TO STEAL MINE
OF COURSE THERE WAS, YOU IDIOT!
NOW I HAVE MINE **AND** YOURS! SOMETIMES I WONDER ABOUT YOU
© 1991 United Feature Syndicate, Inc.
JIM DAVIS 2-2

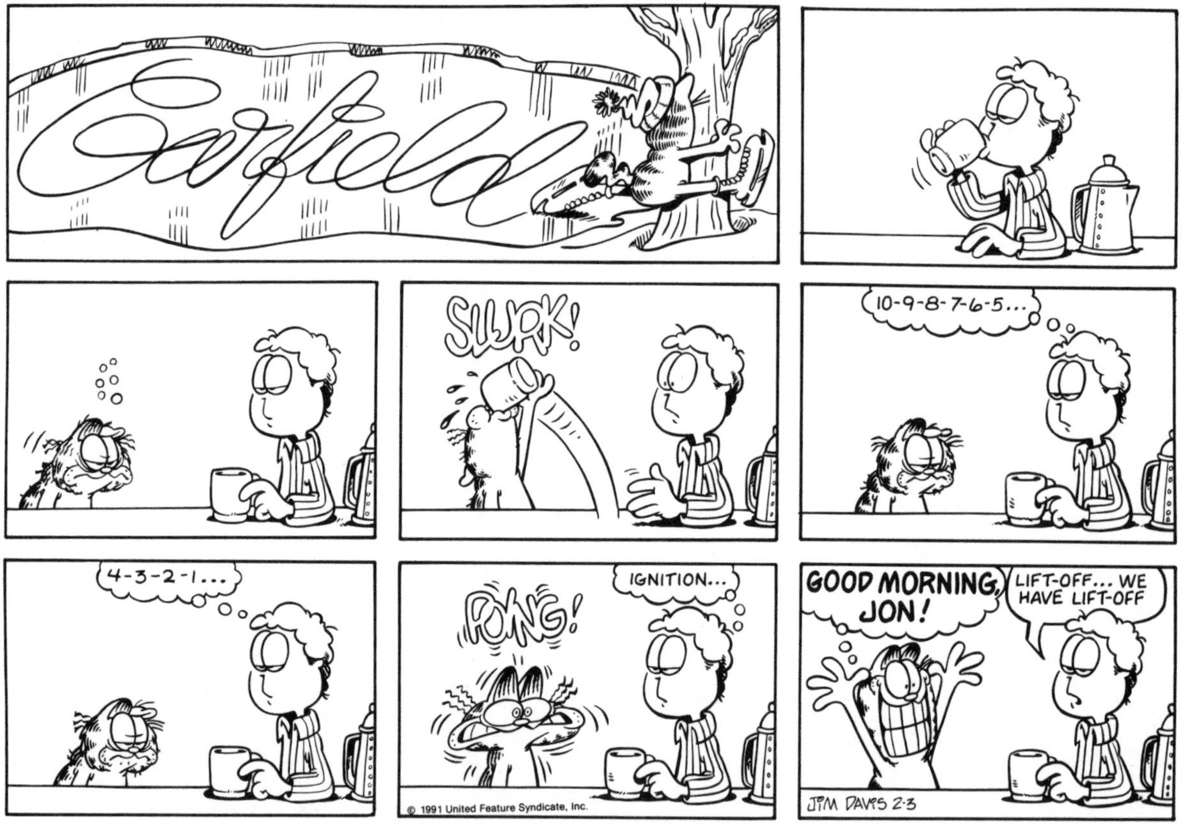
Garfield
SLURK!
10-9-8-7-6-5...
4-3-2-1...
PONG!
IGNITION...
GOOD MORNING, JON!
LIFT-OFF... WE HAVE LIFT-OFF
© 1991 United Feature Syndicate, Inc.
JIM DAVIS 2-3

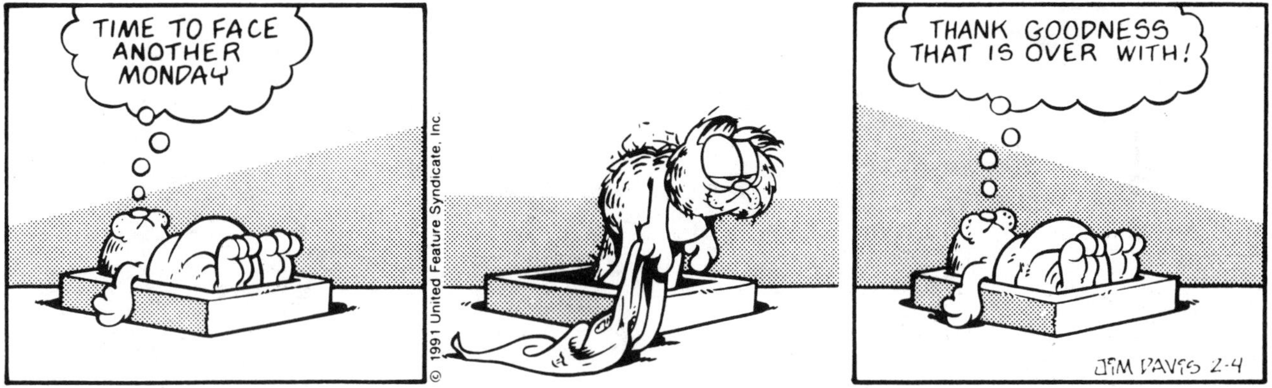
TIME TO FACE ANOTHER MONDAY
THANK GOODNESS THAT IS OVER WITH!
© 1991 United Feature Syndicate, Inc.
JIM DAVIS 2-4

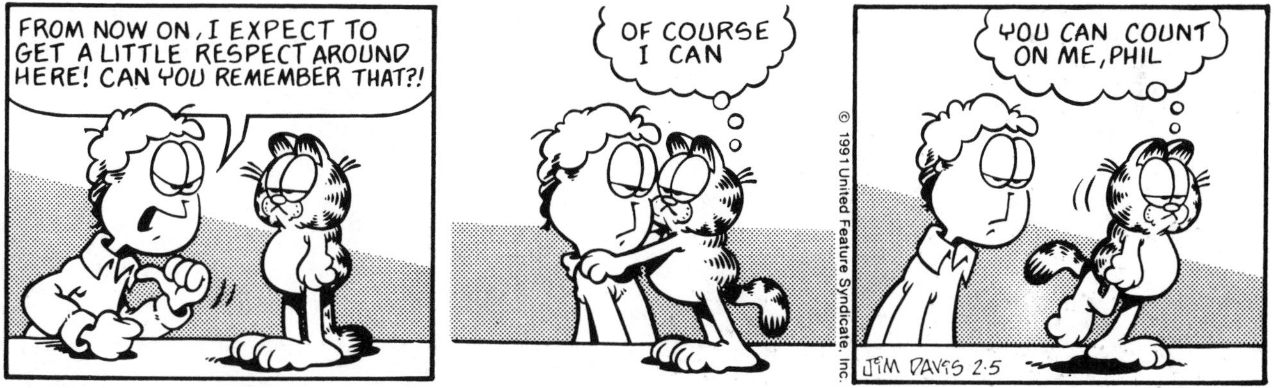
FROM NOW ON, I EXPECT TO GET A LITTLE RESPECT AROUND HERE! CAN YOU REMEMBER THAT?!
OF COURSE I CAN
YOU CAN COUNT ON ME, PHIL
© 1991 United Feature Syndicate, Inc.
JIM DAVIS 2-5

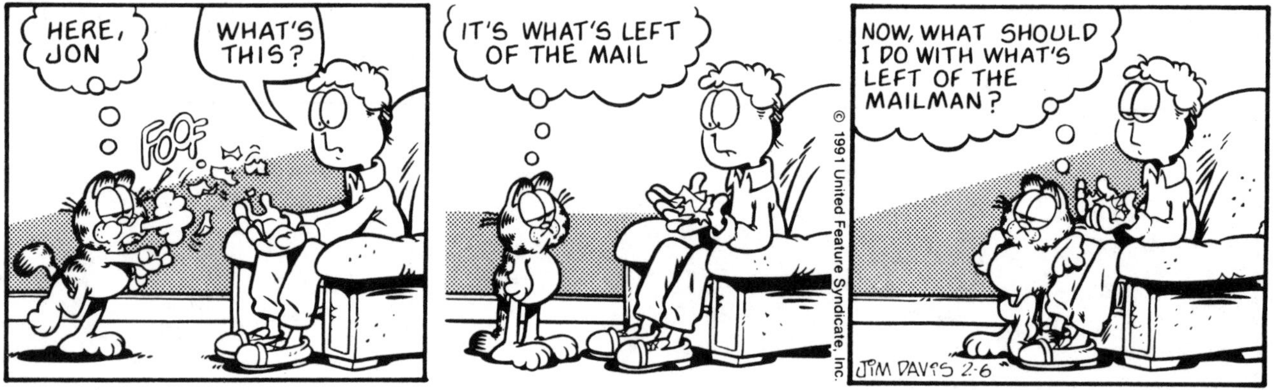
HERE, JON
WHAT'S THIS?
FOOF
IT'S WHAT'S LEFT OF THE MAIL
NOW, WHAT SHOULD I DO WITH WHAT'S LEFT OF THE MAILMAN?
© 1991 United Feature Syndicate, Inc.
JIM DAVIS 2-6

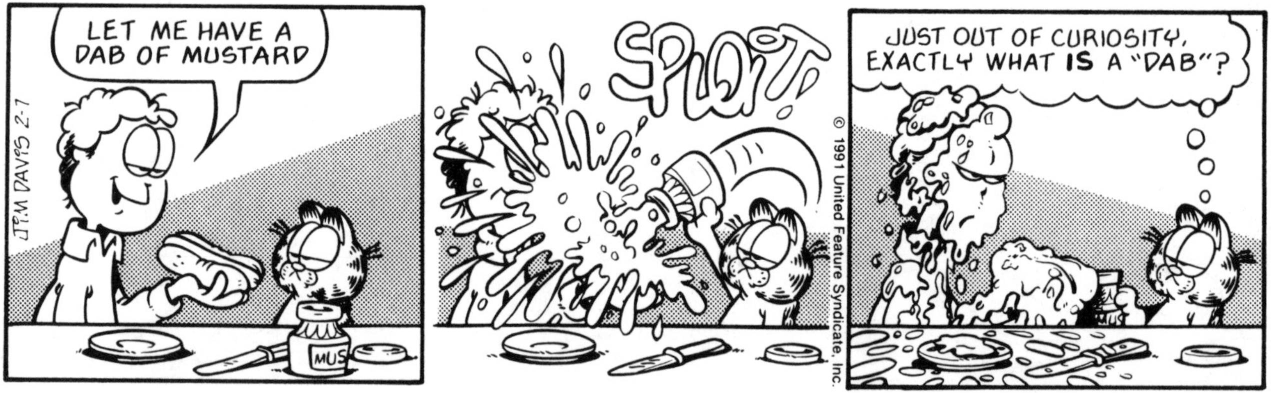
LET ME HAVE A DAB OF MUSTARD
JIM DAVIS 2-7
MUS
SPLOOT
JUST OUT OF CURIOSITY, EXACTLY WHAT **IS** A "DAB"?
© 1991 United Feature Syndicate, Inc.

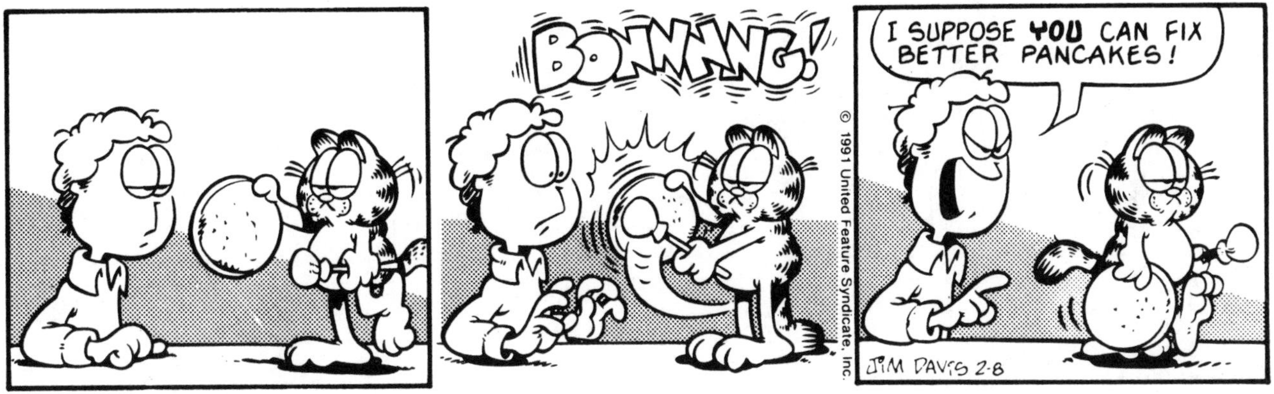
BONNNNG!
I SUPPOSE YOU CAN FIX BETTER PANCAKES!
© 1991 United Feature Syndicate, Inc.
JIM DAVIS 2-8

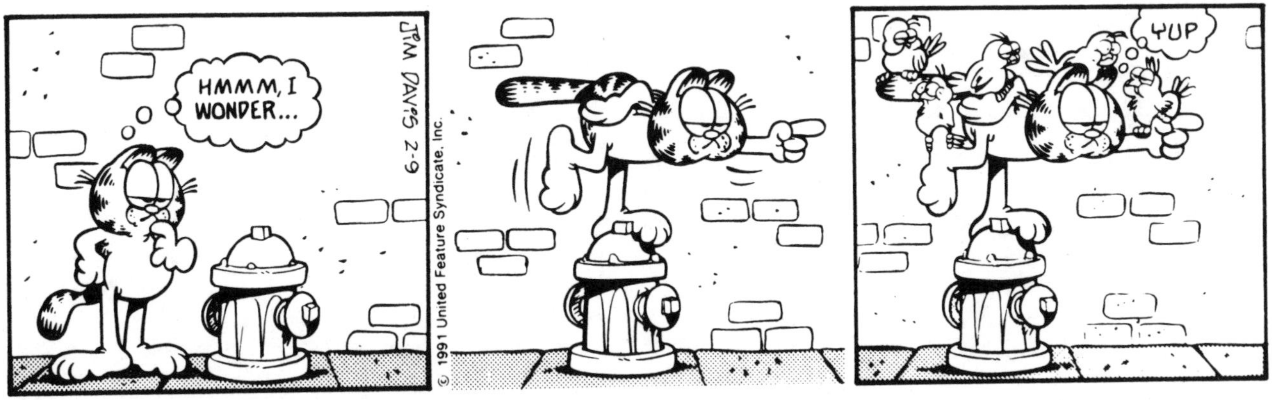
HMMM, I WONDER...
JIM DAVIS 2-9
© 1991 United Feature Syndicate, Inc.
YUP

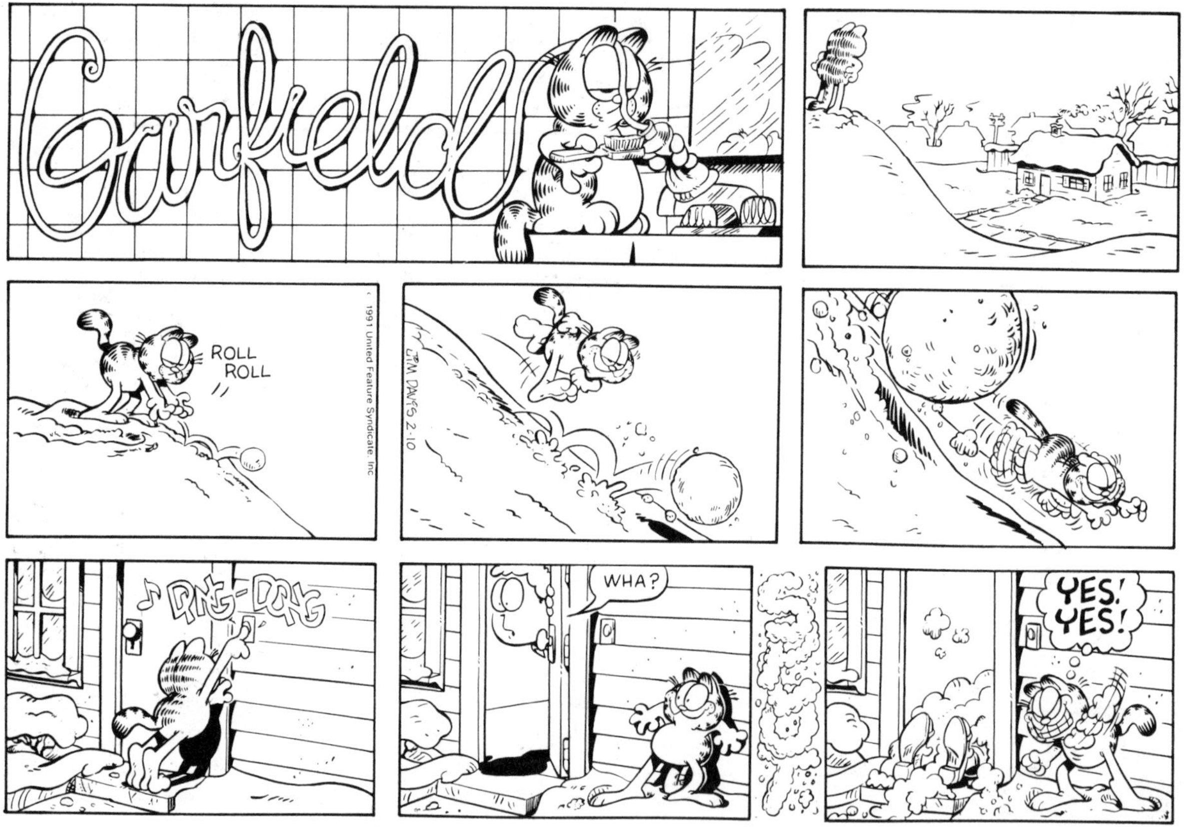
Garfield
ROLL
ROLL
© 1991 United Feature Syndicate, Inc
JIM DAVIS 2-10
DING-DONG
WHA?
YES!
YES!

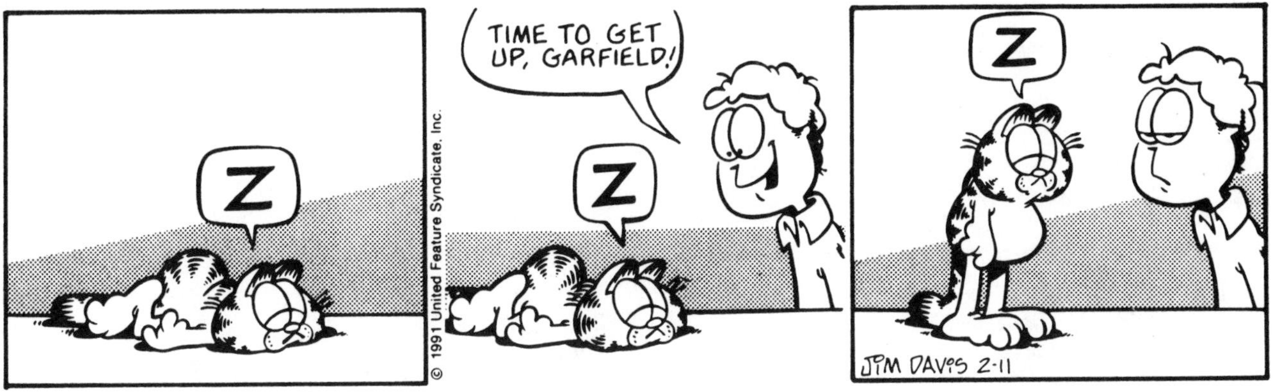
Z
TIME TO GET UP, GARFIELD!
Z
Z
JIM DAVIS 2-11
© 1991 United Feature Syndicate, Inc.

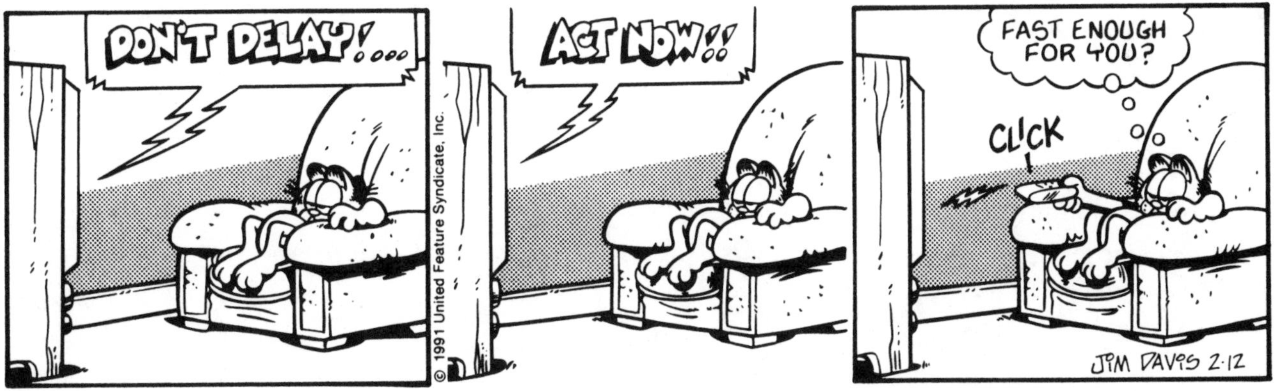
DON'T DELAY!...
ACT NOW!!
CLICK
FAST ENOUGH FOR YOU?
JIM DAVIS 2-12
© 1991 United Feature Syndicate, Inc.

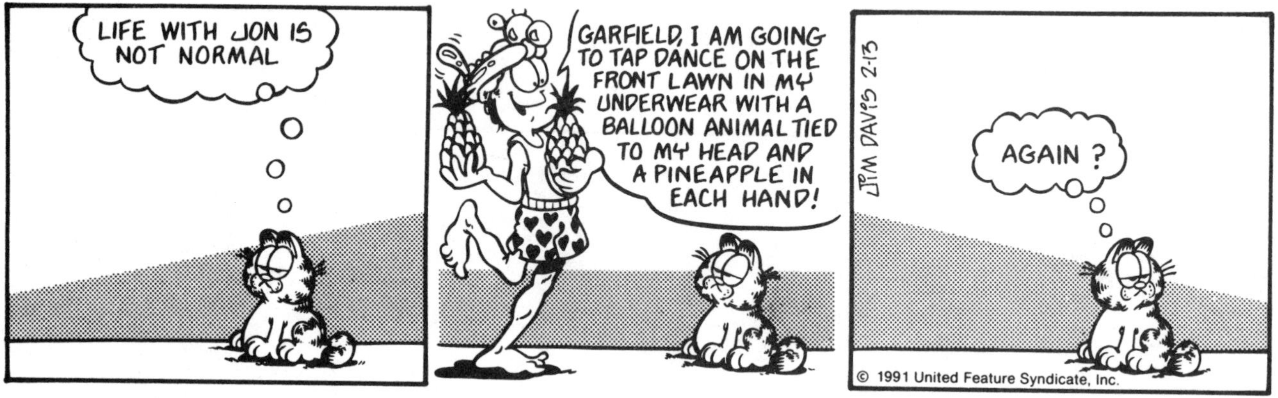
LIFE WITH JON IS NOT NORMAL
GARFIELD, I AM GOING TO TAP DANCE ON THE FRONT LAWN IN MY UNDERWEAR WITH A BALLOON ANIMAL TIED TO MY HEAD AND A PINEAPPLE IN EACH HAND!
AGAIN ?
JIM DAVIS 2-13
© 1991 United Feature Syndicate, Inc.

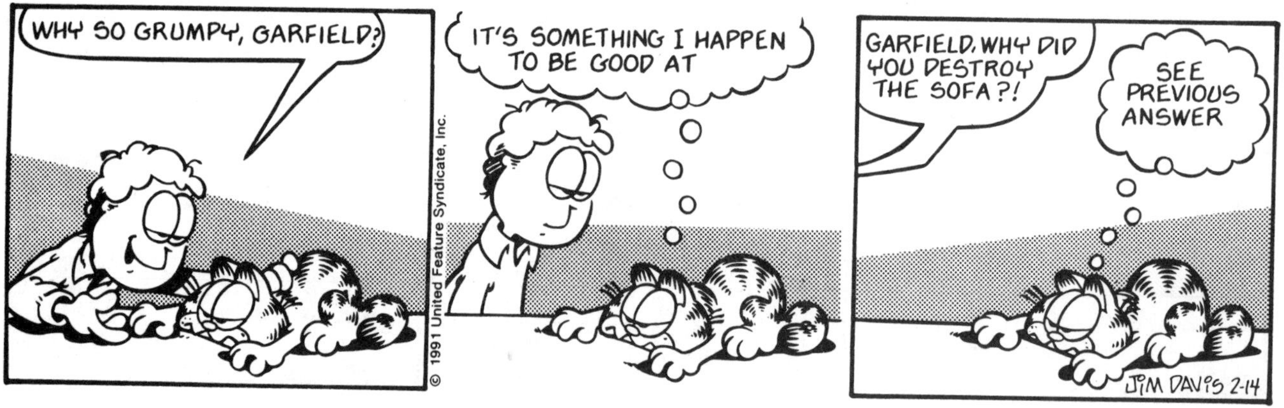
WHY SO GRUMPY, GARFIELD?
© 1991 United Feature Syndicate, Inc.
IT'S SOMETHING I HAPPEN TO BE GOOD AT
GARFIELD, WHY DID YOU DESTROY THE SOFA?!
SEE PREVIOUS ANSWER
JIM DAVIS 2-14

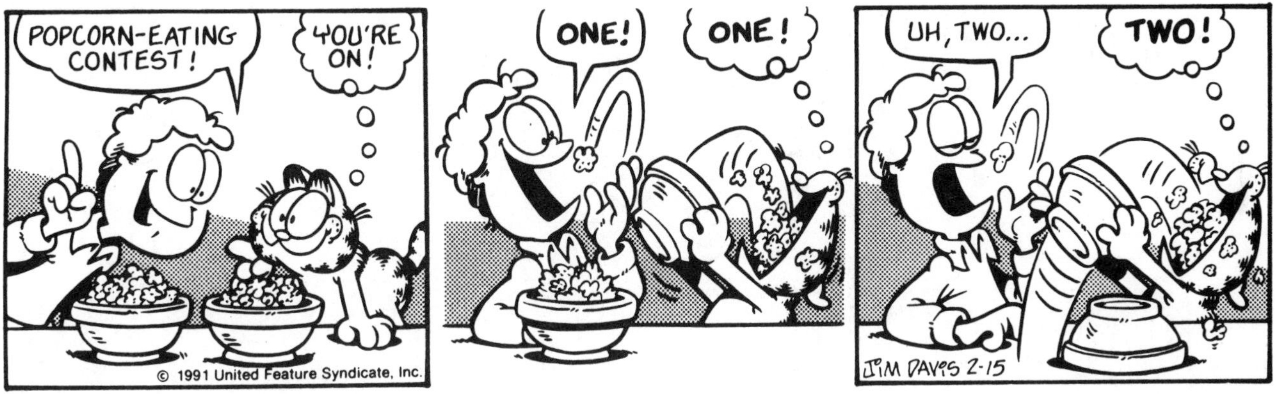
POPCORN-EATING CONTEST!
YOU'RE ON!
© 1991 United Feature Syndicate, Inc.
ONE!
ONE!
UH, TWO...
TWO!
JIM DAVIS 2-15

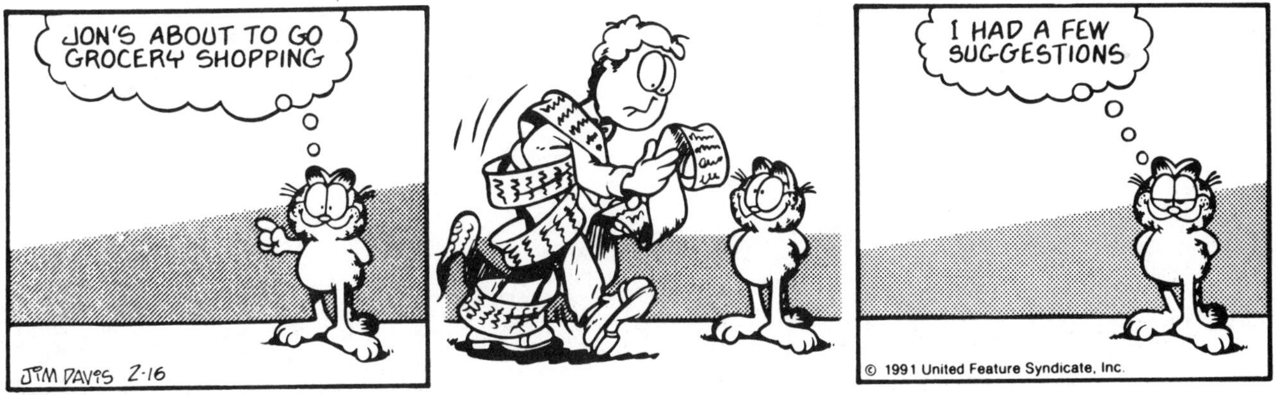
JON'S ABOUT TO GO GROCERY SHOPPING
JIM DAVIS 2-16
I HAD A FEW SUGGESTIONS
© 1991 United Feature Syndicate, Inc.

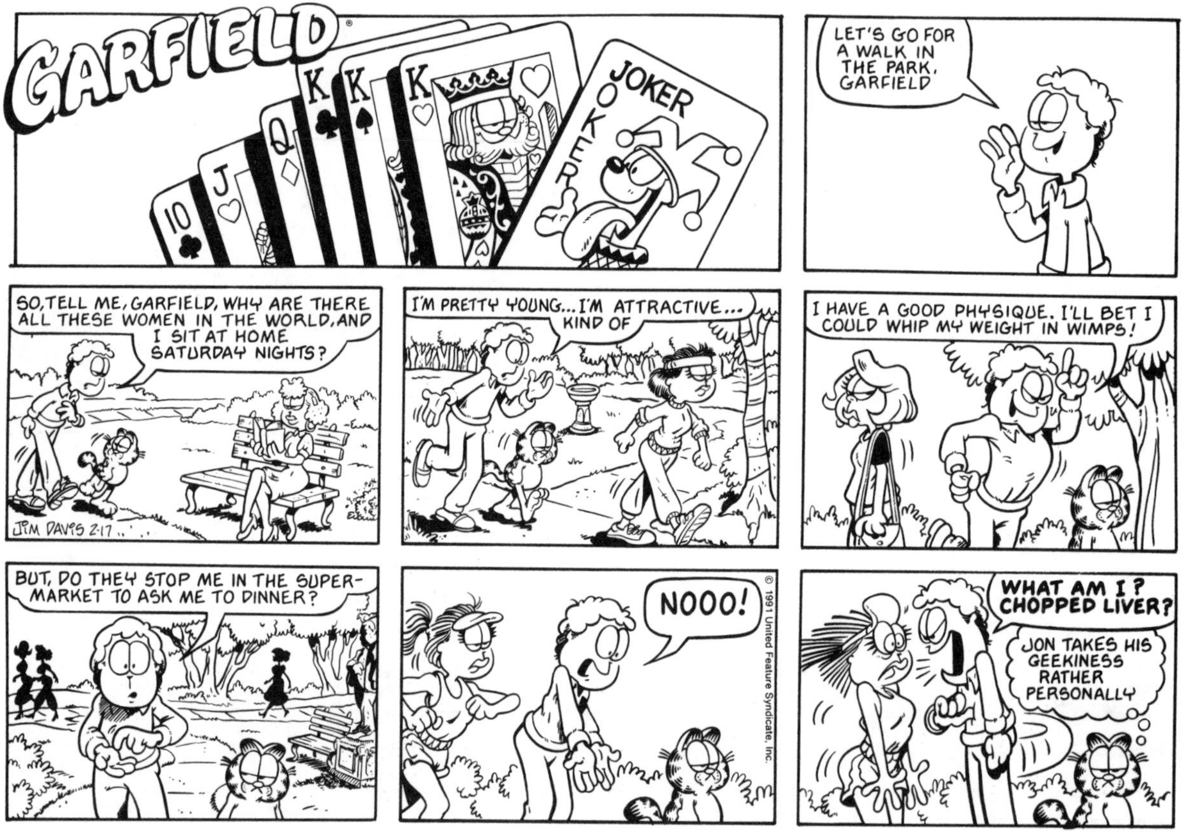
GARFIELD®
10
J
Q
K
K
K
JOKER
JOKER
LET'S GO FOR A WALK IN THE PARK, GARFIELD
SO, TELL ME, GARFIELD, WHY ARE THERE ALL THESE WOMEN IN THE WORLD, AND I SIT AT HOME SATURDAY NIGHTS?
JIM DAVIS 2-17
I'M PRETTY YOUNG... I'M ATTRACTIVE... KIND OF
I HAVE A GOOD PHYSIQUE. I'LL BET I COULD WHIP MY WEIGHT IN WIMPS!
BUT, DO THEY STOP ME IN THE SUPER-MARKET TO ASK ME TO DINNER?
NOOO!
© 1991 United Feature Syndicate, Inc.
WHAT AM I? CHOPPED LIVER?
JON TAKES HIS GEEKINESS RATHER PERSONALLY

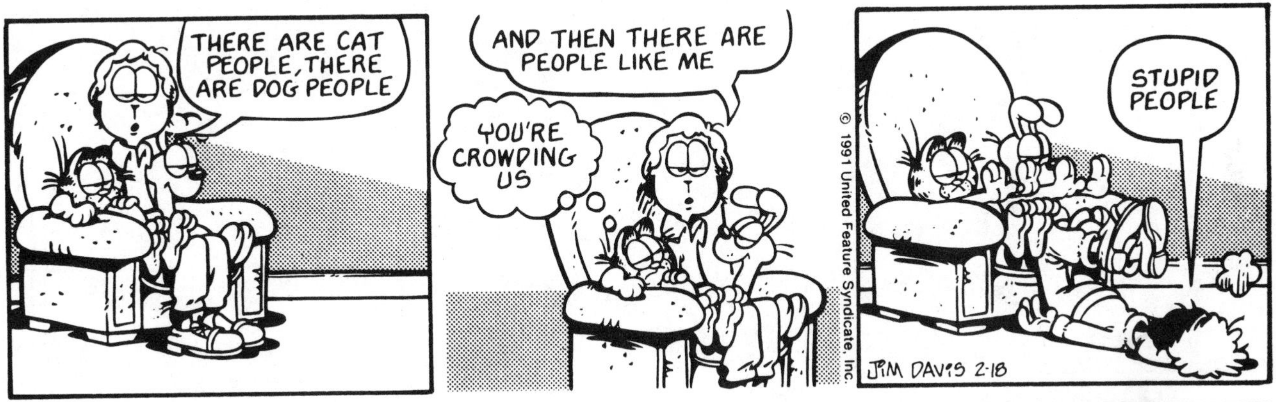
THERE ARE CAT PEOPLE, THERE ARE DOG PEOPLE
AND THEN THERE ARE PEOPLE LIKE ME
YOU'RE CROWDING US
STUPID PEOPLE
© 1991 United Feature Syndicate, Inc.
JIM DAVIS 2-18

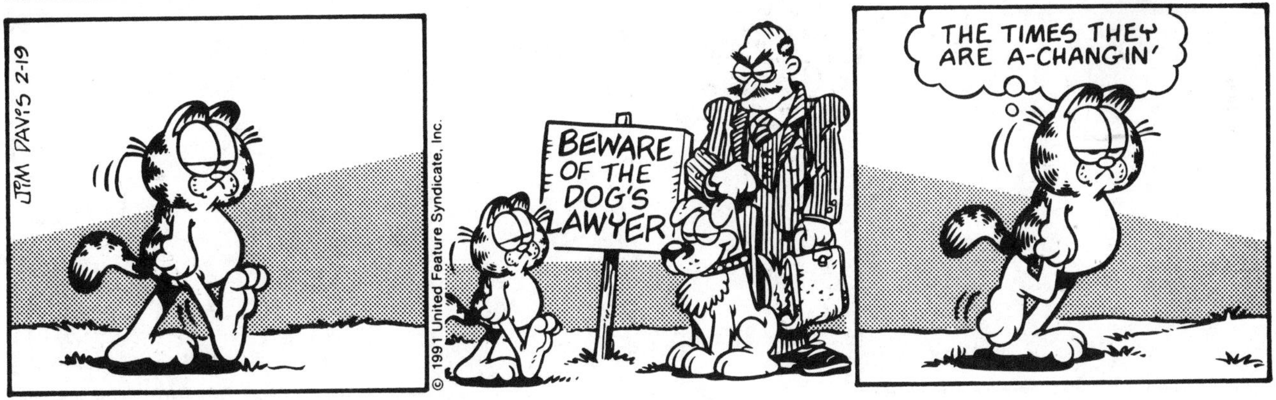
JIM DAVIS 2-19
© 1991 United Feature Syndicate, Inc.
BEWARE OF THE DOG'S LAWYER
THE TIMES THEY ARE A-CHANGIN'

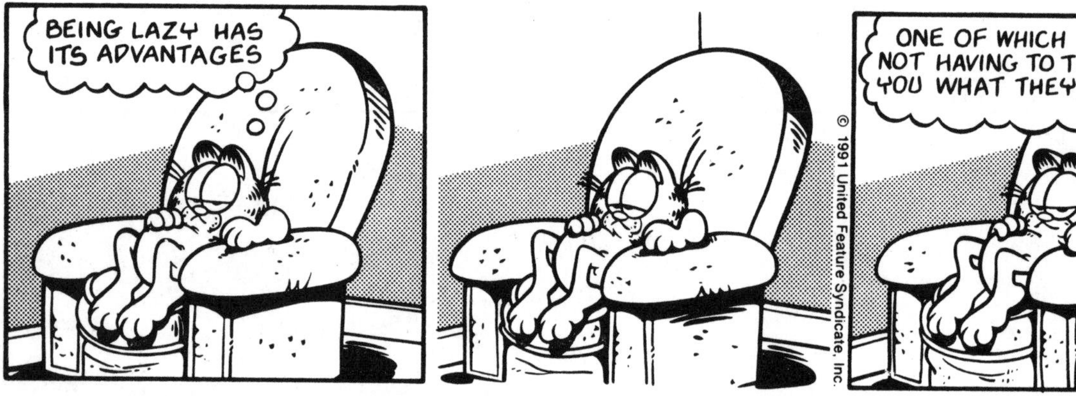
BEING LAZY HAS ITS ADVANTAGES
ONE OF WHICH IS NOT HAVING TO TELL YOU WHAT THEY ARE
JIM DAVIS
© 1991 United Feature Syndicate, Inc.
2-20

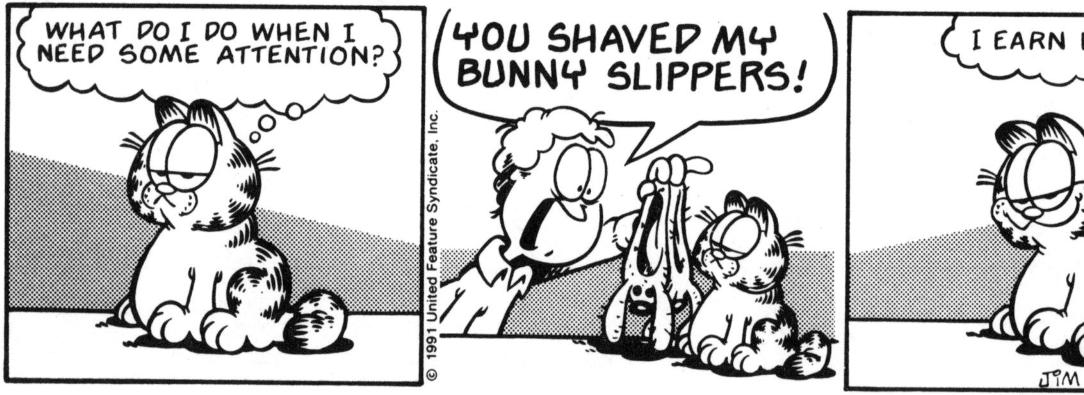
WHAT DO I DO WHEN I NEED SOME ATTENTION?
YOU SHAVED MY BUNNY SLIPPERS!
I EARN IT
© 1991 United Feature Syndicate, Inc.
JIM DAVIS 2-21

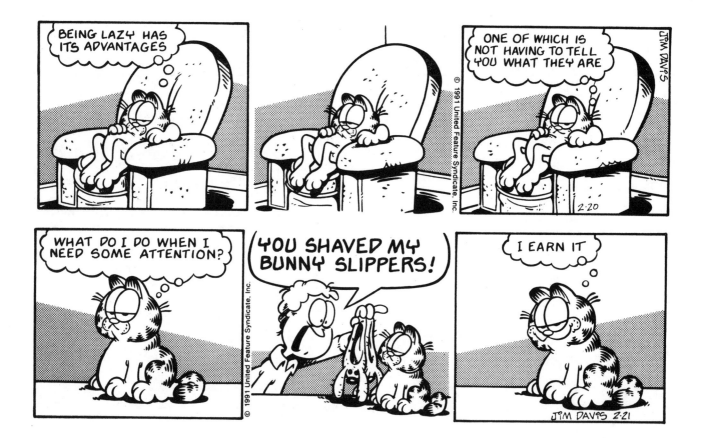

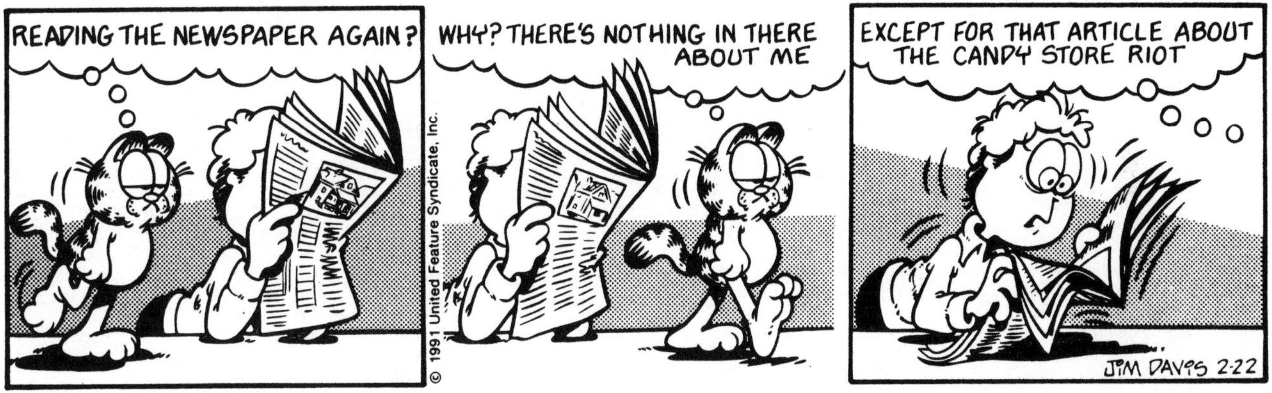
READING THE NEWSPAPER AGAIN?
WHY? THERE'S NOTHING IN THERE ABOUT ME
EXCEPT FOR THAT ARTICLE ABOUT THE CANDY STORE RIOT
© 1991 United Feature Syndicate, Inc.
JIM DAVIS 2-22

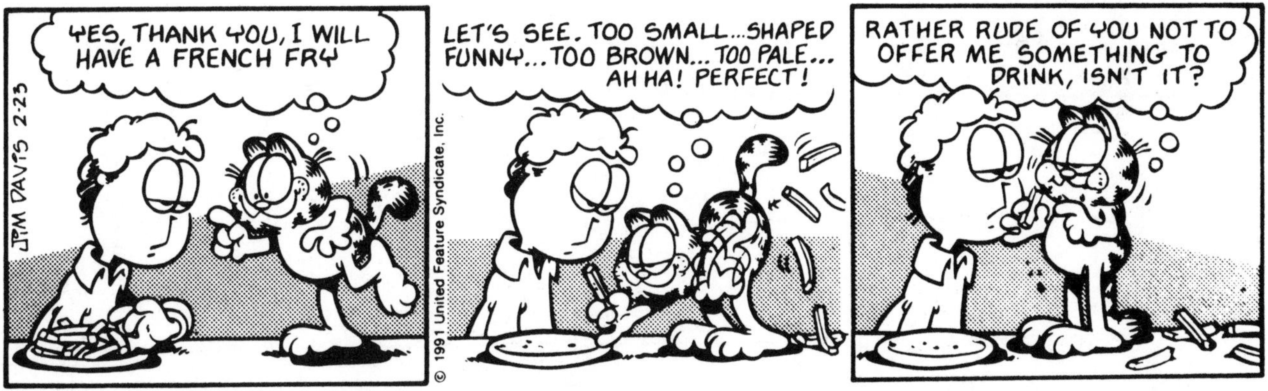
YES, THANK YOU, I WILL HAVE A FRENCH FRY
LET'S SEE. TOO SMALL...SHAPED FUNNY...TOO BROWN...TOO PALE... AH HA! PERFECT!
RATHER RUDE OF YOU NOT TO OFFER ME SOMETHING TO DRINK, ISN'T IT?
© 1991 United Feature Syndicate, Inc.
JIM DAVIS 2-23

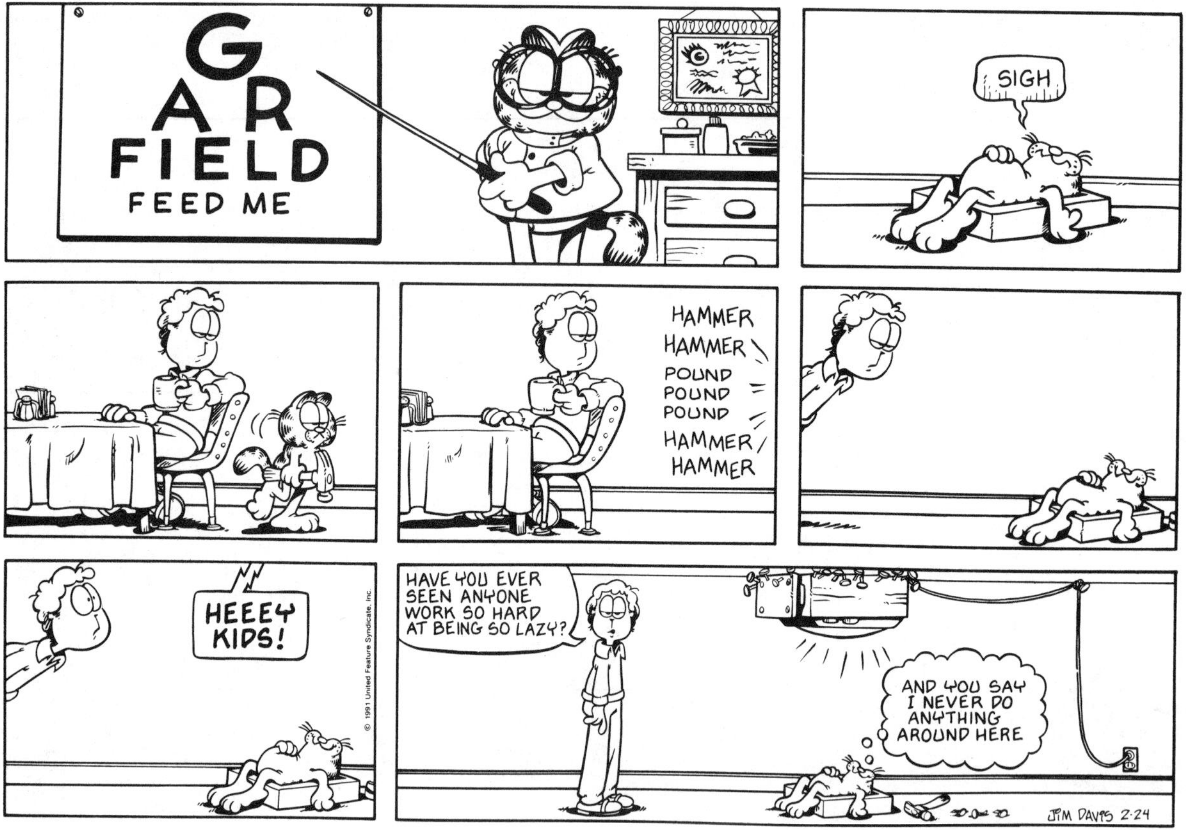
GAR
FIELD
FEED ME
SIGH
HAMMER
HAMMER
POUND
POUND
POUND
HAMMER
HAMMER
HEEEY KIDS!
© 1991 United Feature Syndicate, Inc.
HAVE YOU EVER SEEN ANYONE WORK SO HARD AT BEING SO LAZY?
AND YOU SAY I NEVER DO ANYTHING AROUND HERE
JIM DAVIS 2·24

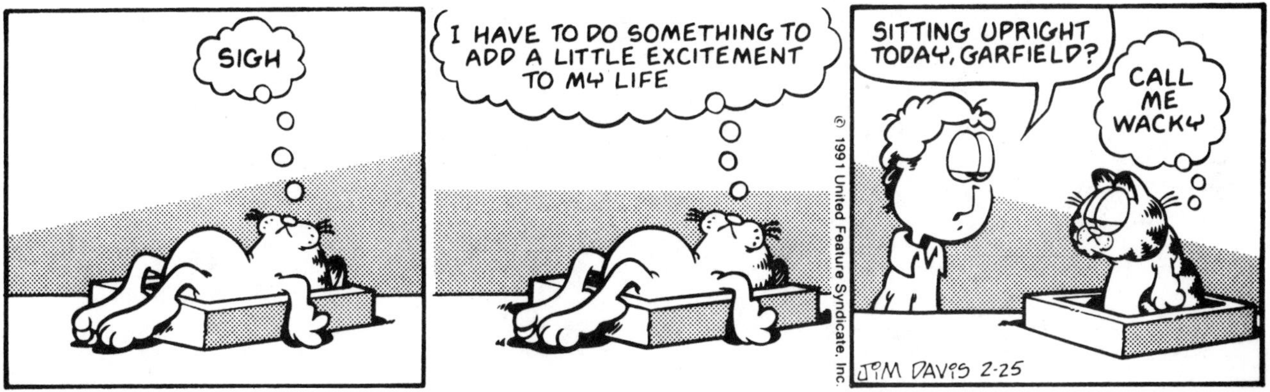
SIGH
I HAVE TO DO SOMETHING TO ADD A LITTLE EXCITEMENT TO MY LIFE
SITTING UPRIGHT TODAY, GARFIELD?
CALL ME WACKY
JIM DAVIS 2-25
© 1991 United Feature Syndicate, Inc.

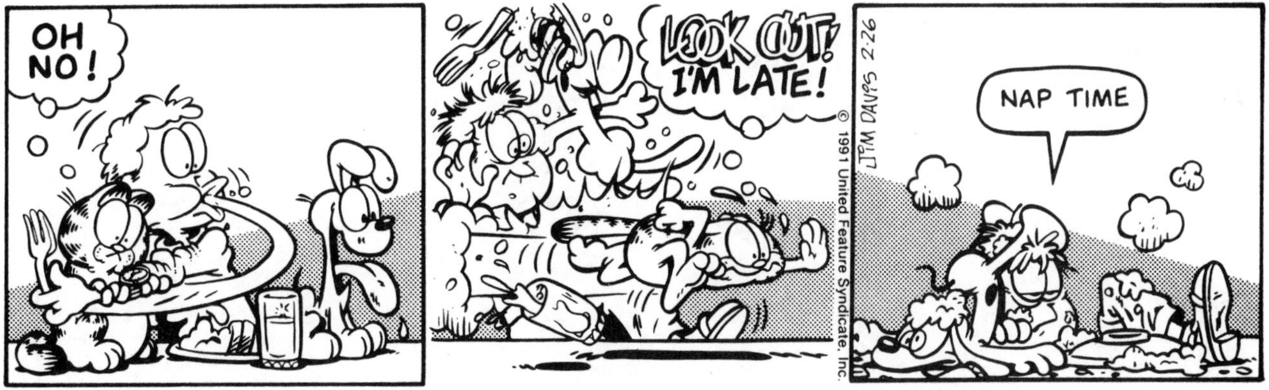
OH NO!
LOOK OUT! I'M LATE!
JIM DAVIS 2-26
© 1991 United Feature Syndicate, Inc.
NAP TIME

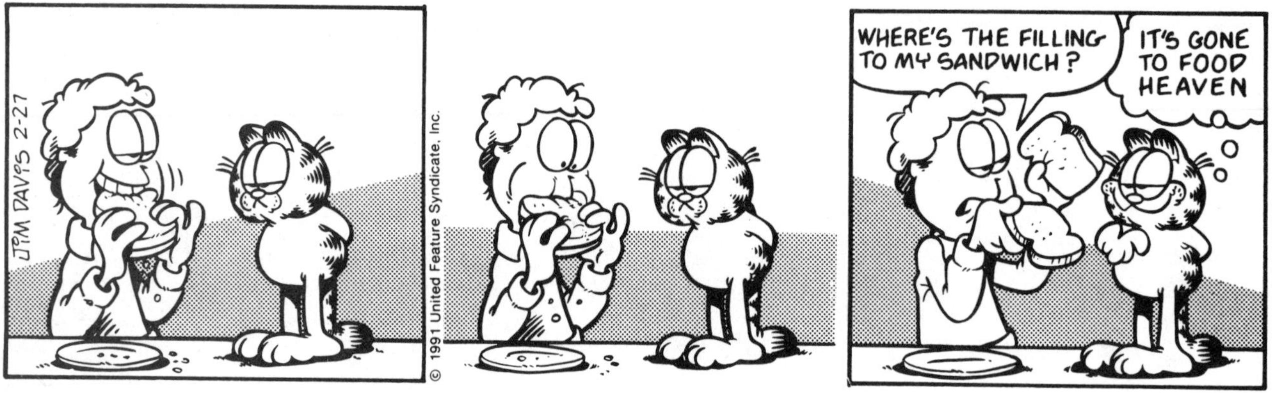
JIM DAVIS 2-27
© 1991 United Feature Syndicate, Inc.
WHERE'S THE FILLING TO MY SANDWICH?
IT'S GONE TO FOOD HEAVEN

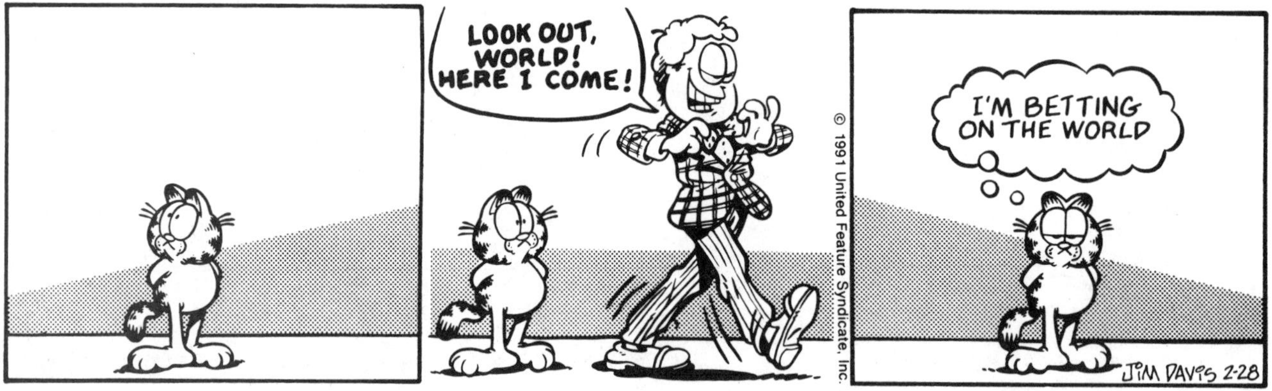
LOOK OUT, WORLD! HERE I COME!
© 1991 United Feature Syndicate, Inc.
I'M BETTING ON THE WORLD
JIM DAVIS 2-28

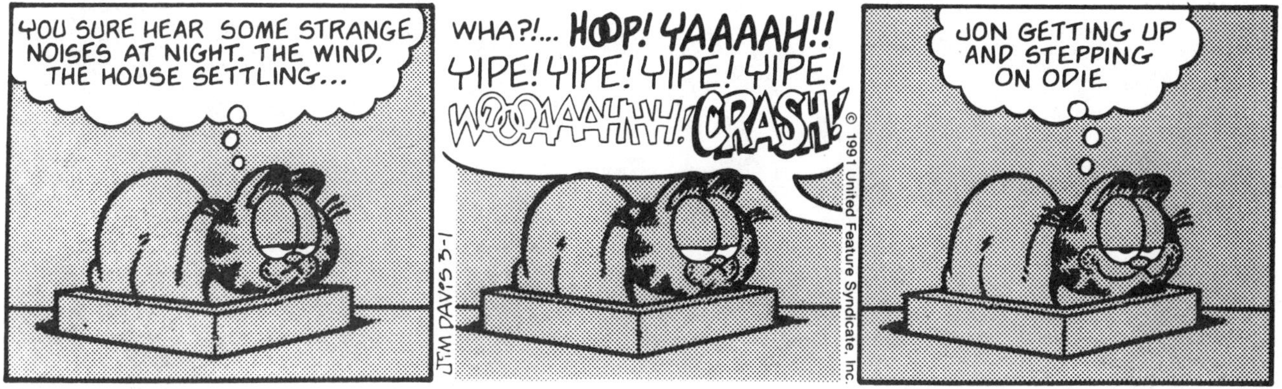
YOU SURE HEAR SOME STRANGE NOISES AT NIGHT. THE WIND, THE HOUSE SETTLING...
WHA?!... HOOP! YAAAAH!! YIPE! YIPE! YIPE! YIPE! WOOAAAHHH! CRASH!
JON GETTING UP AND STEPPING ON ODIE
JIM DAVIS 3-1
© 1991 United Feature Syndicate, Inc.

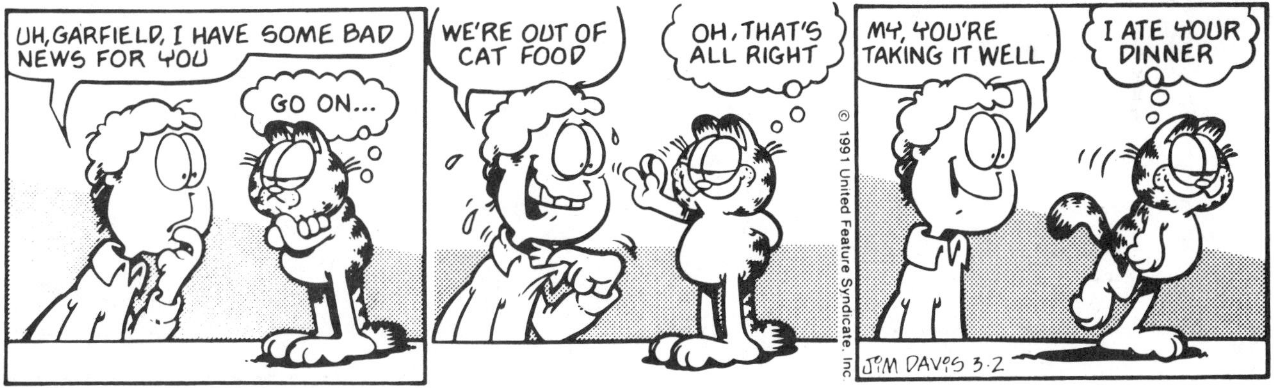
UH, GARFIELD, I HAVE SOME BAD NEWS FOR YOU
GO ON...
WE'RE OUT OF CAT FOOD
OH, THAT'S ALL RIGHT
MY, YOU'RE TAKING IT WELL
I ATE YOUR DINNER
JIM DAVIS 3-2
© 1991 United Feature Syndicate, Inc.

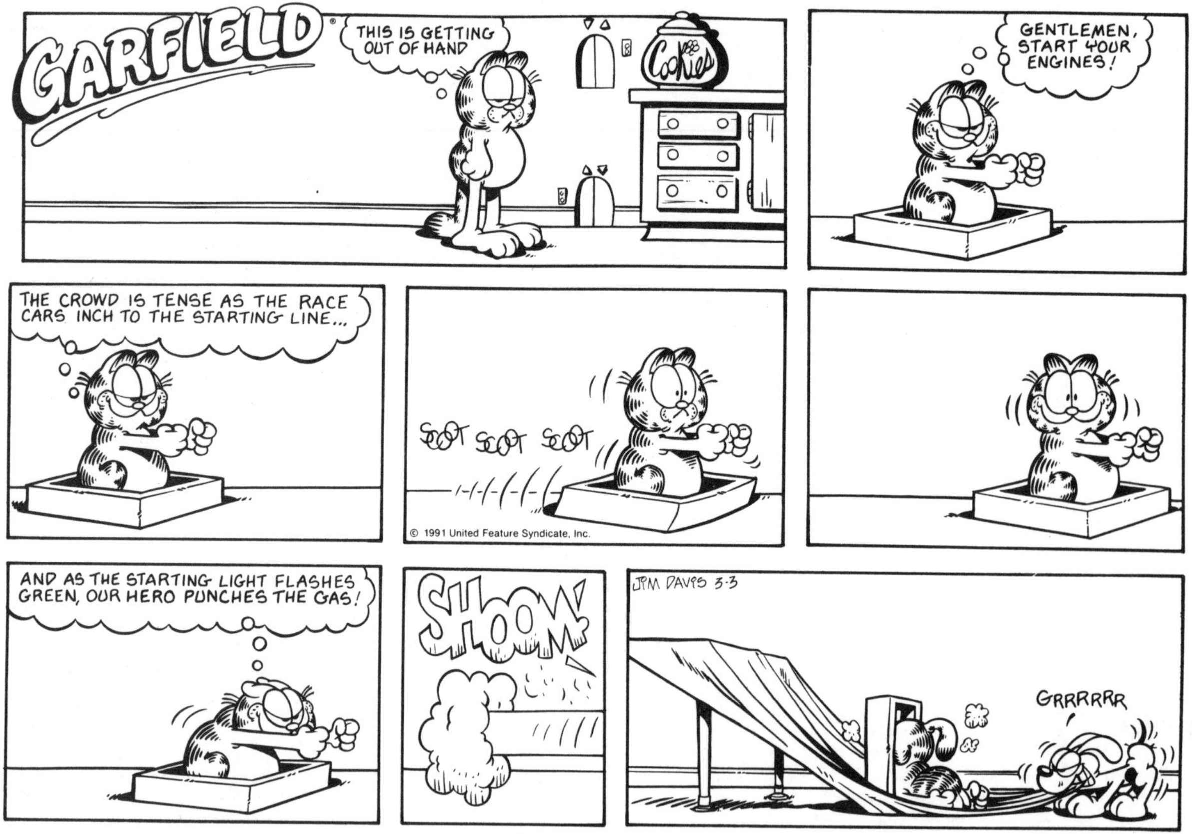

GARFIELD
THIS IS GETTING OUT OF HAND
COOKIES
GENTLEMEN, START YOUR ENGINES!
THE CROWD IS TENSE AS THE RACE CARS INCH TO THE STARTING LINE...
SCOOT SCOOT SCOOT
© 1991 United Feature Syndicate, Inc.
AND AS THE STARTING LIGHT FLASHES GREEN, OUR HERO PUNCHES THE GAS!
SHOOM!
JIM DAVIS 3-3
GRRRRRR

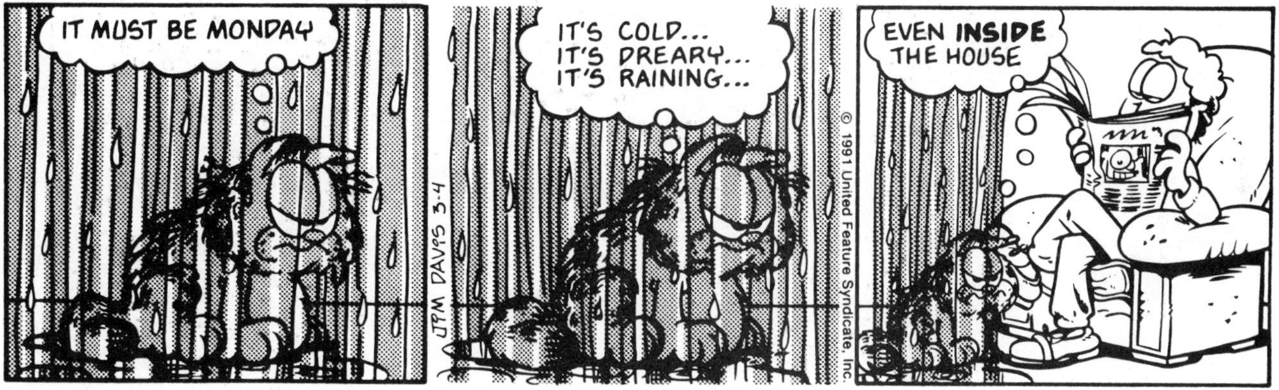
IT MUST BE MONDAY
JIM DAVIS 3-4
IT'S COLD...
IT'S DREARY...
IT'S RAINING...
© 1991 United Feature Syndicate, Inc.
EVEN **INSIDE** THE HOUSE

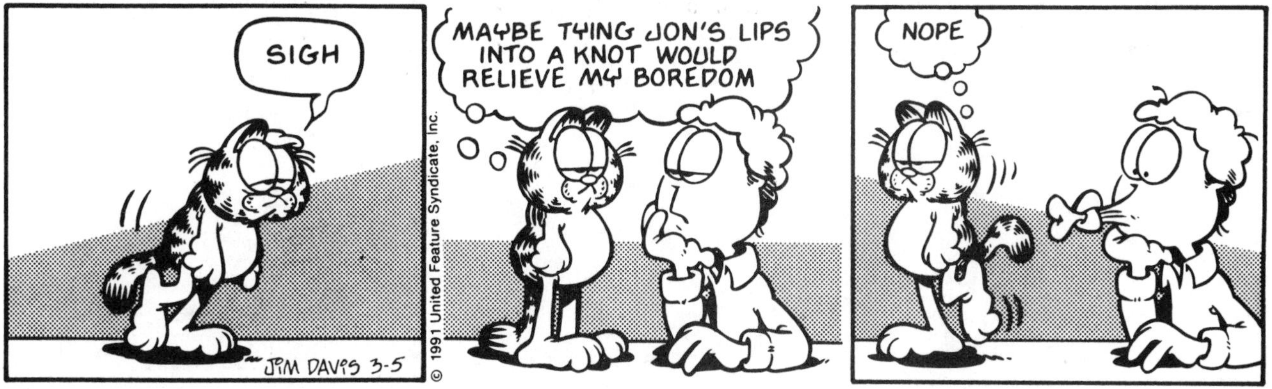
SIGH
JIM DAVIS 3-5
© 1991 United Feature Syndicate, Inc.
MAYBE TYING JON'S LIPS INTO A KNOT WOULD RELIEVE MY BOREDOM
NOPE

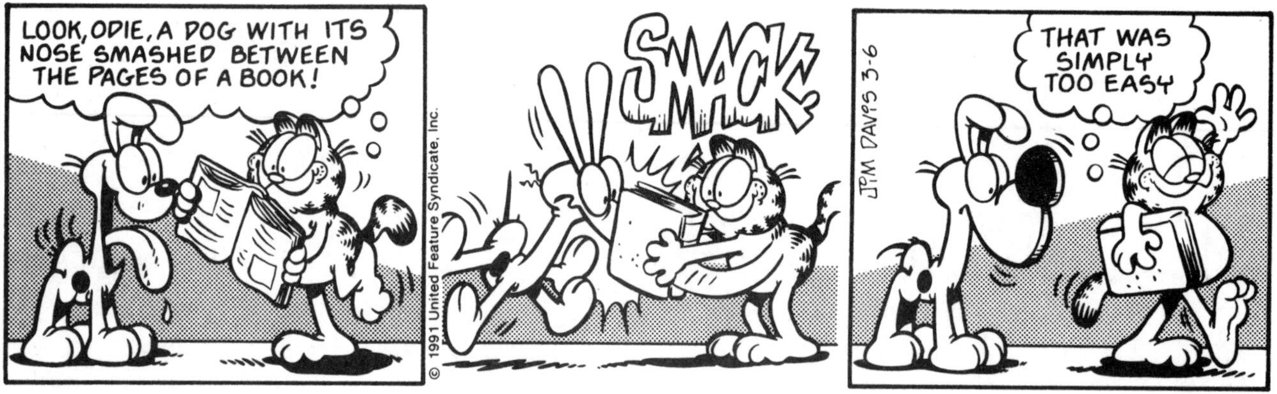
LOOK, ODIE, A DOG WITH ITS NOSE SMASHED BETWEEN THE PAGES OF A BOOK!
SMACK!
THAT WAS SIMPLY TOO EASY
JIM DAVIS 3-6
© 1991 United Feature Syndicate, Inc.

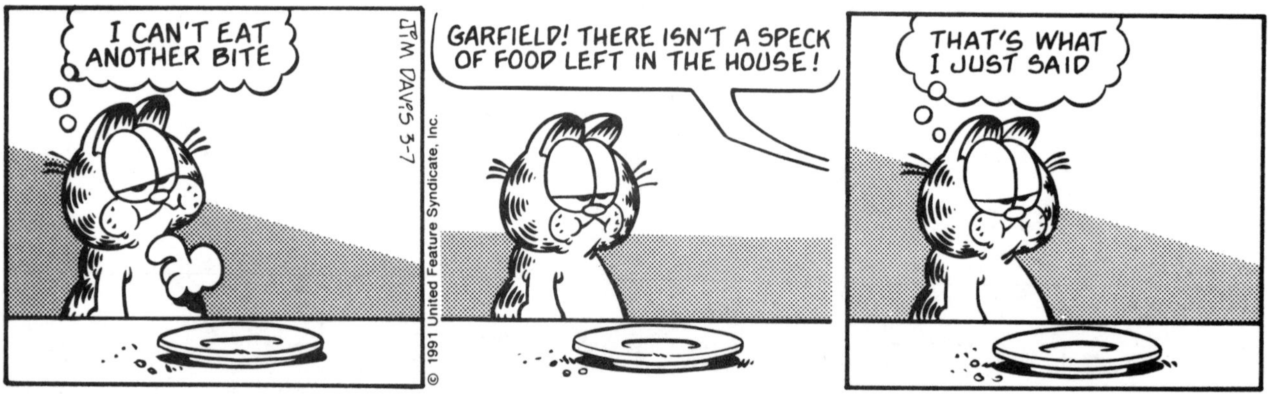
I CAN'T EAT ANOTHER BITE
GARFIELD! THERE ISN'T A SPECK OF FOOD LEFT IN THE HOUSE!
THAT'S WHAT I JUST SAID
JIM DAVIS 3-7
© 1991 United Feature Syndicate, Inc.

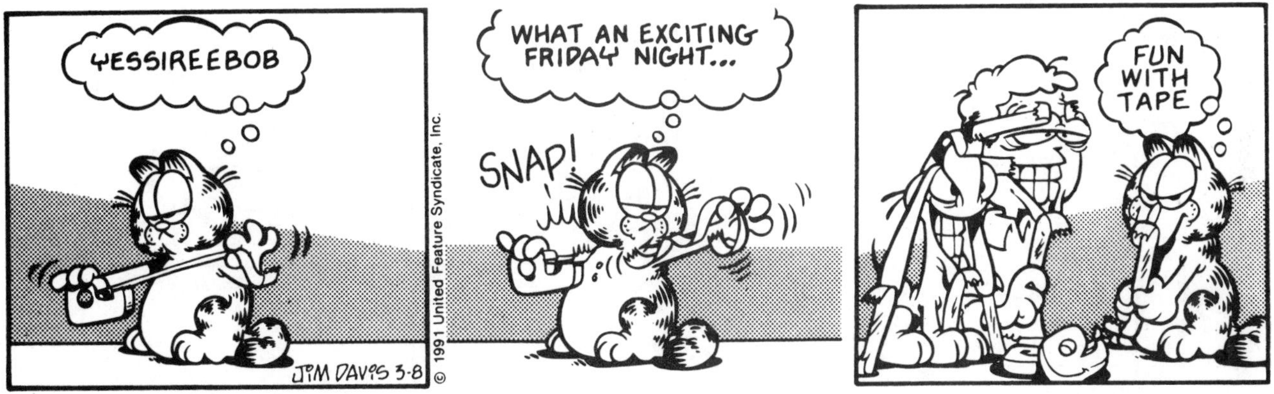
YESSIREEBOB
JIM DAVIS 3-8
© 1991 United Feature Syndicate, Inc.
WHAT AN EXCITING FRIDAY NIGHT...
SNAP!
FUN WITH TAPE

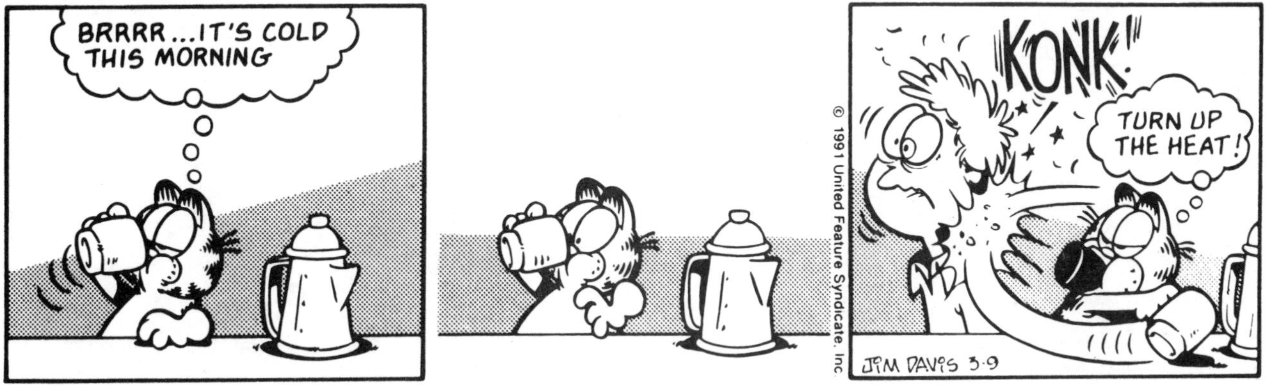
BRRRR...IT'S COLD THIS MORNING
© 1991 United Feature Syndicate, Inc.
KONK!
TURN UP THE HEAT!
JIM DAVIS 3-9

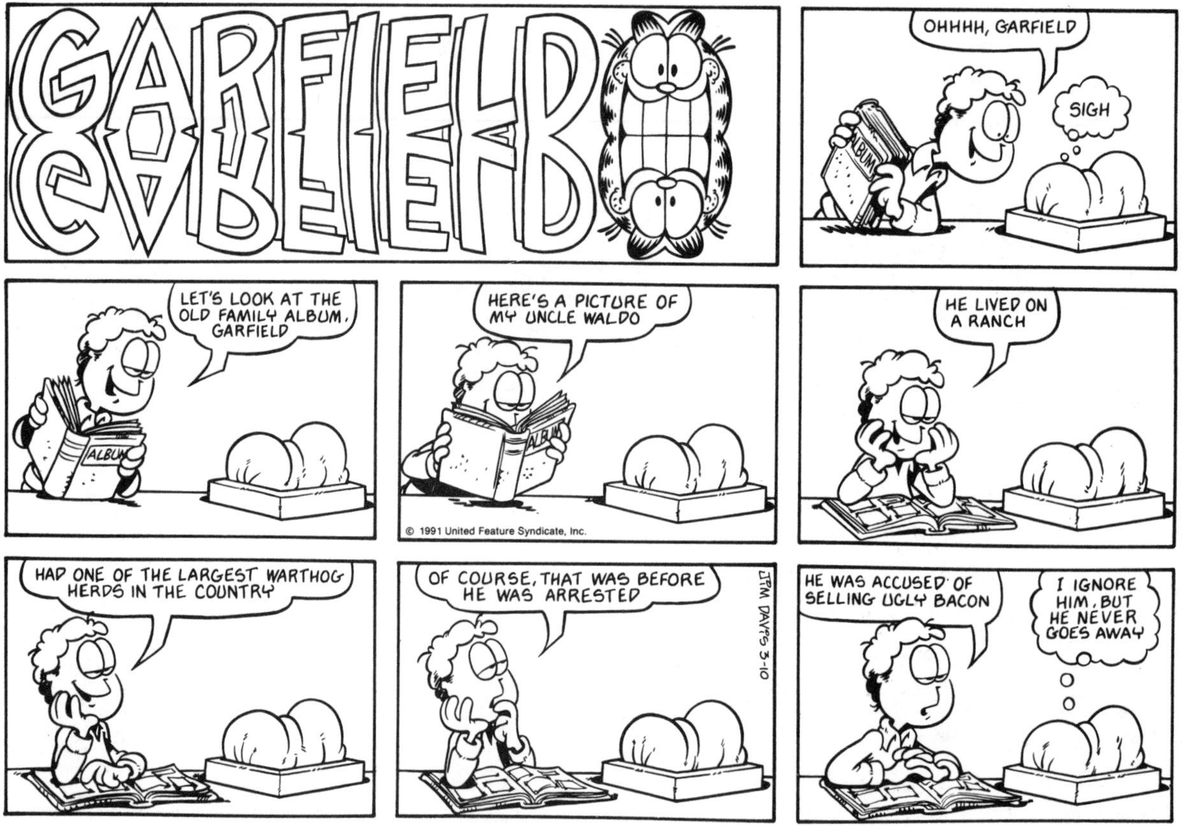
GARFIELD
OHHHH, GARFIELD
ALBUM
SIGH
LET'S LOOK AT THE OLD FAMILY ALBUM, GARFIELD
HERE'S A PICTURE OF MY UNCLE WALDO
© 1991 United Feature Syndicate, Inc.
HE LIVED ON A RANCH
HAD ONE OF THE LARGEST WARTHOG HERDS IN THE COUNTRY
OF COURSE, THAT WAS BEFORE HE WAS ARRESTED
JIM DAVIS 3-10
HE WAS ACCUSED OF SELLING UGLY BACON
I IGNORE HIM, BUT HE NEVER GOES AWAY

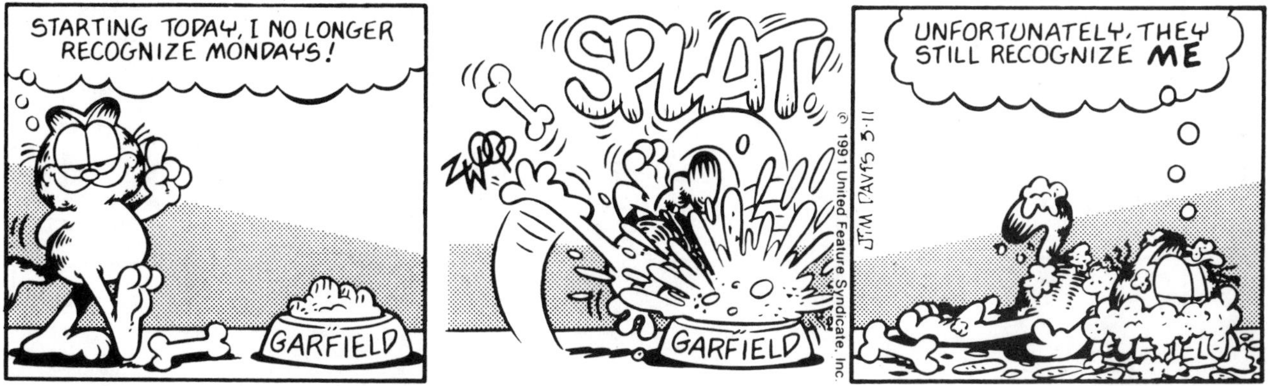
STARTING TODAY, I NO LONGER RECOGNIZE MONDAYS!
GARFIELD
ZWOOP
SPLAT!
GARFIELD
© 1991 United Feature Syndicate, Inc.
JIM DAVIS 3-11
UNFORTUNATELY, THEY STILL RECOGNIZE ME

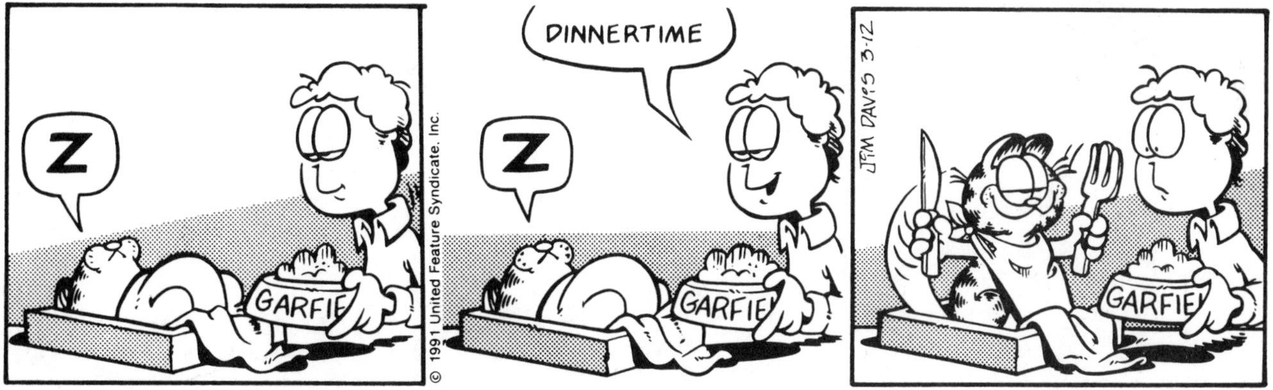
Z
GARFIE
© 1991 United Feature Syndicate, Inc.
DINNERTIME
Z
GARFIE
JIM DAVIS 3-12
GARFIE

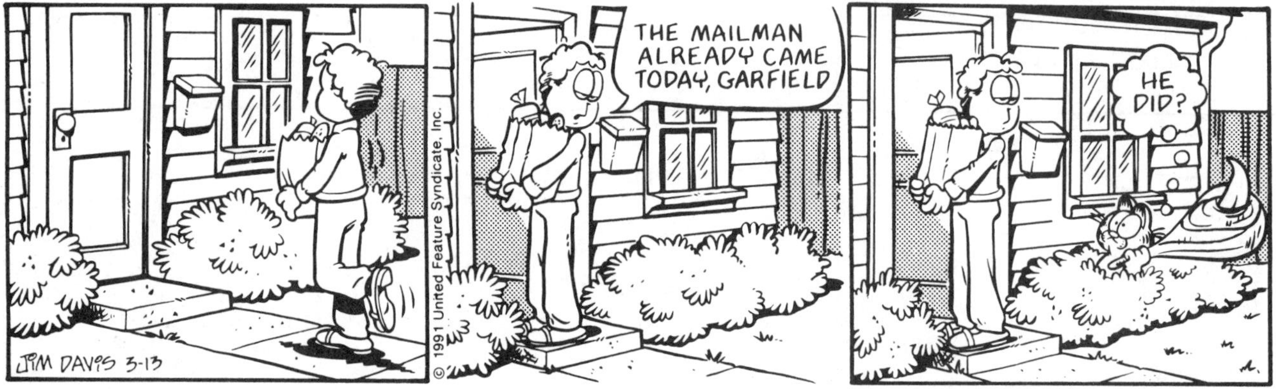
JIM DAVIS 3-13
© 1991 United Feature Syndicate, Inc.
THE MAILMAN ALREADY CAME TODAY, GARFIELD
HE DID?

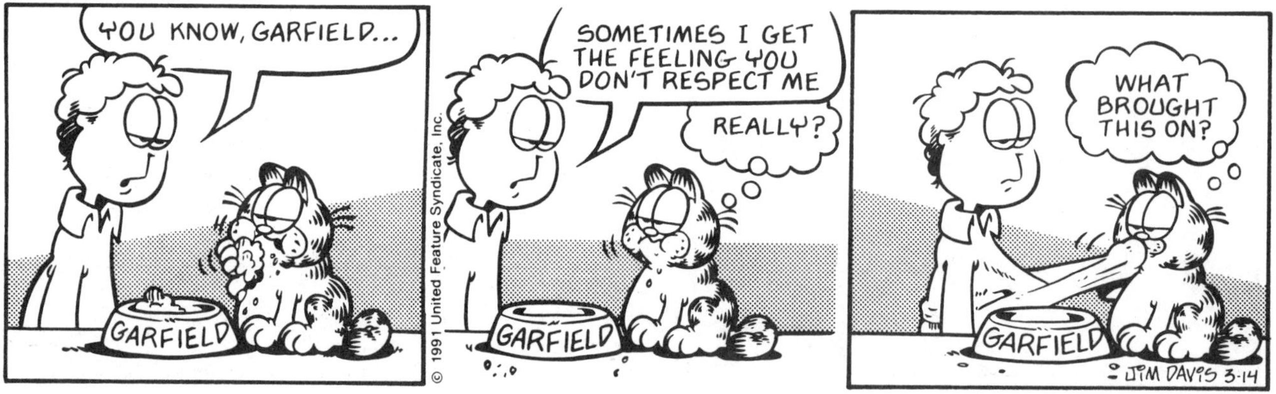
YOU KNOW, GARFIELD...
GARFIELD
© 1991 United Feature Syndicate, Inc.
SOMETIMES I GET THE FEELING YOU DON'T RESPECT ME
REALLY?
GARFIELD
WHAT BROUGHT THIS ON?
GARFIELD
JIM DAVIS 3-14

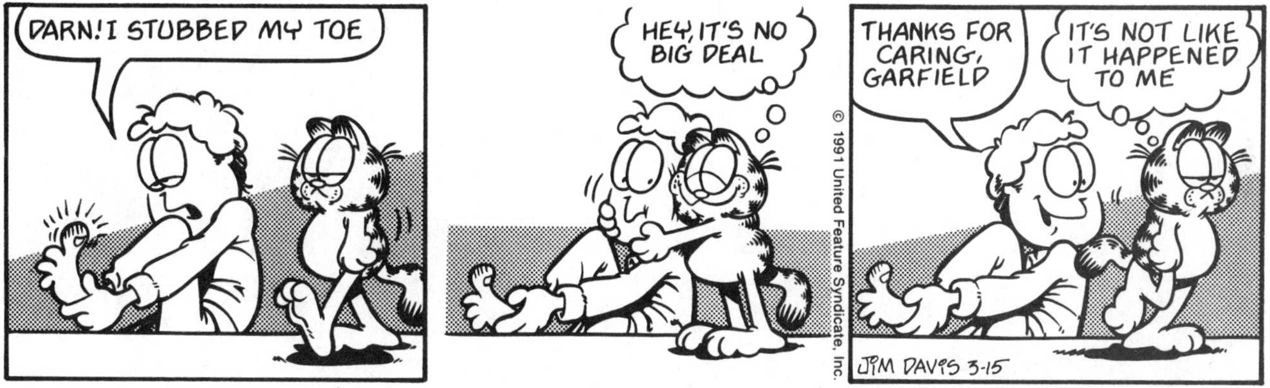
DARN! I STUBBED MY TOE
HEY, IT'S NO BIG DEAL
THANKS FOR CARING, GARFIELD
IT'S NOT LIKE IT HAPPENED TO ME
JIM DAVIS 3-15

© 1991 United Feature Syndicate, Inc.

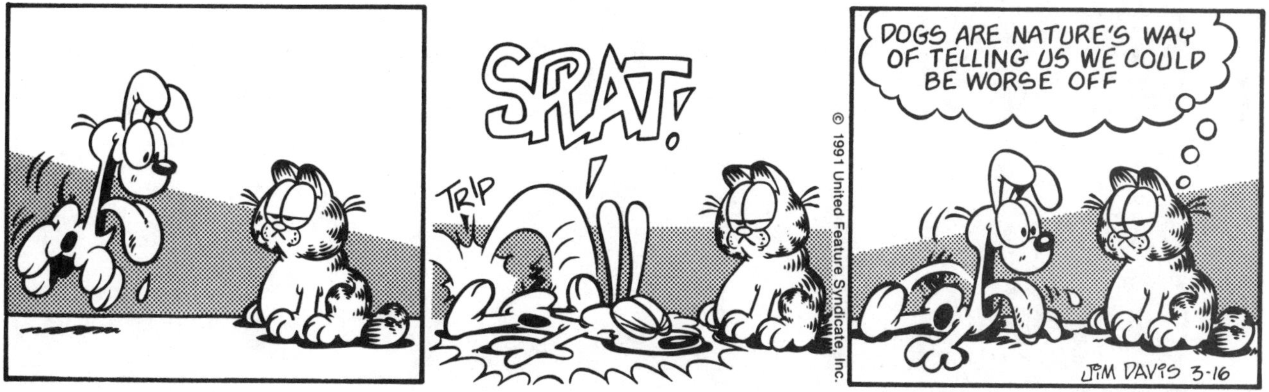
SPLAT!
TRIP
DOGS ARE NATURE'S WAY OF TELLING US WE COULD BE WORSE OFF
JIM DAVIS 3-16

© 1991 United Feature Syndicate, Inc.

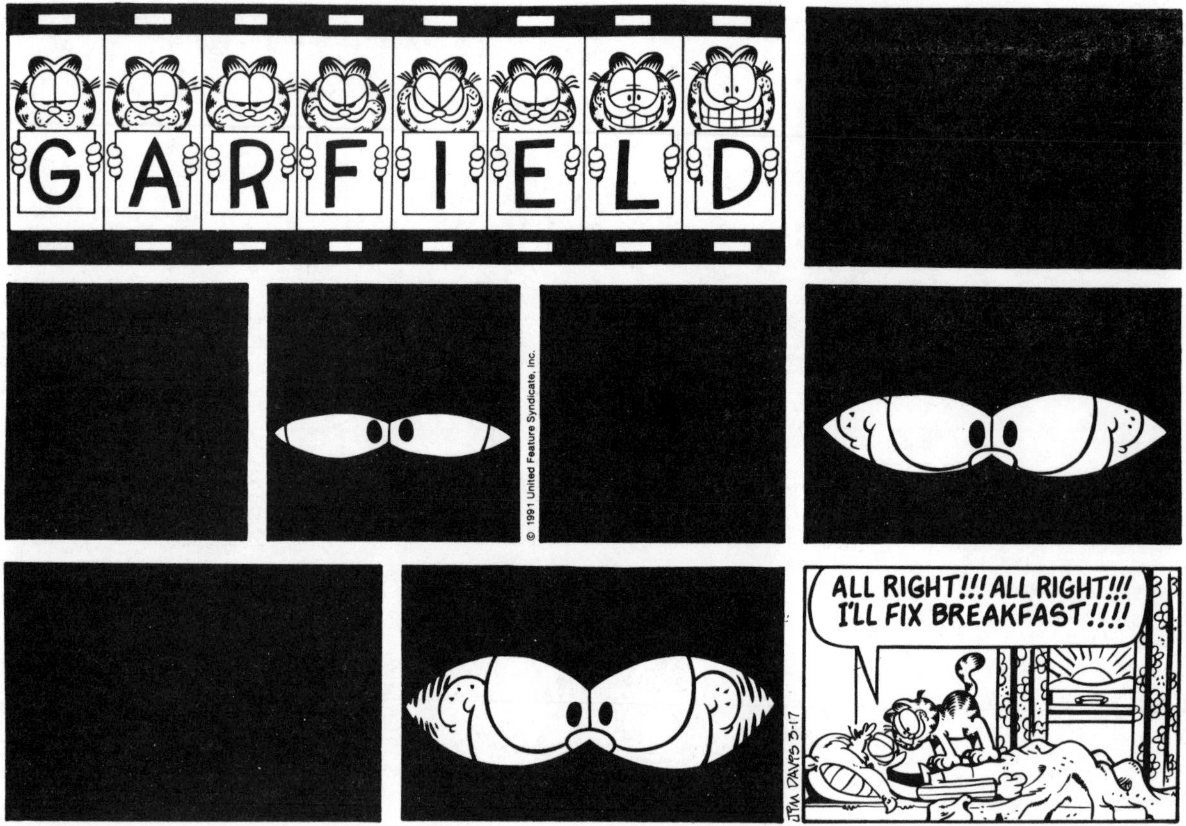
GARFIELD
© 1991 United Feature Syndicate, Inc.
ALL RIGHT!!! ALL RIGHT!!!
I'LL FIX BREAKFAST!!!!
JIM DAVIS 3-17

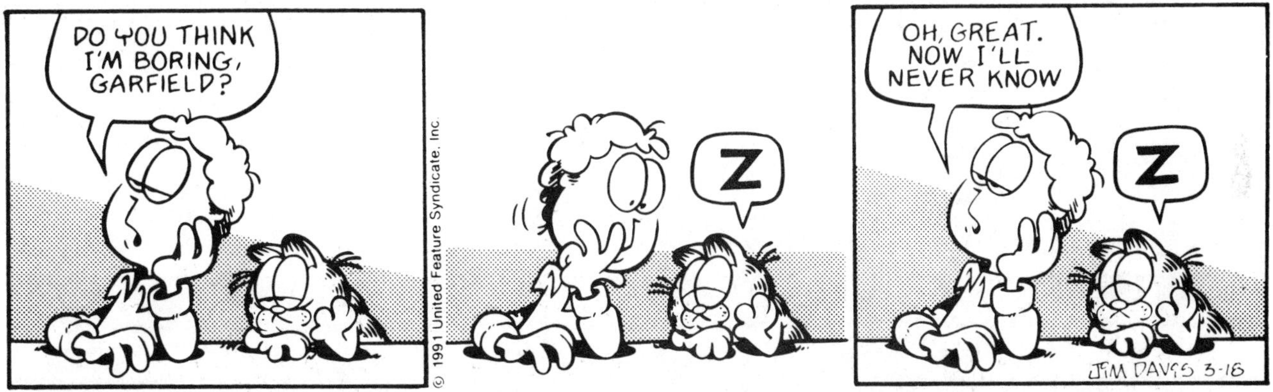
DO YOU THINK I'M BORING, GARFIELD?
Z
OH, GREAT. NOW I'LL NEVER KNOW
Z
JIM DAVIS 3-18

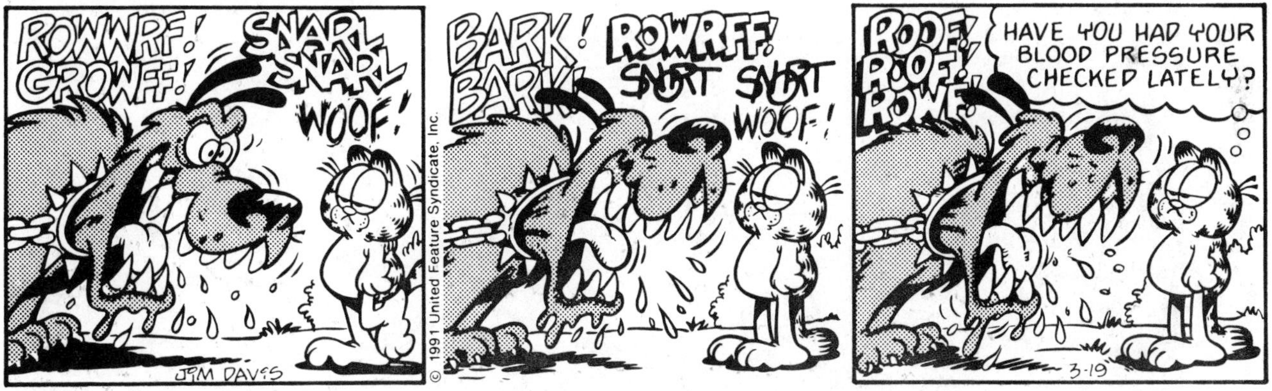
ROWWRF! GROWFF!
SNARL SNARL
WOOF!
JIM DAVIS
BARK! BARK!
ROWRFF!
SNORT SNORT
WOOF!
ROOF! ROOF! ROWF!
HAVE YOU HAD YOUR BLOOD PRESSURE CHECKED LATELY?
3-19

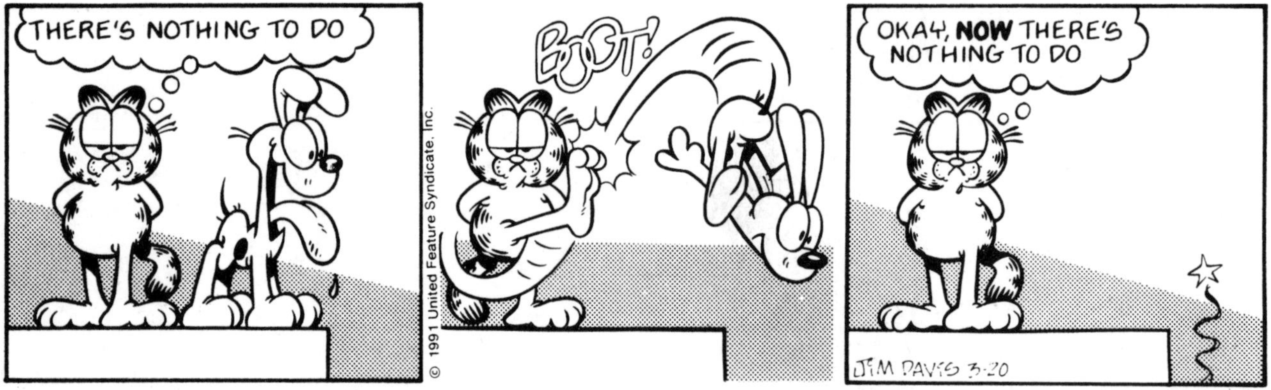
THERE'S NOTHING TO DO
BOOT!
OKAY, **NOW** THERE'S NOTHING TO DO
JIM DAVIS 3-20
© 1991 United Feature Syndicate, Inc.

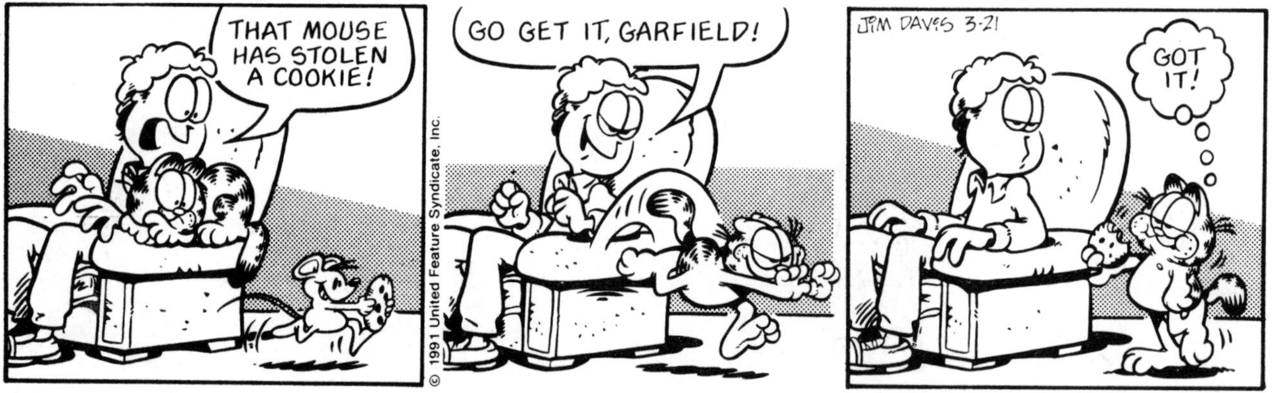
THAT MOUSE HAS STOLEN A COOKIE!
GO GET IT, GARFIELD!
GOT IT!
JIM DAVIS 3-21
© 1991 United Feature Syndicate, Inc.

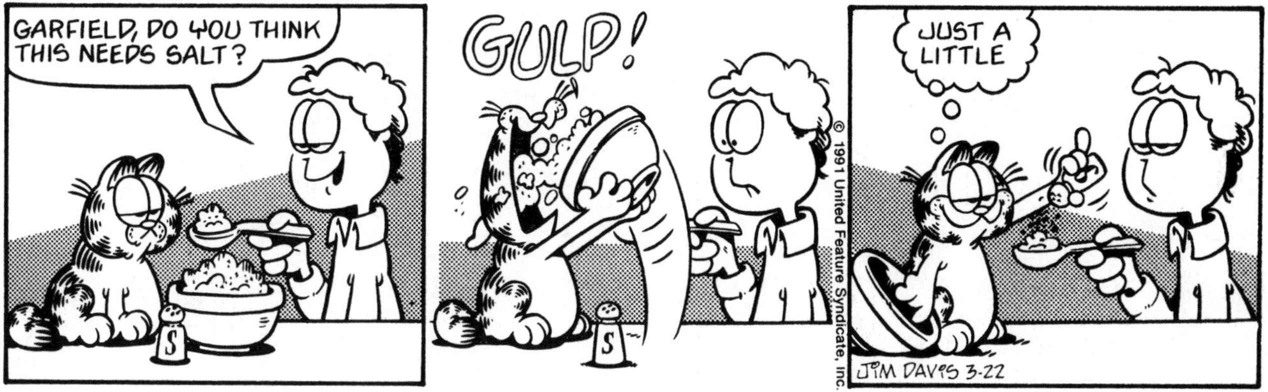
GARFIELD, DO YOU THINK THIS NEEDS SALT?
GULP!
JUST A LITTLE
© 1991 United Feature Syndicate, Inc.
JIM DAVIS 3-22

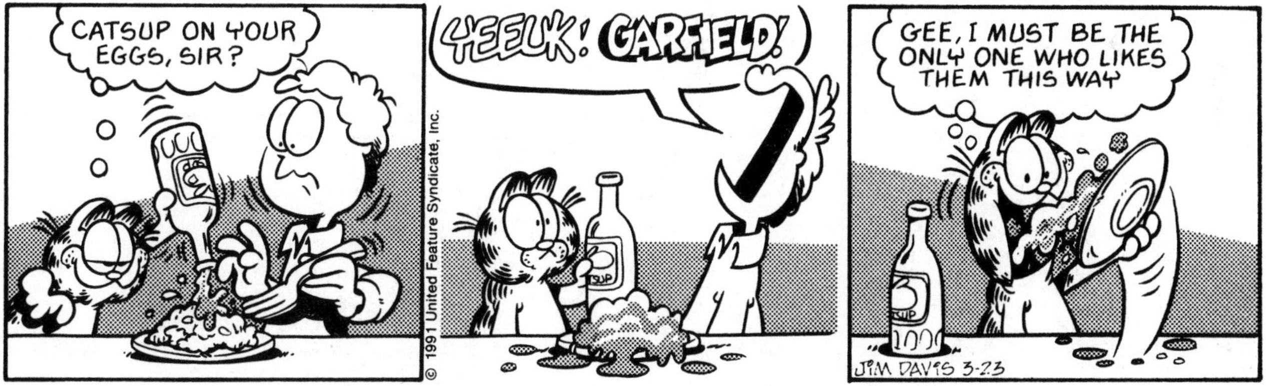
CATSUP ON YOUR EGGS, SIR?
© 1991 United Feature Syndicate, Inc.
YEEUK! GARFIELD!
GEE, I MUST BE THE ONLY ONE WHO LIKES THEM THIS WAY
JIM DAVIS 3-23

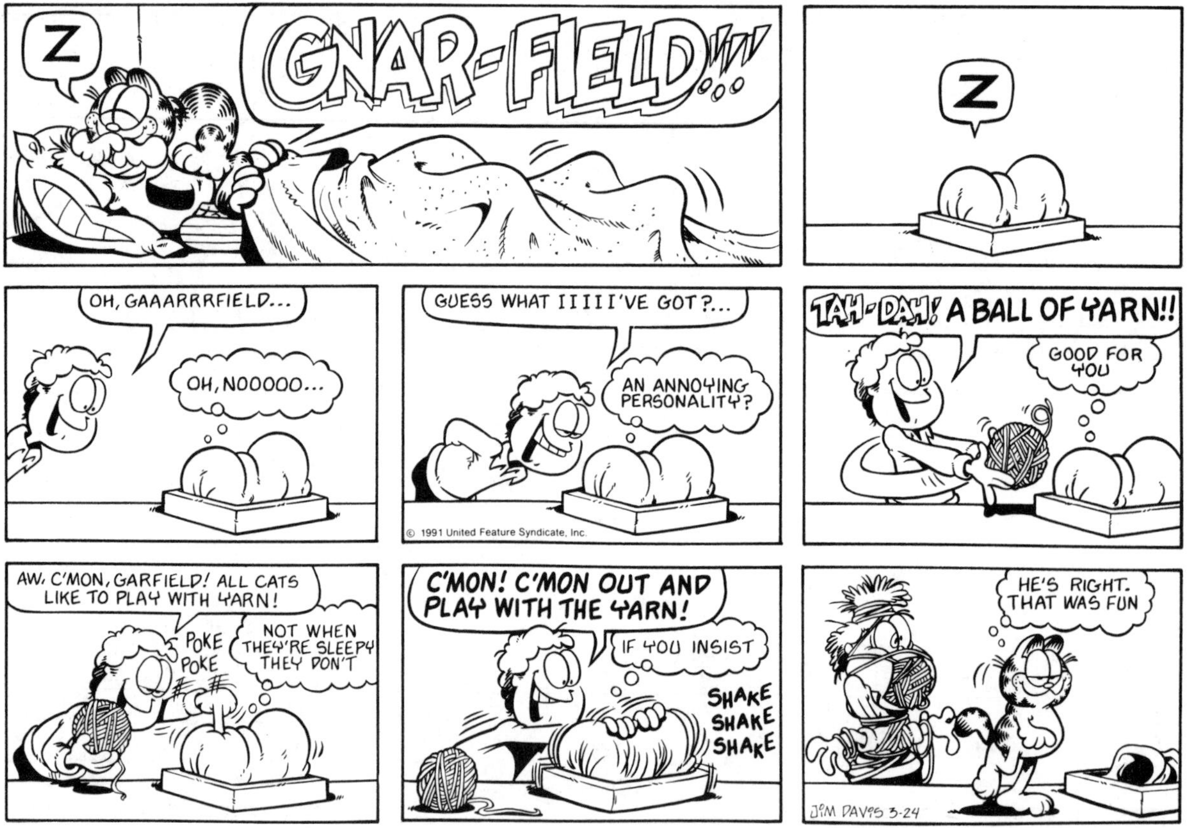
Z
GNAR-FIELD!!!
Z
OH, GAAARRRFIELD...
OH, NOOOOO...
GUESS WHAT IIIII'VE GOT?...
AN ANNOYING PERSONALITY?
TAH-DAH! A BALL OF YARN!!
GOOD FOR YOU
AW, C'MON, GARFIELD! ALL CATS LIKE TO PLAY WITH YARN!
POKE POKE
NOT WHEN THEY'RE SLEEPY THEY DON'T
C'MON! C'MON OUT AND PLAY WITH THE YARN!
IF YOU INSIST
SHAKE SHAKE SHAKE
HE'S RIGHT. THAT WAS FUN
JIM DAVIS 3-24

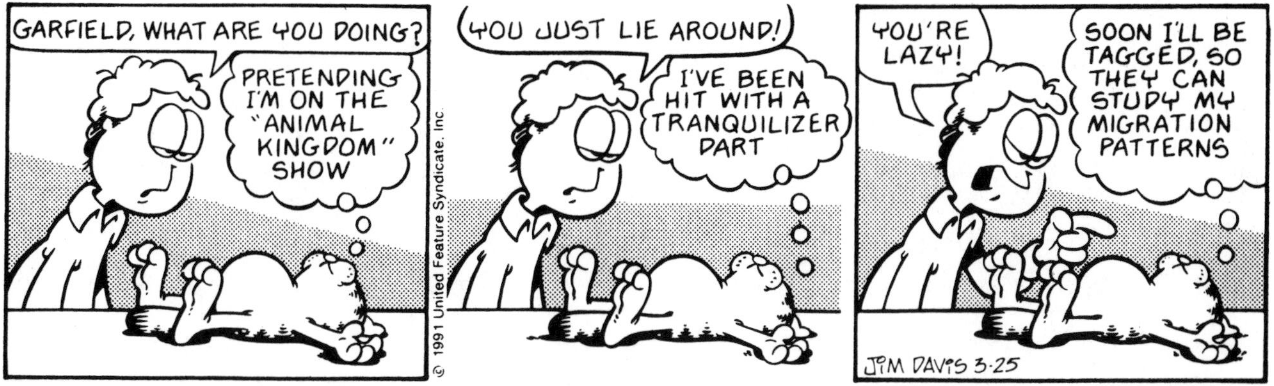
GARFIELD, WHAT ARE YOU DOING?
PRETENDING I'M ON THE "ANIMAL KINGDOM" SHOW
© 1991 United Feature Syndicate, Inc.
YOU JUST LIE AROUND!
I'VE BEEN HIT WITH A TRANQUILIZER DART
YOU'RE LAZY!
SOON I'LL BE TAGGED, SO THEY CAN STUDY MY MIGRATION PATTERNS
JIM DAVIS 3-25

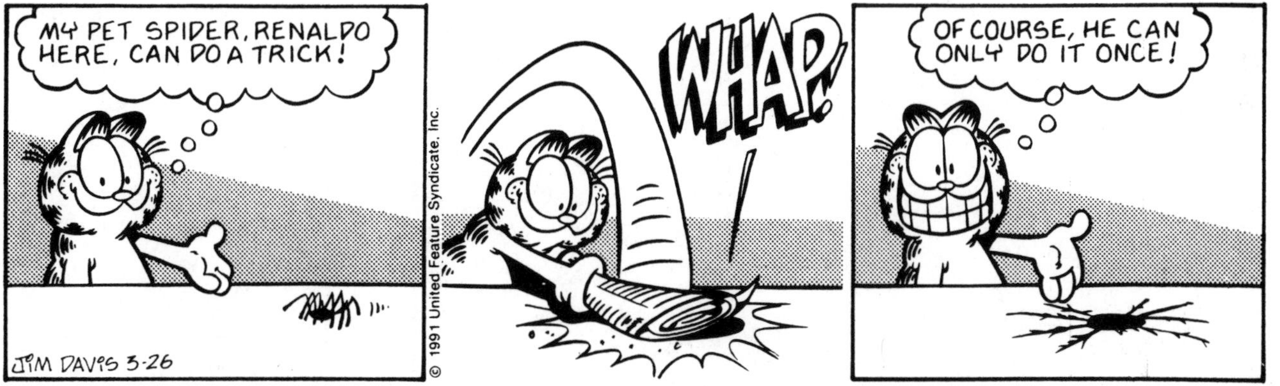
MY PET SPIDER, RENALDO HERE, CAN DO A TRICK!
JIM DAVIS 3-26
© 1991 United Feature Syndicate, Inc.
WHAP!
OF COURSE, HE CAN ONLY DO IT ONCE!

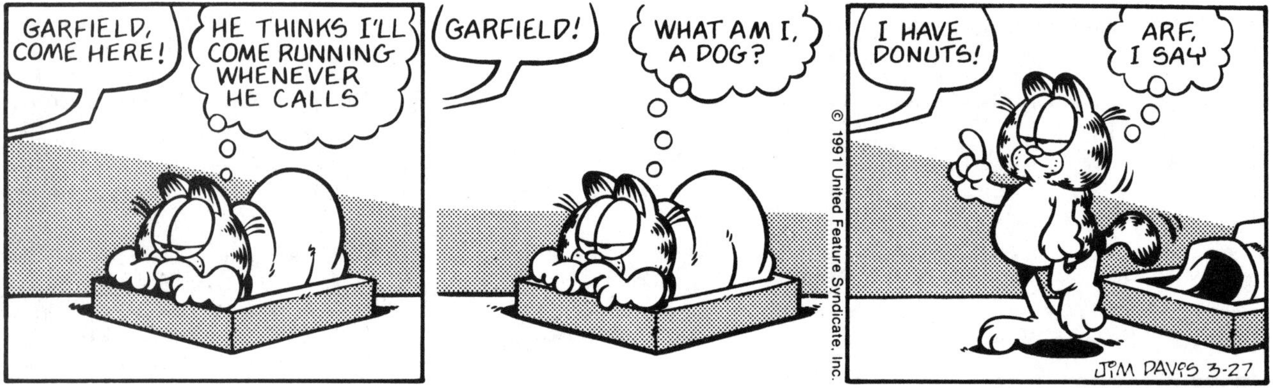
GARFIELD, COME HERE!
HE THINKS I'LL COME RUNNING WHENEVER HE CALLS
GARFIELD!
WHAT AM I, A DOG?
I HAVE DONUTS!
ARF, I SAY
© 1991 United Feature Syndicate, Inc.
JIM DAVIS 3-27

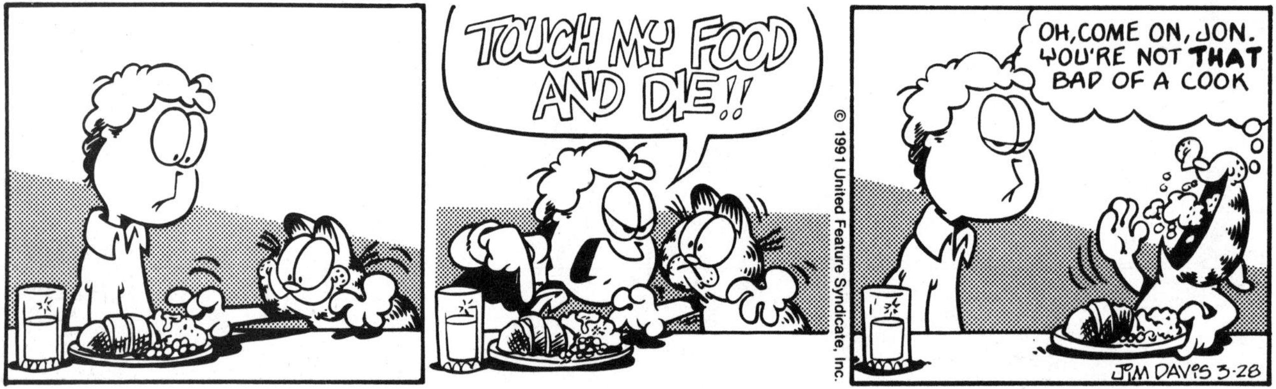
TOUCH MY FOOD AND DIE!!
OH, COME ON, JON. YOU'RE NOT **THAT** BAD OF A COOK
© 1991 United Feature Syndicate, Inc.
JIM DAVIS 3-28

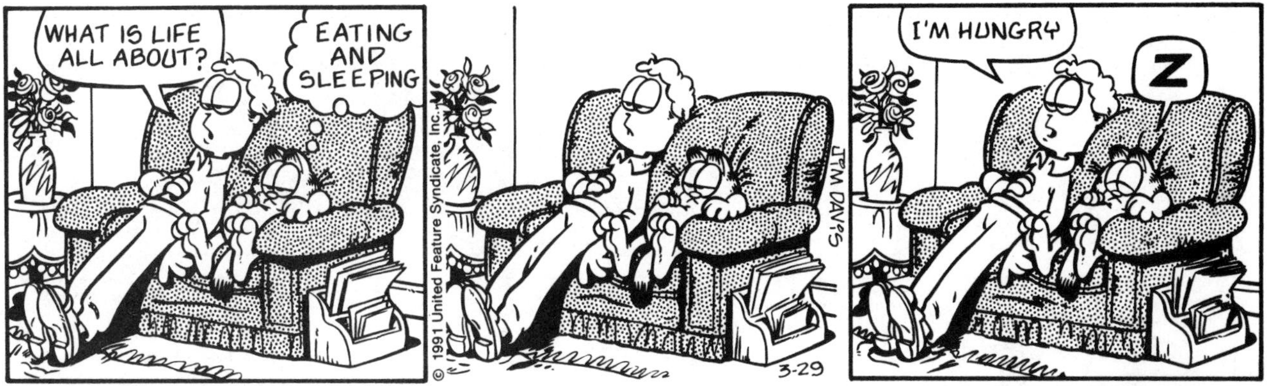
WHAT IS LIFE ALL ABOUT?
EATING AND SLEEPING
I'M HUNGRY
Z
JIM DAVIS
3-29
© 1991 United Feature Syndicate, Inc.

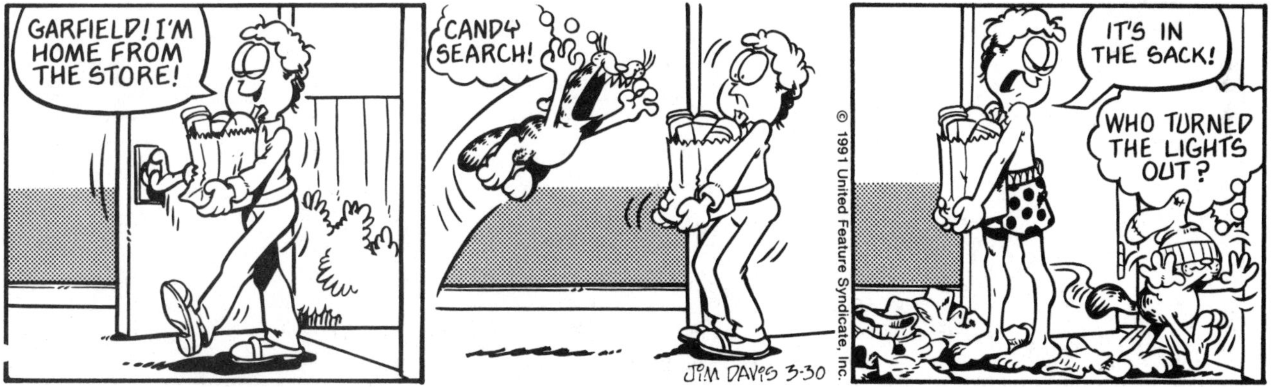
GARFIELD! I'M HOME FROM THE STORE!
CANDY SEARCH!
IT'S IN THE SACK!
WHO TURNED THE LIGHTS OUT?
JIM DAVIS 3-30
© 1991 United Feature Syndicate, Inc.

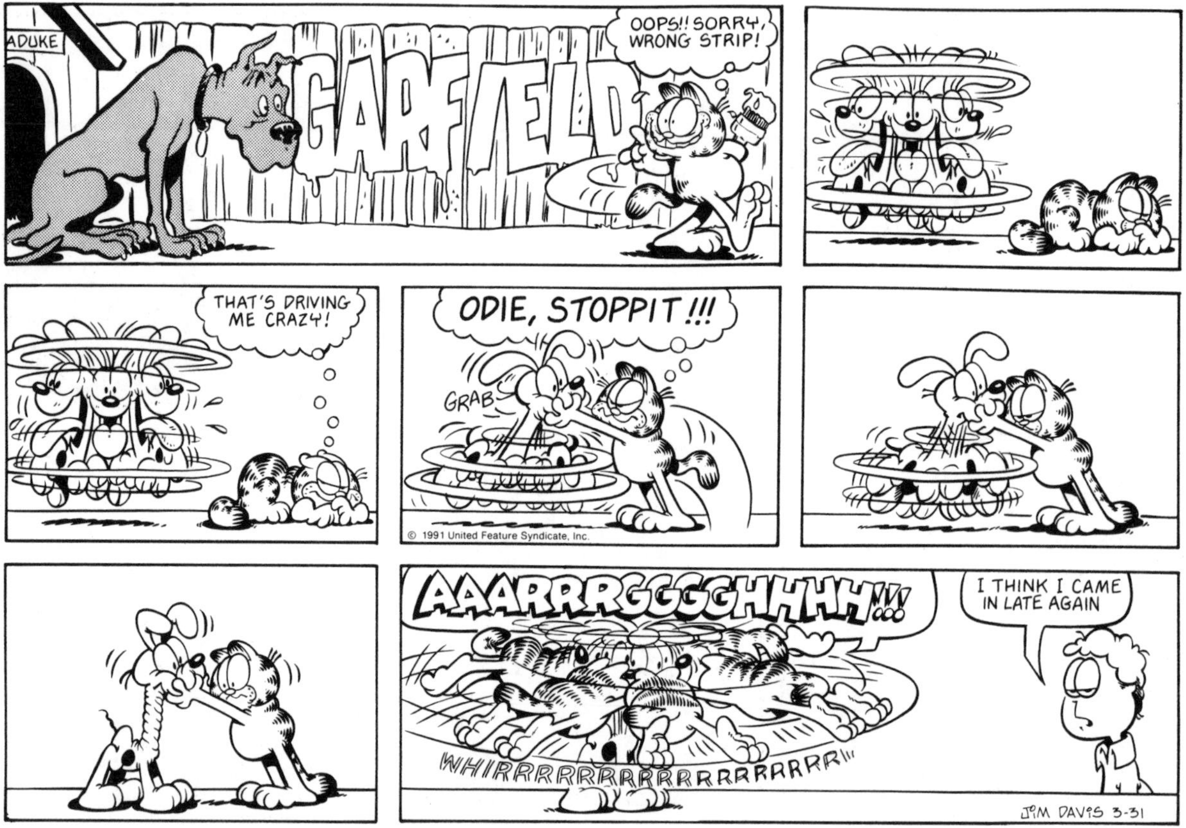
ADUKE
GARFIELD
OOPS!! SORRY, WRONG STRIP!
THAT'S DRIVING ME CRAZY!
ODIE, STOPPIT!!!
GRAB
© 1991 United Feature Syndicate, Inc.
AAARRRGGGGHHHH!!!
WHIRRRRRRRRRRRRRRRRRRRR
I THINK I CAME IN LATE AGAIN
JIM DAVIS 3-31

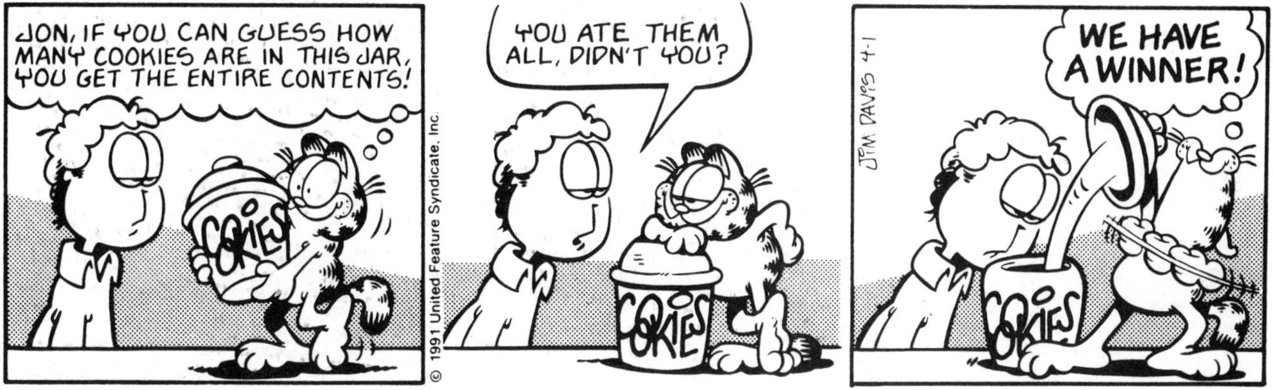
JON, IF YOU CAN GUESS HOW MANY COOKIES ARE IN THIS JAR, YOU GET THE ENTIRE CONTENTS!
COOKIES
© 1991 United Feature Syndicate, Inc.
YOU ATE THEM ALL, DIDN'T YOU?
COOKIES
JIM DAVIS 4-1
WE HAVE A WINNER!
COOKIES

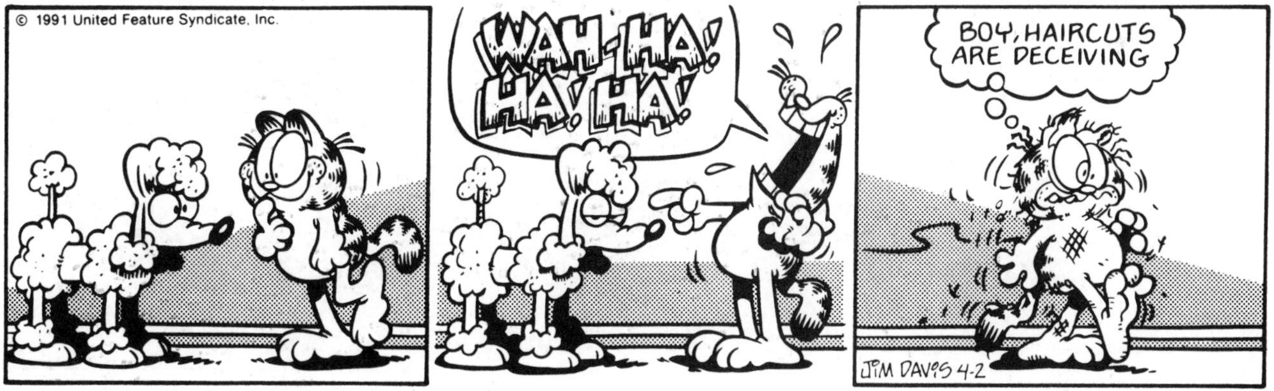
© 1991 United Feature Syndicate, Inc.
WAH-HA! HA! HA!
BOY, HAIRCUTS ARE DECEIVING
JIM DAVIS 4-2

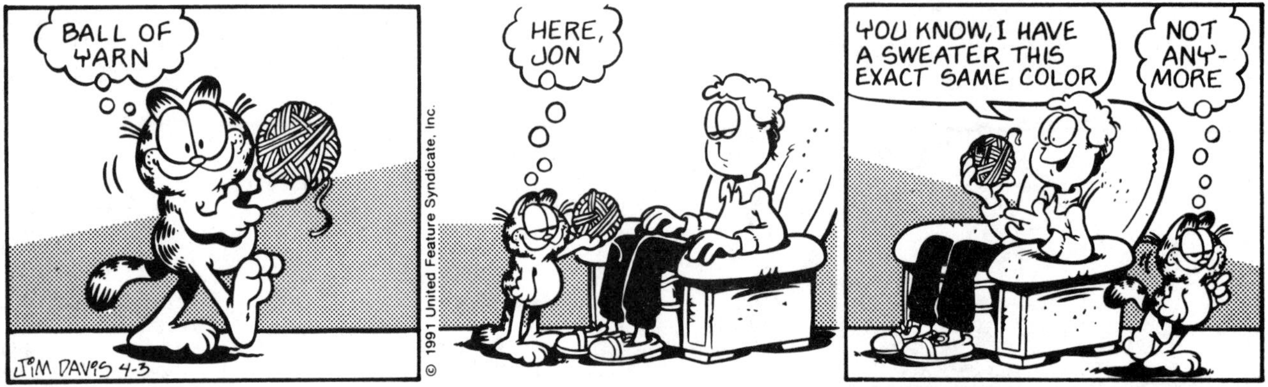
BALL OF YARN
JIM DAVIS 4-3
HERE, JON
YOU KNOW, I HAVE A SWEATER THIS EXACT SAME COLOR
NOT ANY-MORE

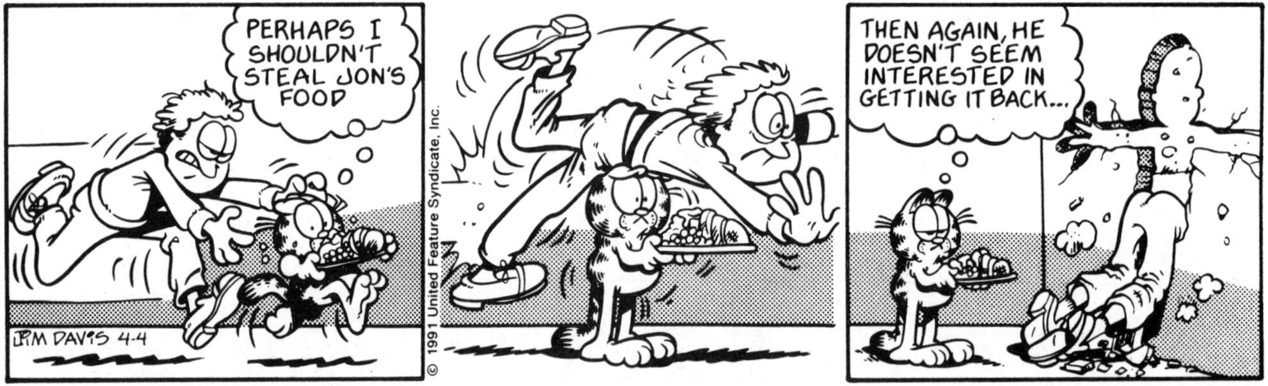
PERHAPS I SHOULDN'T STEAL JON'S FOOD
JIM DAVIS 4-4
THEN AGAIN, HE DOESN'T SEEM INTERESTED IN GETTING IT BACK...

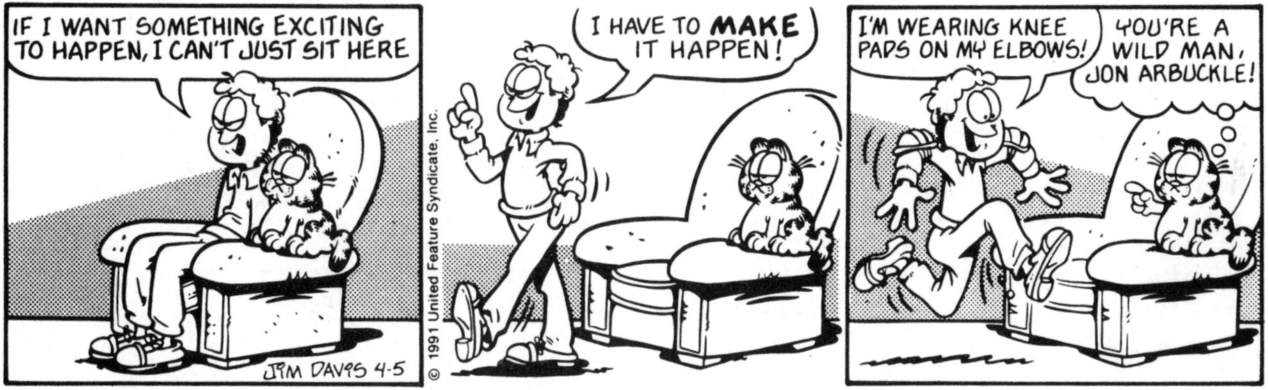
IF I WANT SOMETHING EXCITING TO HAPPEN, I CAN'T JUST SIT HERE
JIM DAVIS 4-5
© 1991 United Feature Syndicate, Inc.
I HAVE TO **MAKE** IT HAPPEN!
I'M WEARING KNEE PADS ON MY ELBOWS!
YOU'RE A WILD MAN, JON ARBUCKLE!

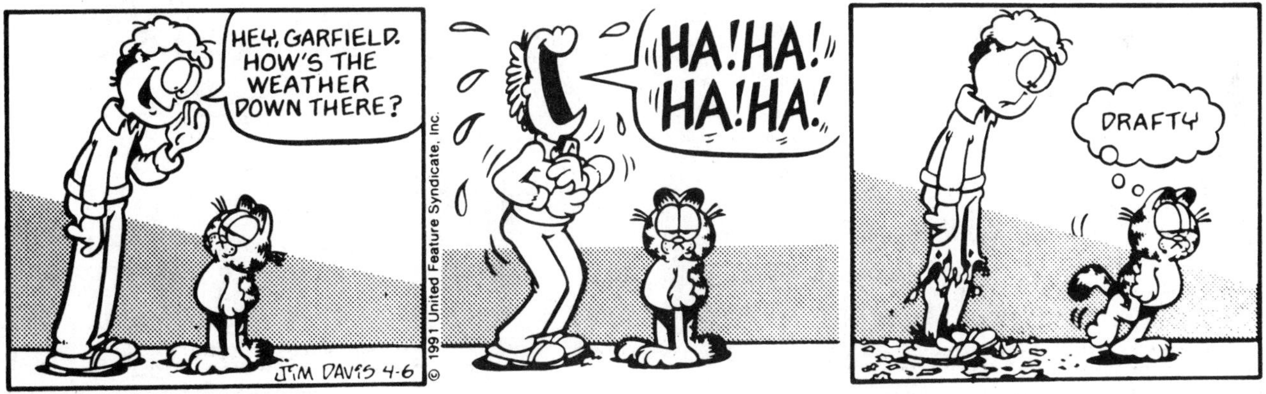
HEY, GARFIELD. HOW'S THE WEATHER DOWN THERE?
JIM DAVIS 4-6
© 1991 United Feature Syndicate, Inc.
HA! HA! HA! HA!
DRAFTY

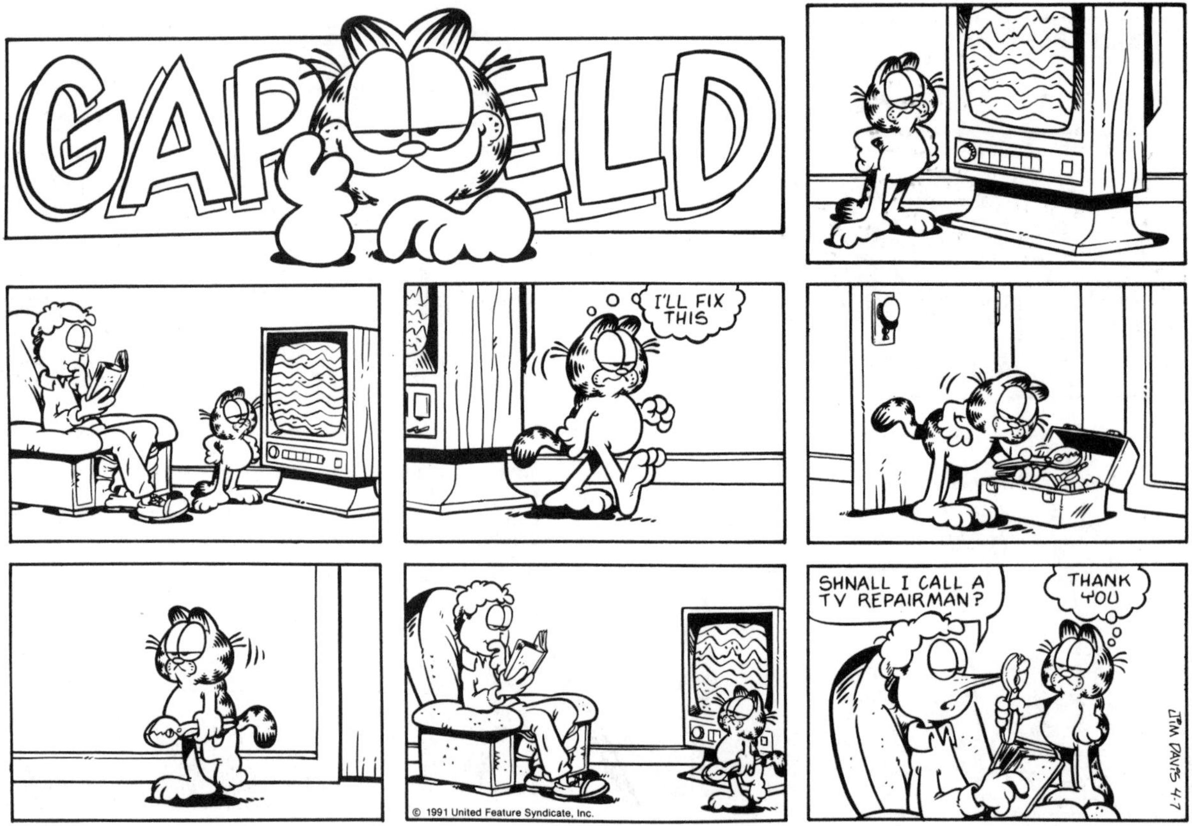
GARFIELD
I'LL FIX THIS
SHNALL I CALL A TV REPAIRMAN?
THANK YOU
JIM DAVIS 4-7
© 1991 United Feature Syndicate, Inc.

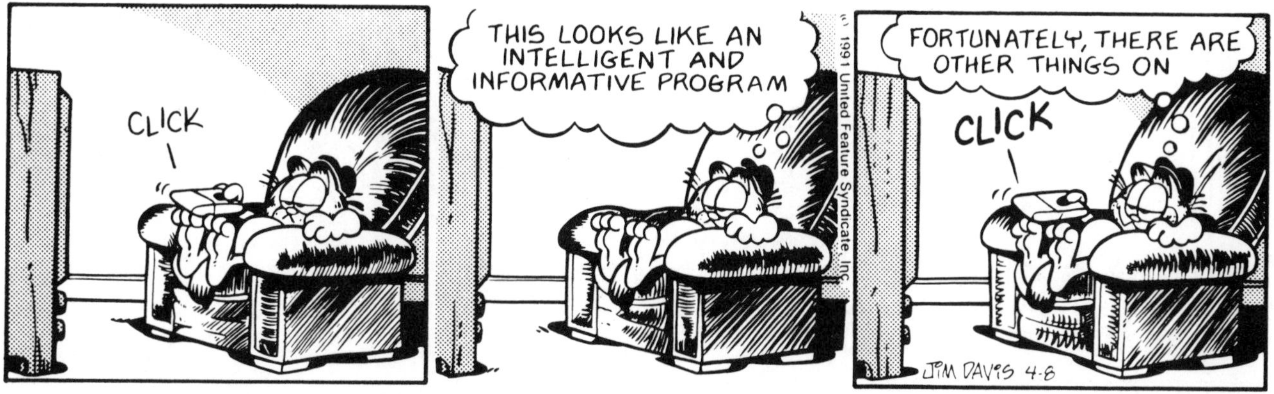
CLICK
THIS LOOKS LIKE AN INTELLIGENT AND INFORMATIVE PROGRAM
© 1991 United Feature Syndicate, Inc.
FORTUNATELY, THERE ARE OTHER THINGS ON
CLICK
JIM DAVIS 4-8

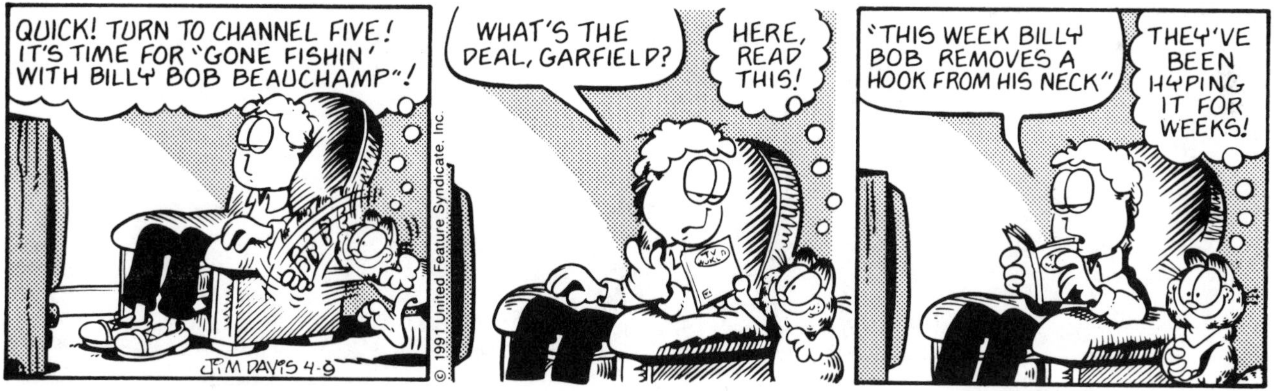
QUICK! TURN TO CHANNEL FIVE! IT'S TIME FOR "GONE FISHIN' WITH BILLY BOB BEAUCHAMP"!
JIM DAVIS 4-9
© 1991 United Feature Syndicate, Inc.
WHAT'S THE DEAL, GARFIELD?
HERE, READ THIS!
"THIS WEEK BILLY BOB REMOVES A HOOK FROM HIS NECK"
THEY'VE BEEN HYPING IT FOR WEEKS!

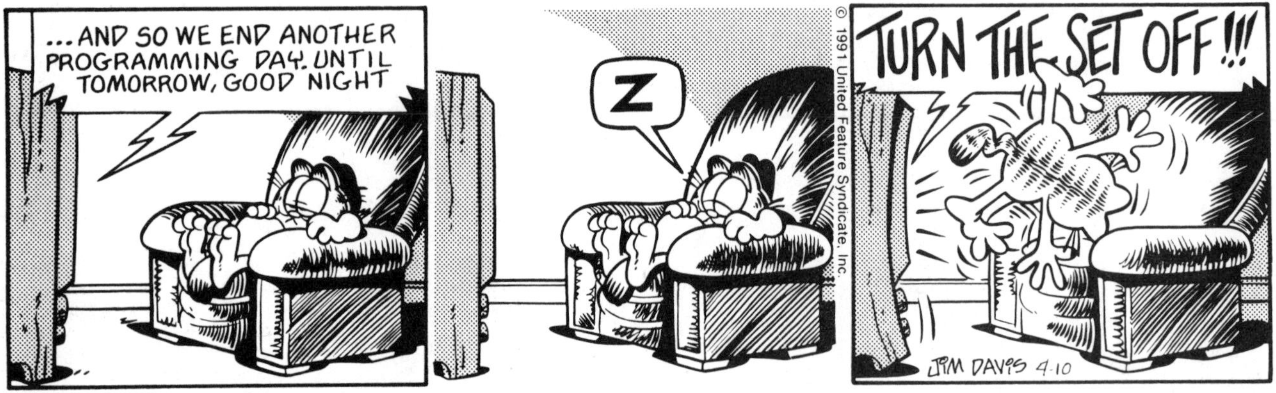
...AND SO WE END ANOTHER PROGRAMMING DAY. UNTIL TOMORROW, GOOD NIGHT
Z
© 1991 United Feature Syndicate, Inc.
TURN THE SET OFF!!!
JIM DAVIS 4-10

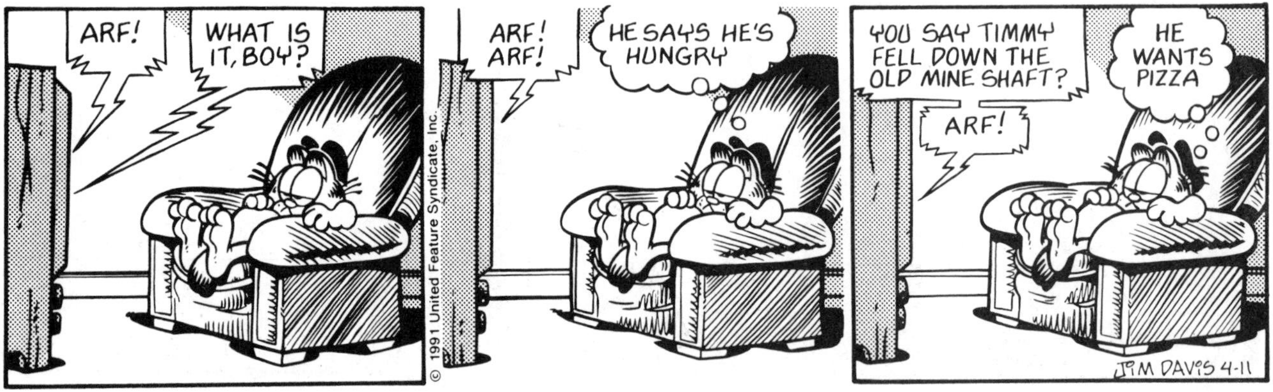
ARF!
WHAT IS IT, BOY?
© 1991 United Feature Syndicate, Inc.
ARF! ARF!
HE SAYS HE'S HUNGRY
YOU SAY TIMMY FELL DOWN THE OLD MINE SHAFT?
ARF!
HE WANTS PIZZA
JIM DAVIS 4-11

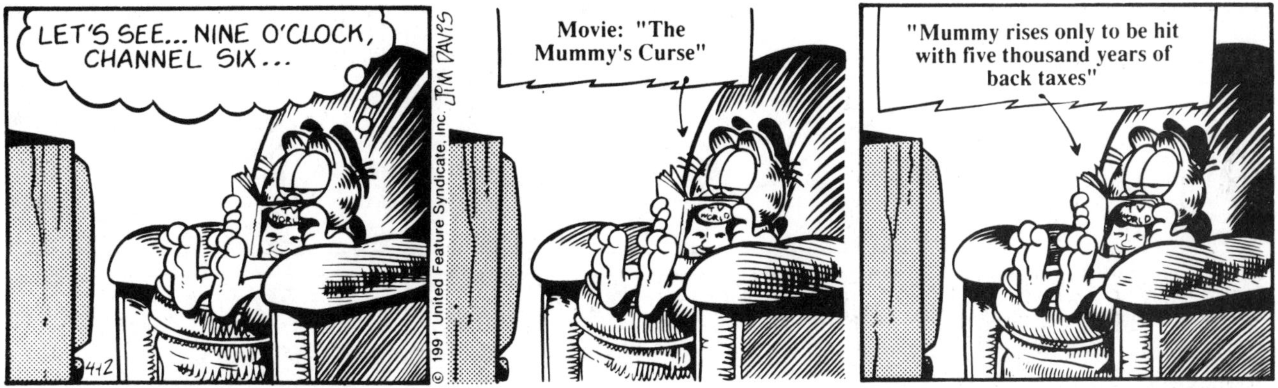
LET'S SEE... NINE O'CLOCK, CHANNEL SIX...
Movie: "The Mummy's Curse"
"Mummy rises only to be hit with five thousand years of back taxes"
© 1991 United Feature Syndicate, Inc.
JIM DAVIS

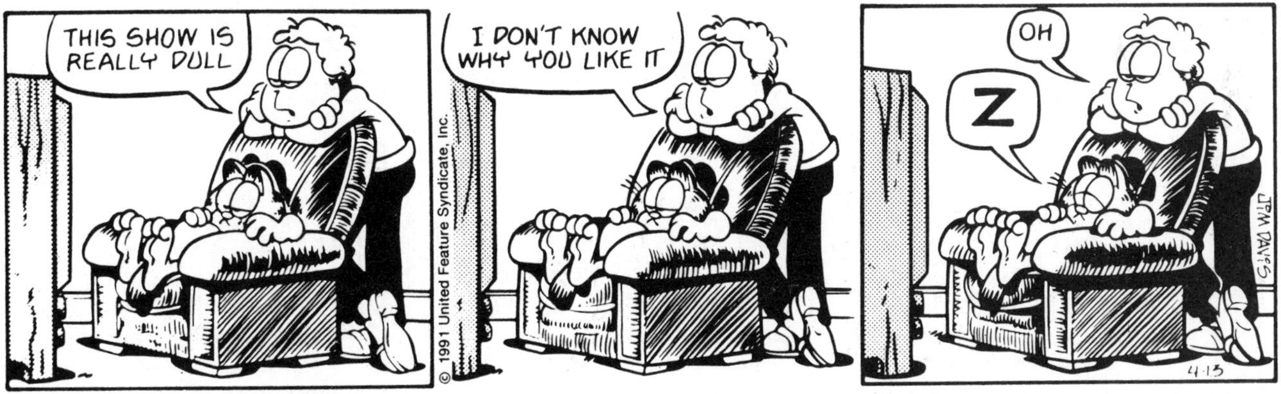
THIS SHOW IS REALLY DULL
I DON'T KNOW WHY YOU LIKE IT
Z
OH
© 1991 United Feature Syndicate, Inc.
JIM DAVIS

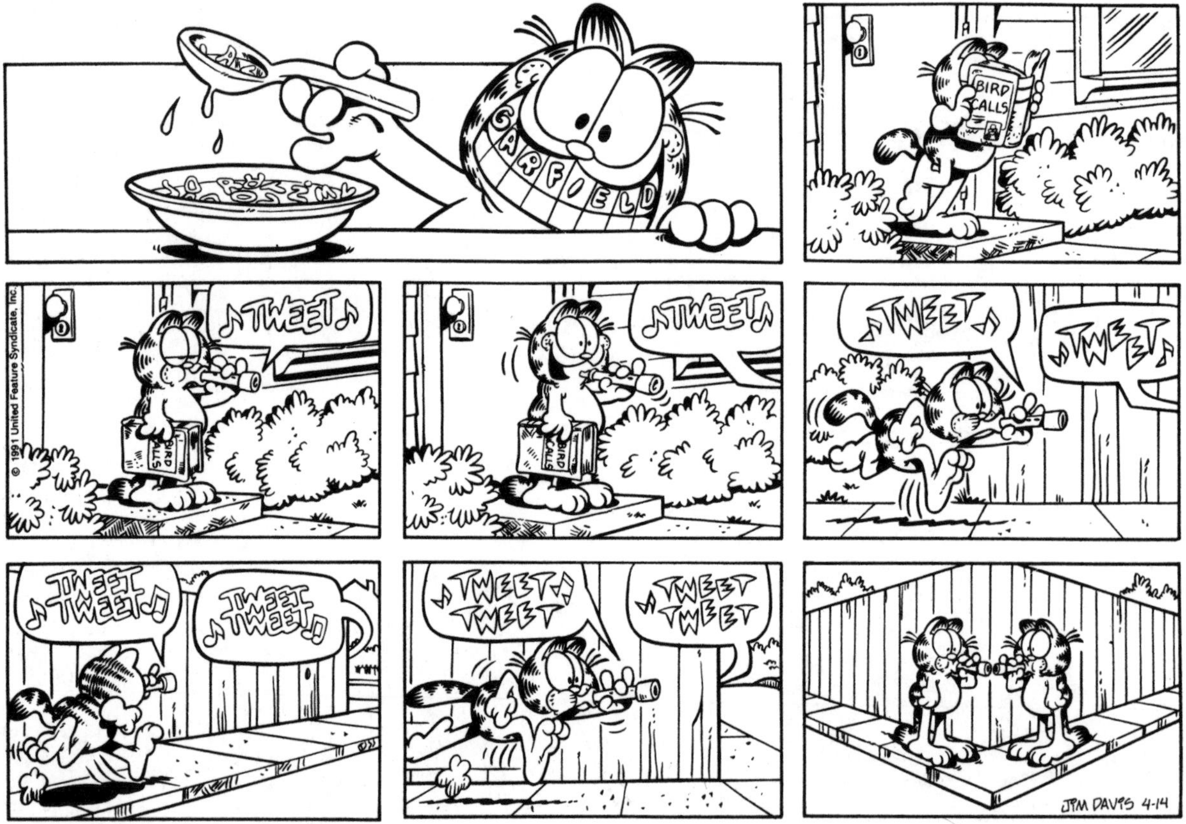
GARFIELD
BIRD CALLS
© 1991 United Feature Syndicate, Inc.
♪TWEET♪
BIRD CALLS
♪TWEET♪
BIRD CALLS
♪TWEET♪
♪TWEET♪
♪TWEET TWEET♫
♪TWEET TWEET♫
♪TWEET♪ TWEET
♪TWEET TWEET
JIM DAVIS 4-14

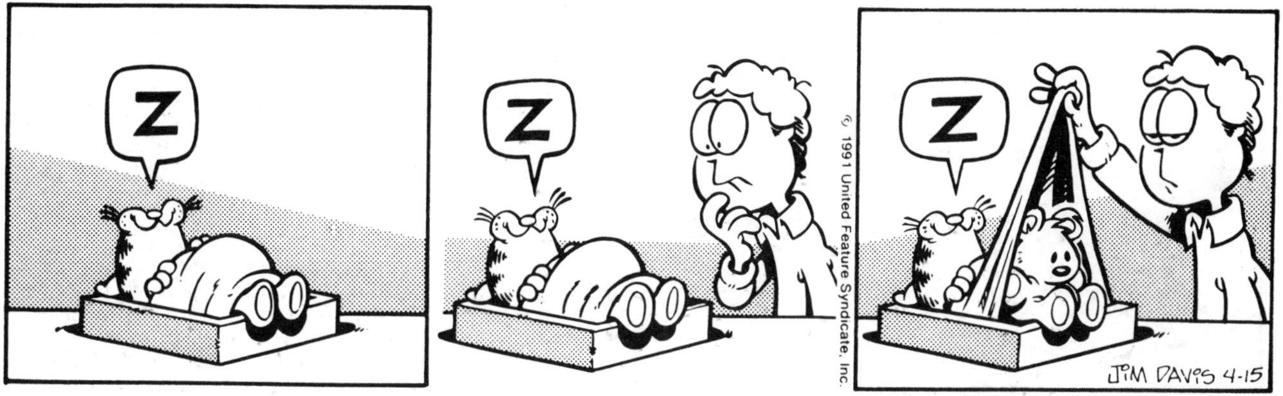
Z
Z
Z
© 1991 United Feature Syndicate, Inc.
JIM DAVIS 4-15

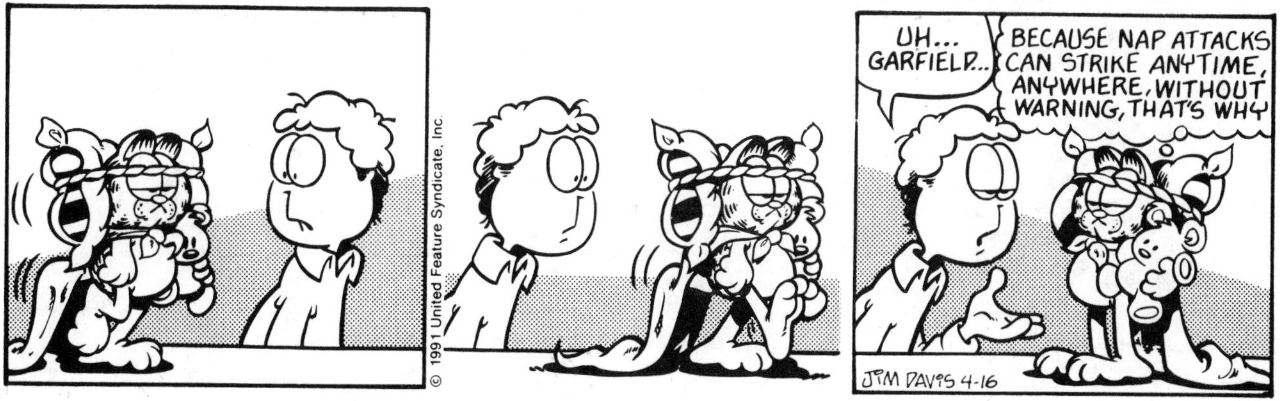
© 1991 United Feature Syndicate, Inc.
UH... GARFIELD...
BECAUSE NAP ATTACKS CAN STRIKE ANYTIME, ANYWHERE, WITHOUT WARNING, THAT'S WHY
JIM DAVIS 4-16

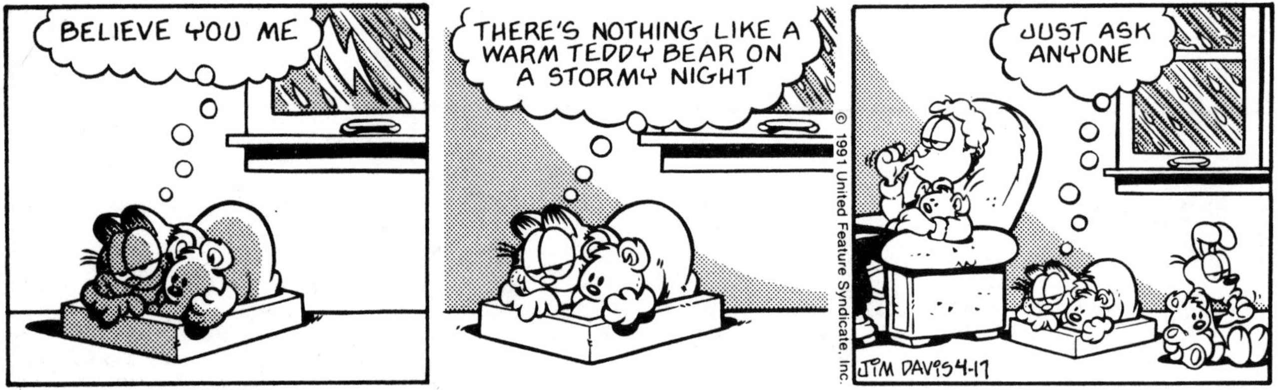
BELIEVE YOU ME
THERE'S NOTHING LIKE A WARM TEDDY BEAR ON A STORMY NIGHT
JUST ASK ANYONE
JIM DAVIS 4-17

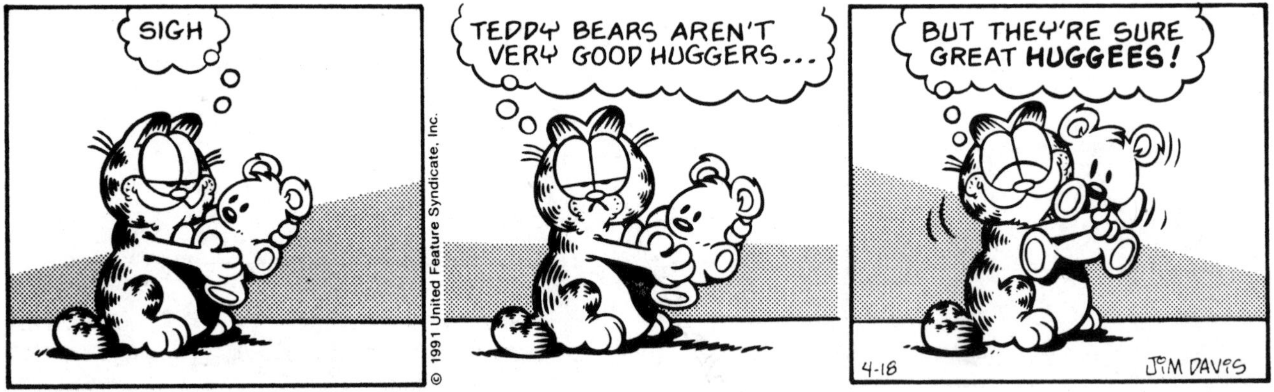
SIGH
TEDDY BEARS AREN'T VERY GOOD HUGGERS...
BUT THEY'RE SURE GREAT **HUGGEES**!
4-18
JIM DAVIS

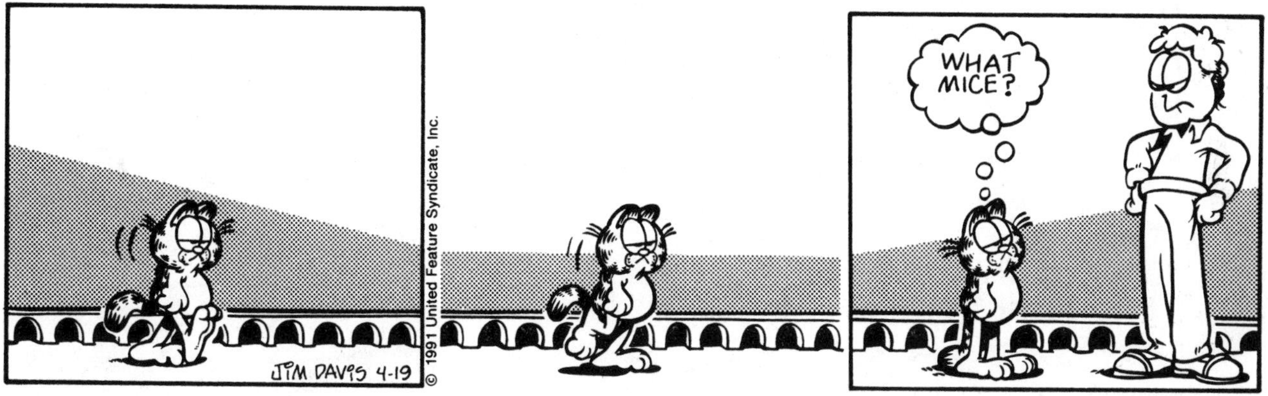
JIM DAVIS 4-19
WHAT MICE?

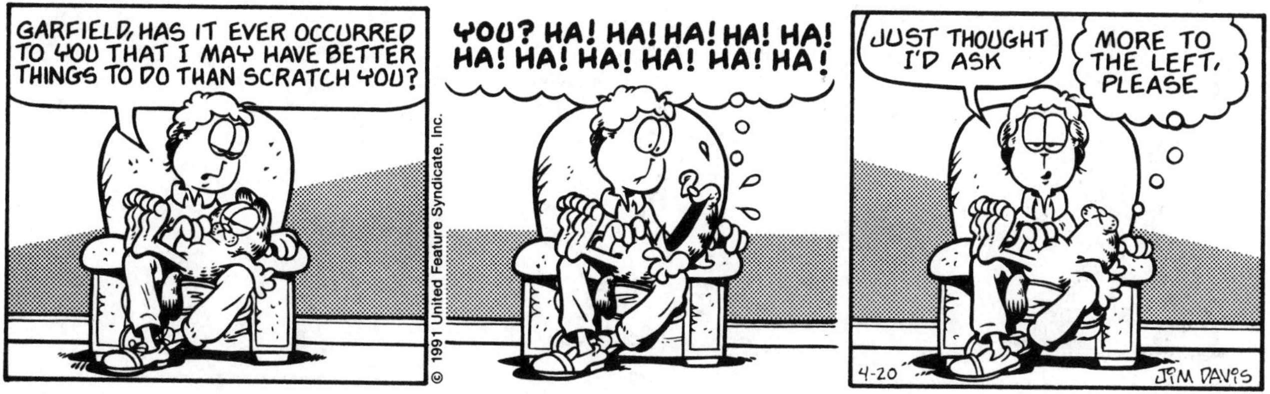
GARFIELD, HAS IT EVER OCCURRED TO YOU THAT I MAY HAVE BETTER THINGS TO DO THAN SCRATCH YOU?
YOU? HA! HA! HA! HA! HA! HA! HA! HA! HA! HA! HA!
JUST THOUGHT I'D ASK
MORE TO THE LEFT, PLEASE
4-20
JIM DAVIS

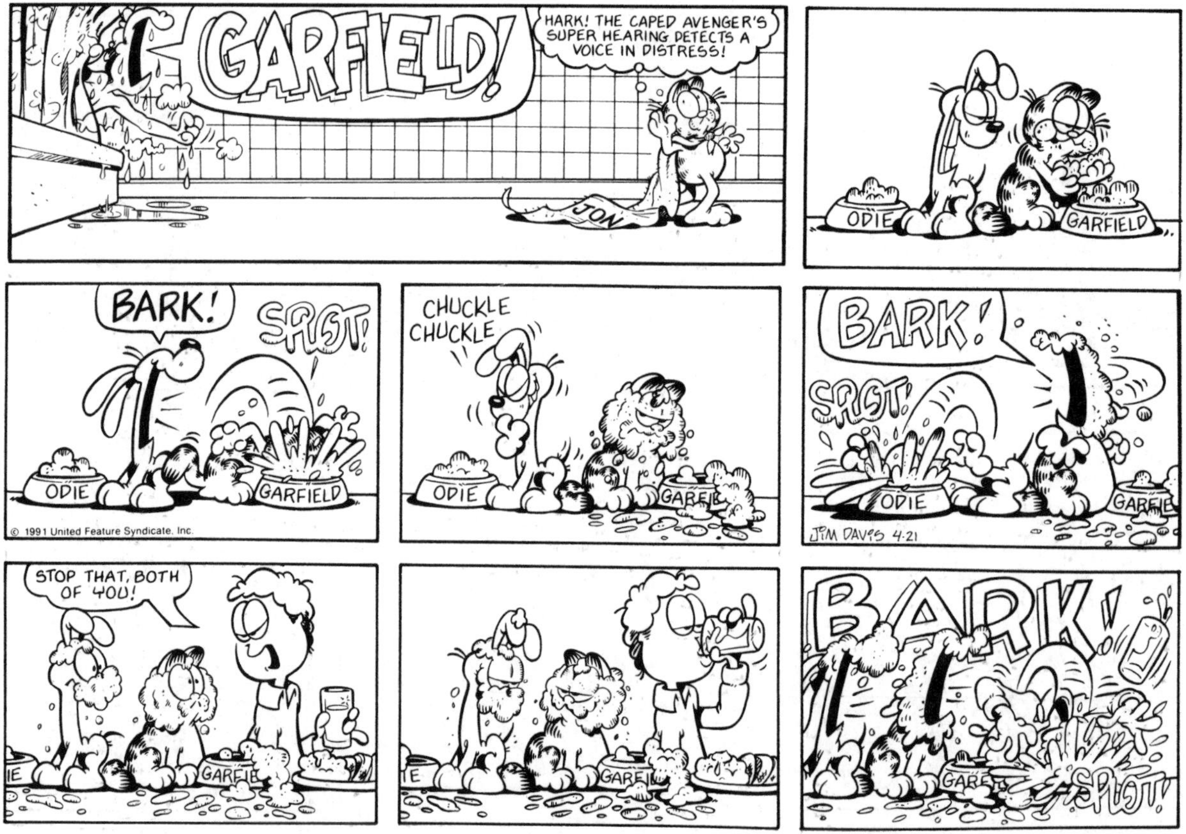
GARFIELD!
HARK! THE CAPED AVENGER'S SUPER HEARING DETECTS A VOICE IN DISTRESS!
JON
ODIE
GARFIELD
BARK!
SPLOT!
© 1991 United Feature Syndicate, Inc.
CHUCKLE CHUCKLE
BARK!
SPLOT!
JIM DAVIS 4-21
STOP THAT, BOTH OF YOU!
BARK!
SPLOT!

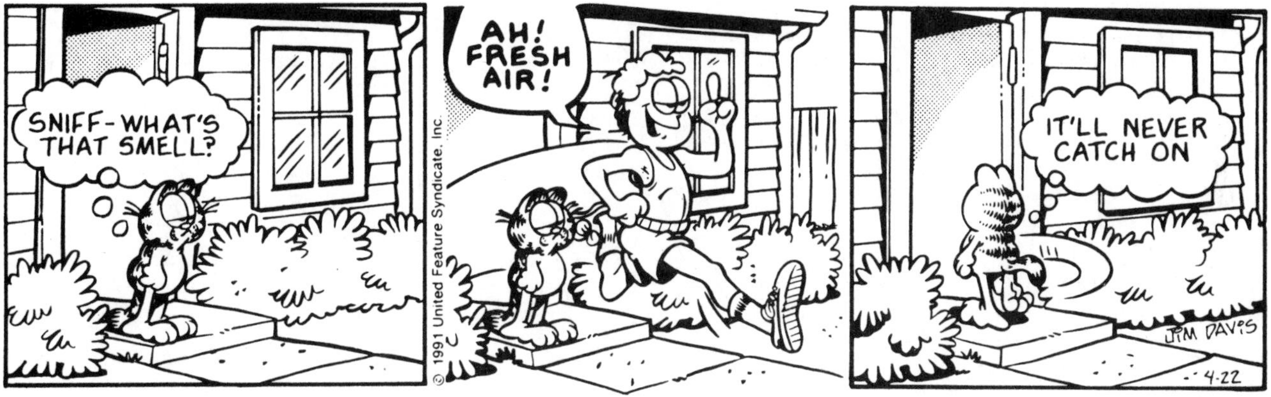
SNIFF- WHAT'S THAT SMELL?
AH! FRESH AIR!
IT'LL NEVER CATCH ON
JIM DAVIS
4-22

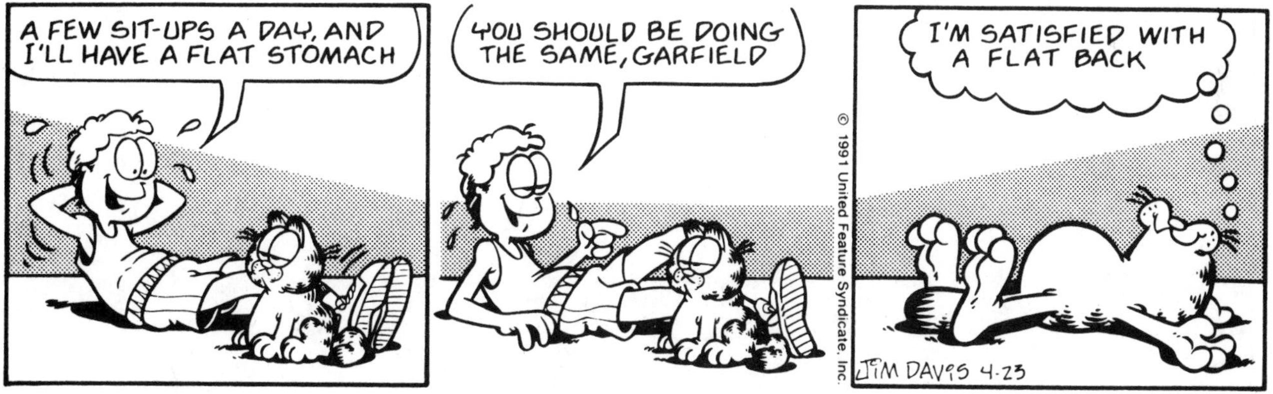
A FEW SIT-UPS A DAY, AND I'LL HAVE A FLAT STOMACH
YOU SHOULD BE DOING THE SAME, GARFIELD
I'M SATISFIED WITH A FLAT BACK
JIM DAVIS 4-23

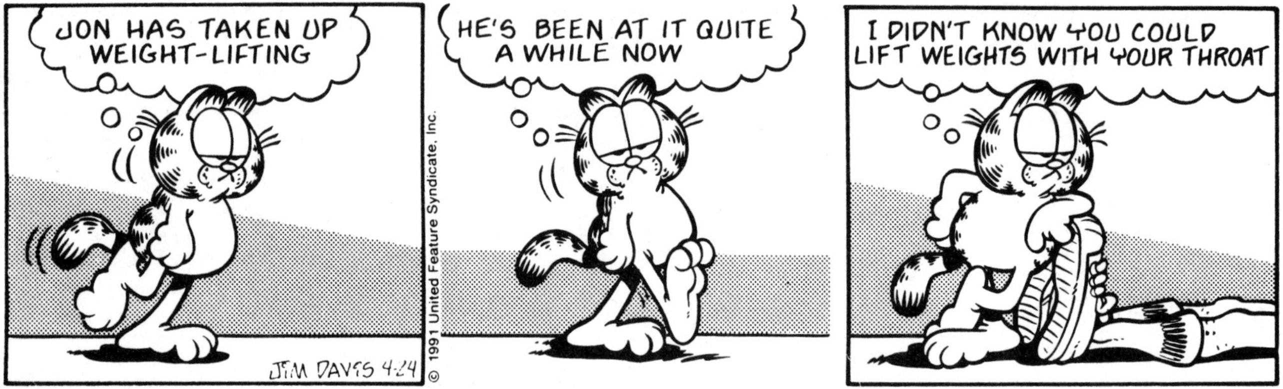
JON HAS TAKEN UP WEIGHT-LIFTING
JIM DAVIS 4-24
HE'S BEEN AT IT QUITE A WHILE NOW
I DIDN'T KNOW YOU COULD LIFT WEIGHTS WITH YOUR THROAT

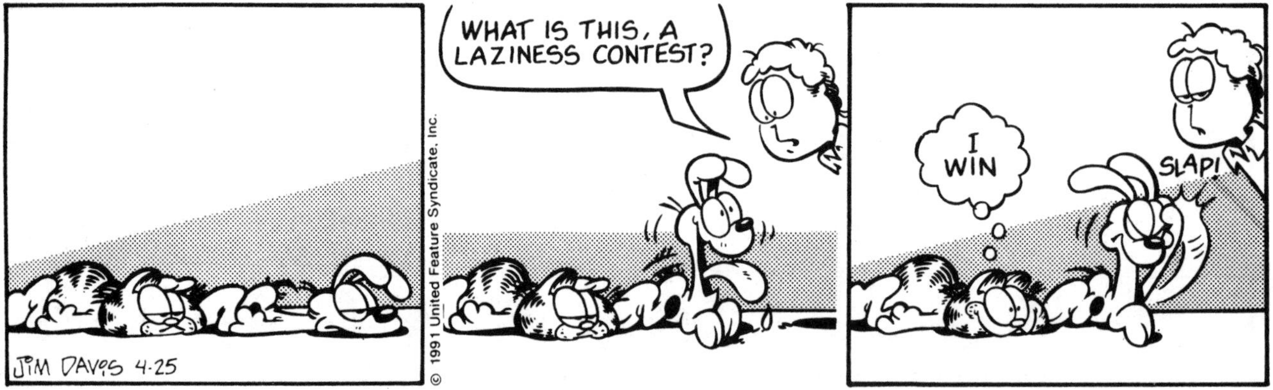
JIM DAVIS 4-25
WHAT IS THIS, A LAZINESS CONTEST?
I WIN
SLAP!

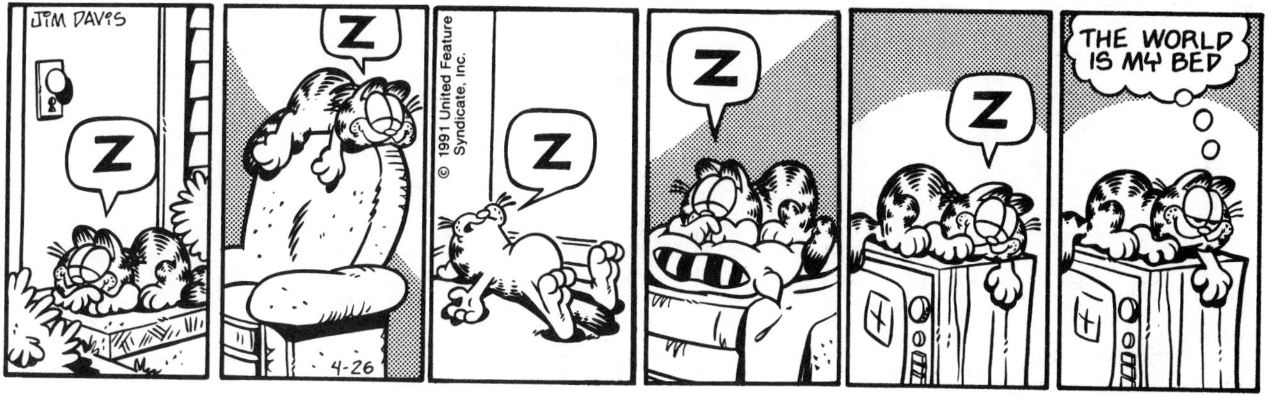
JIM DAVIS
Z
Z
4-26
© 1991 United Feature Syndicate, Inc.
Z
Z
Z
THE WORLD IS MY BED

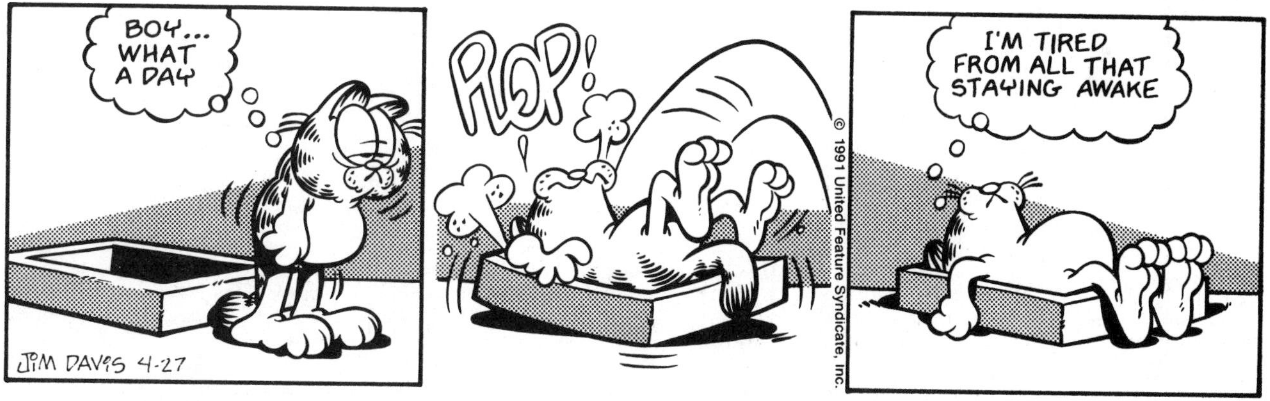
BOY... WHAT A DAY
JIM DAVIS 4-27
PLOP!
© 1991 United Feature Syndicate, Inc.
I'M TIRED FROM ALL THAT STAYING AWAKE

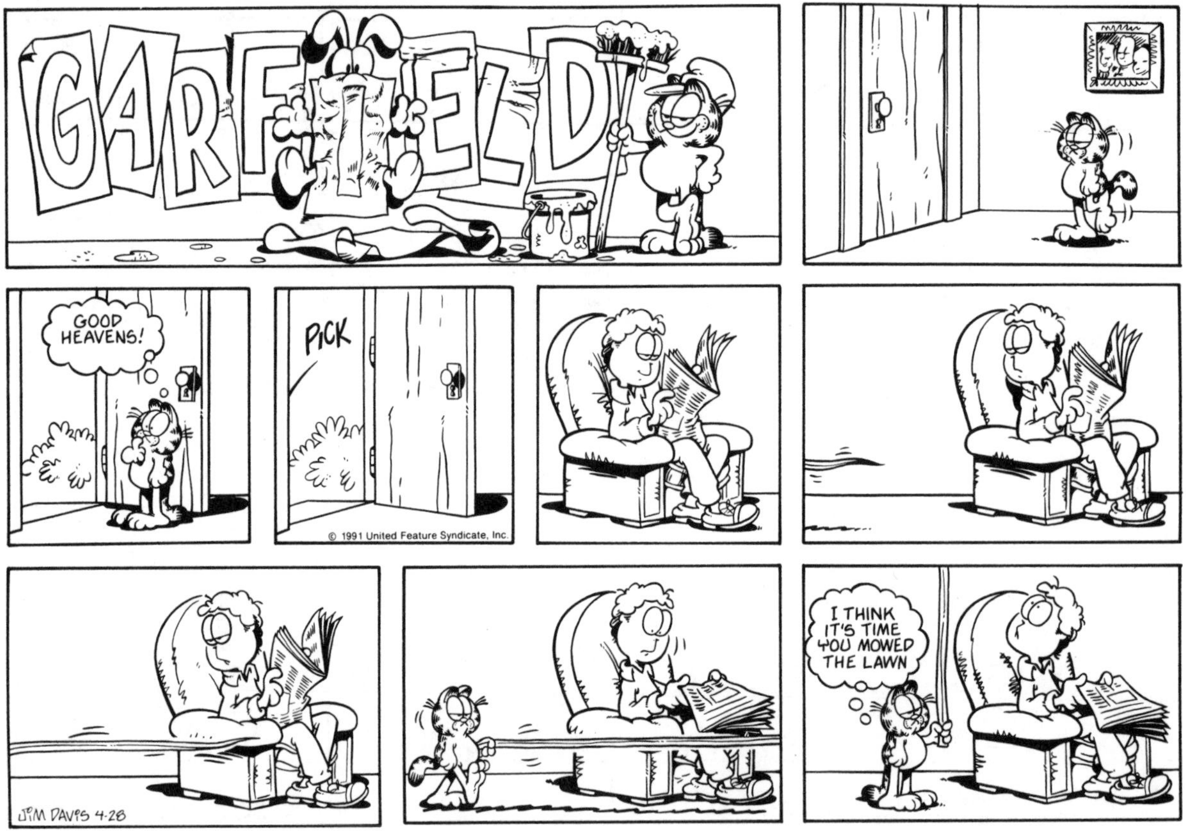
GARFIELD
GOOD HEAVENS!
PICK
© 1991 United Feature Syndicate, Inc.
JIM DAVIS 4-28
I THINK IT'S TIME YOU MOWED THE LAWN

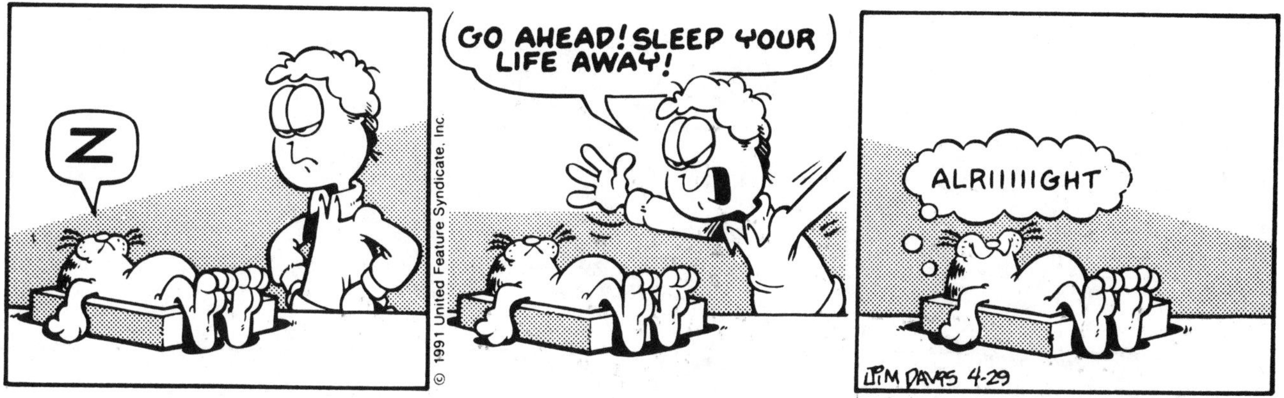
Z
GO AHEAD! SLEEP YOUR LIFE AWAY!
ALRIIIIIGHT
© 1991 United Feature Syndicate, Inc.
JIM DAVIS 4-29

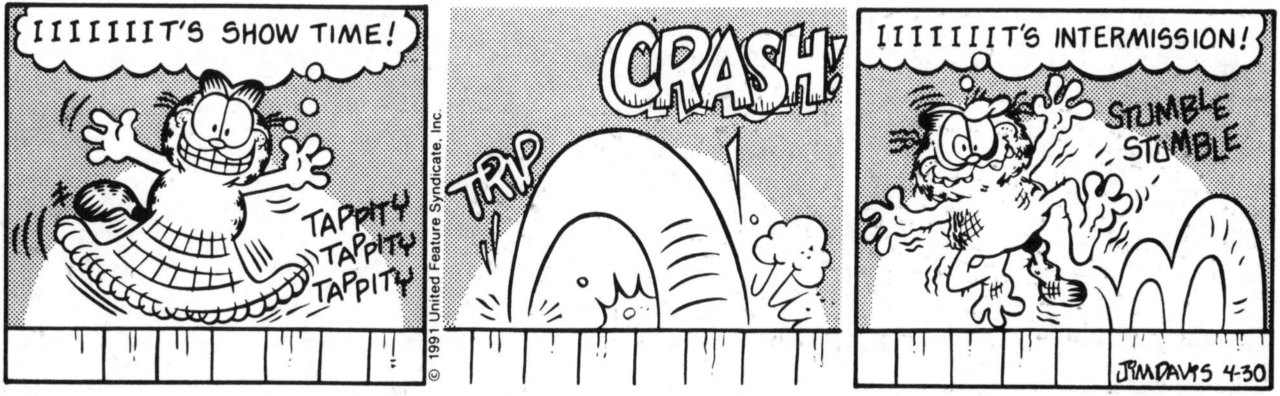
IIIIIIIT'S SHOW TIME!
TAPPITY TAPPITY TAPPITY
TRIP
CRASH!
IIIIIIIT'S INTERMISSION!
STUMBLE STUMBLE
© 1991 United Feature Syndicate, Inc.
JIM DAVIS 4-30

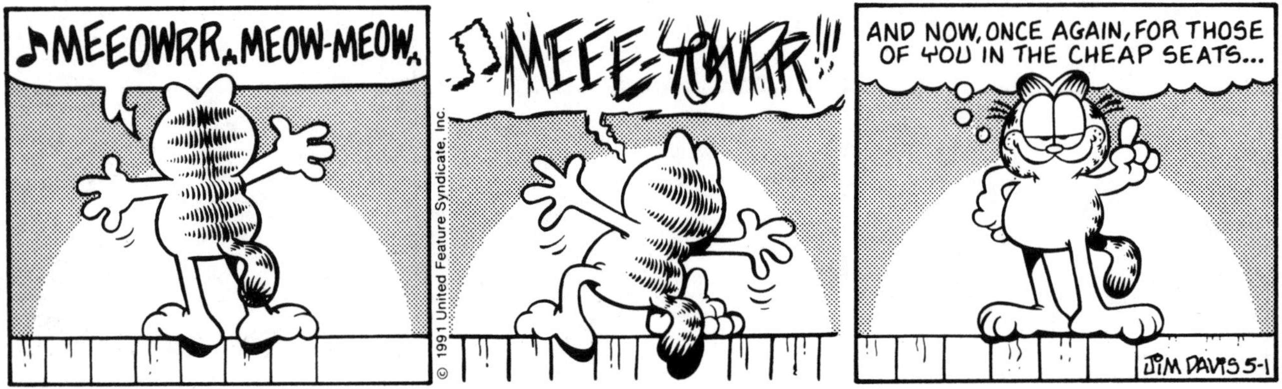
♪MEEOWRR MEOW-MEOW
MEEE-YOWRR!!!
© 1991 United Feature Syndicate, Inc.
AND NOW, ONCE AGAIN, FOR THOSE OF YOU IN THE CHEAP SEATS...
JIM DAVIS 5-1

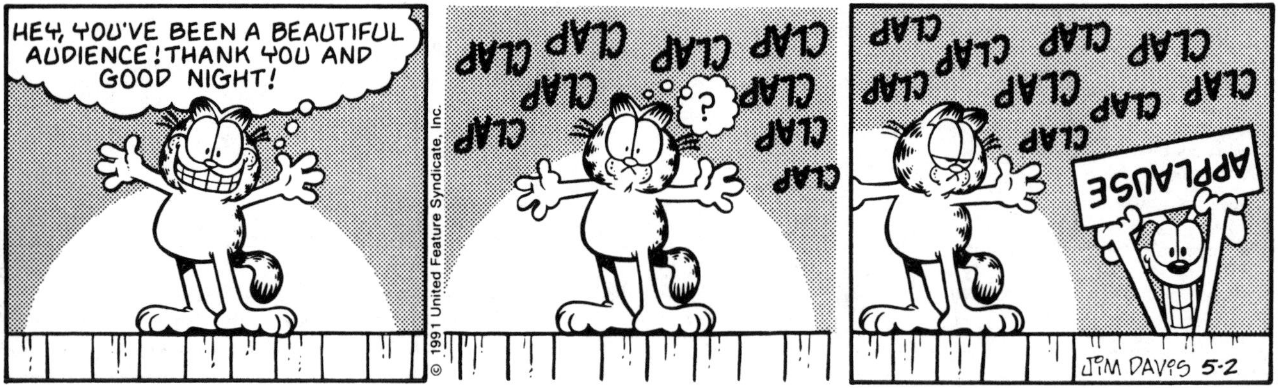
HEY, YOU'VE BEEN A BEAUTIFUL AUDIENCE! THANK YOU AND GOOD NIGHT!
© 1991 United Feature Syndicate, Inc.
CLAP CLAP CLAP CLAP CLAP CLAP CLAP CLAP CLAP
?
CLAP CLAP CLAP CLAP CLAP CLAP CLAP CLAP CLAP CLAP
APPLAUSE
JIM DAVIS 5-2

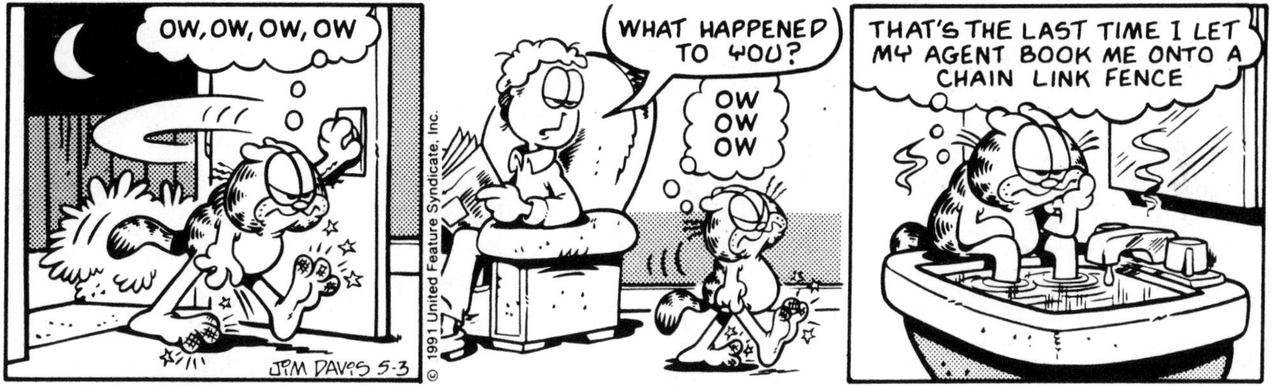
OW, OW, OW, OW
JIM DAVIS 5-3
© 1991 United Feature Syndicate, Inc.
WHAT HAPPENED TO YOU?
OW OW OW
THAT'S THE LAST TIME I LET MY AGENT BOOK ME ONTO A CHAIN LINK FENCE

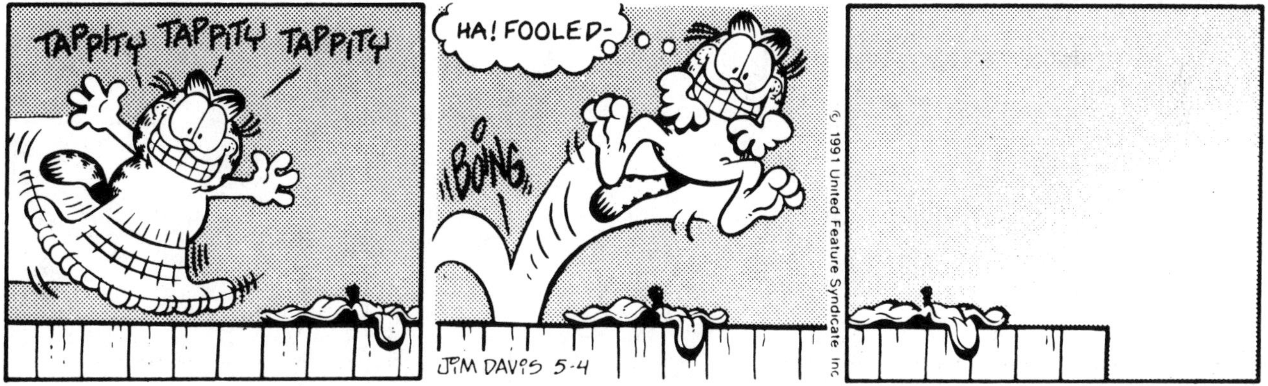
TAPPITY TAPPITY TAPPITY
HA! FOOLED-
BOING
JIM DAVIS 5-4
© 1991 United Feature Syndicate, Inc.

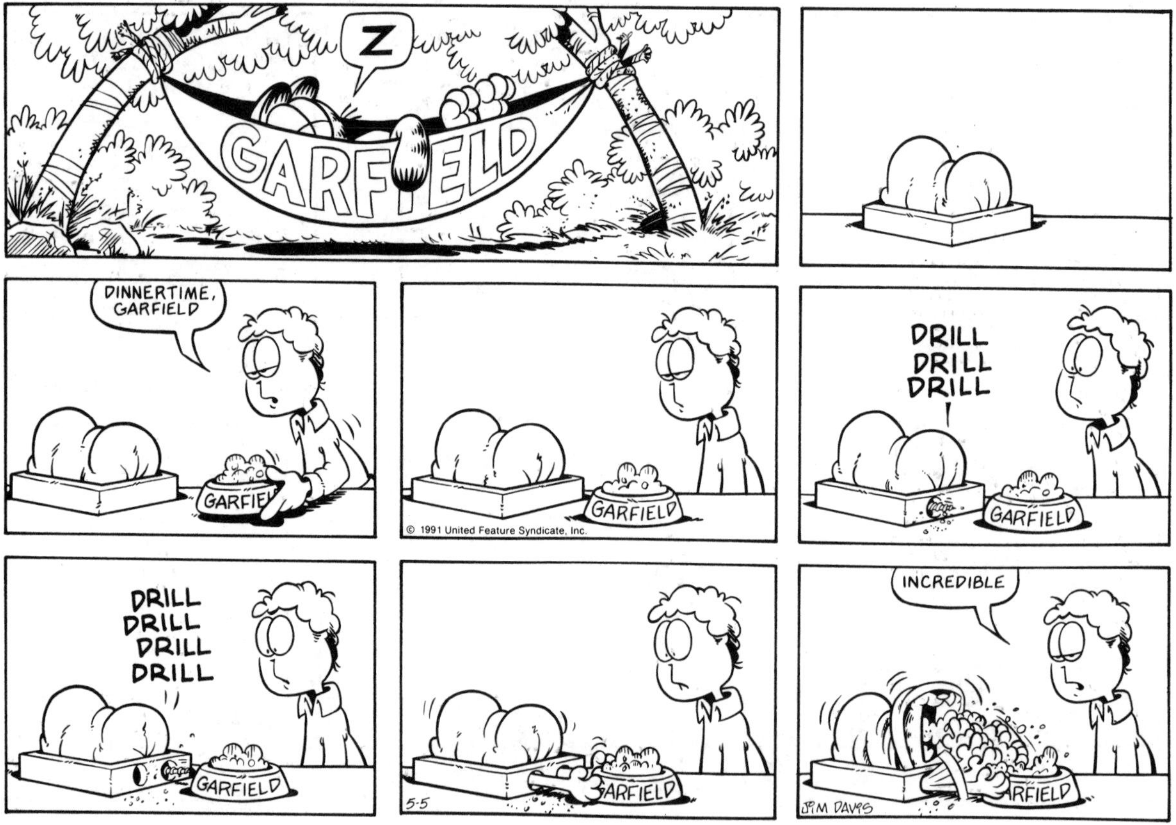
GARFIELD
Z
DINNERTIME, GARFIELD
GARFIELD
GARFIELD
© 1991 United Feature Syndicate, Inc.
DRILL DRILL DRILL
GARFIELD
DRILL DRILL DRILL DRILL
GARFIELD
5-5
INCREDIBLE
JIM DAVIS

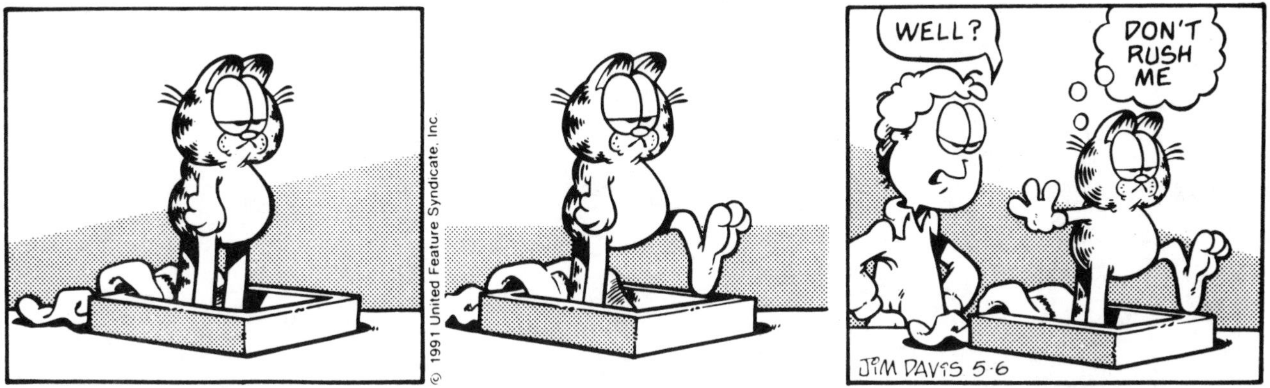
WELL?
DON'T RUSH ME
JIM DAVIS 5-6

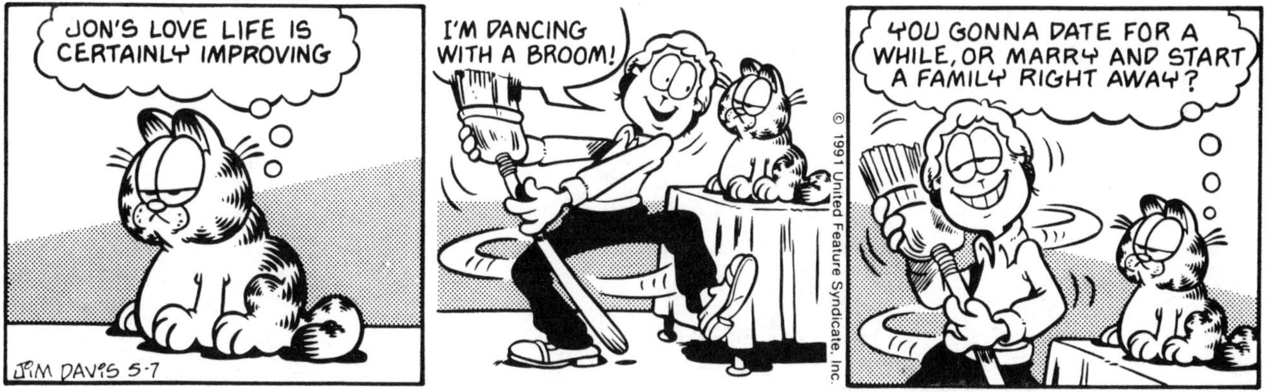
JON'S LOVE LIFE IS CERTAINLY IMPROVING
JIM DAVIS 5-7
I'M DANCING WITH A BROOM!
YOU GONNA DATE FOR A WHILE, OR MARRY AND START A FAMILY RIGHT AWAY?

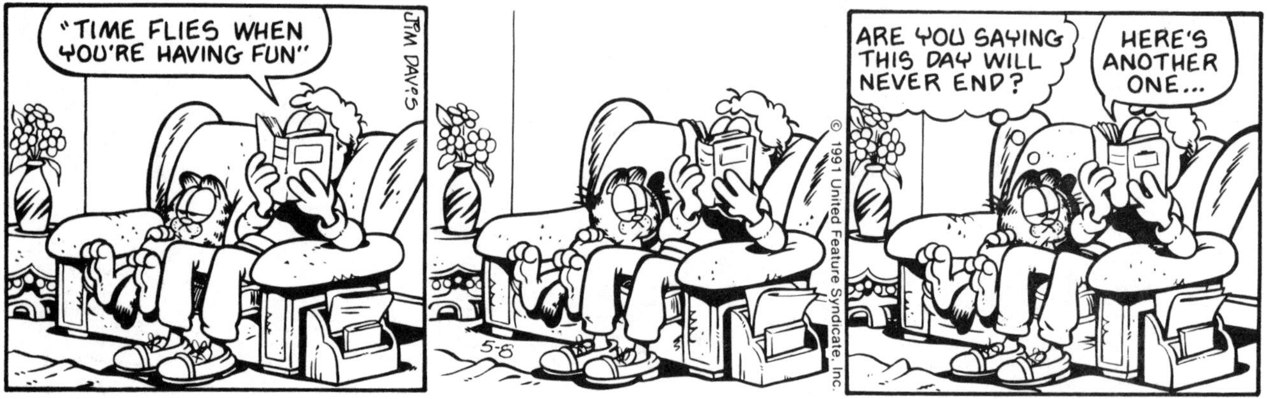
"TIME FLIES WHEN YOU'RE HAVING FUN"
JIM DAVIS
5-8
ARE YOU SAYING THIS DAY WILL NEVER END?
HERE'S ANOTHER ONE...
© 1991 United Feature Syndicate, Inc.

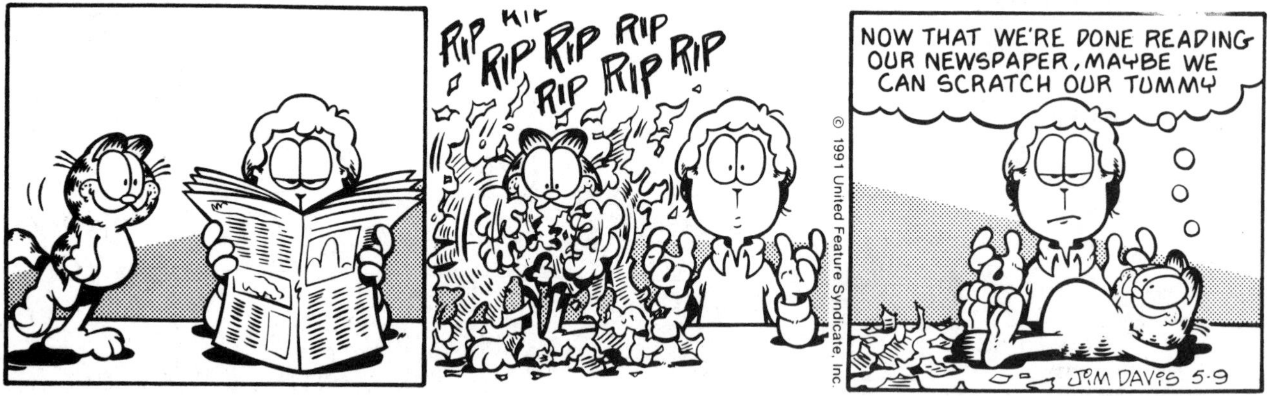
RIP RIP RIP RIP RIP RIP RIP RIP
NOW THAT WE'RE DONE READING OUR NEWSPAPER, MAYBE WE CAN SCRATCH OUR TUMMY
JIM DAVIS 5-9
© 1991 United Feature Syndicate, Inc.

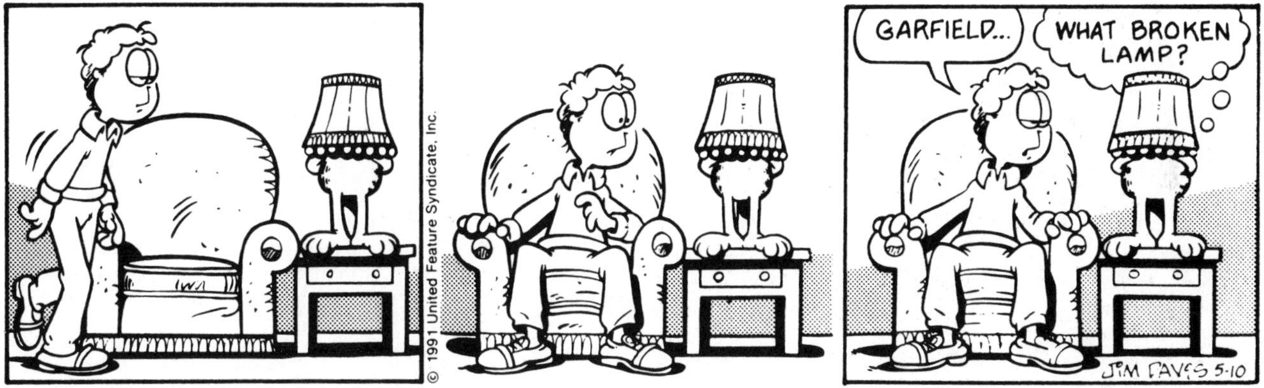
© 1991 United Feature Syndicate, Inc.
GARFIELD...
WHAT BROKEN LAMP?
JIM DAVIS 5-10

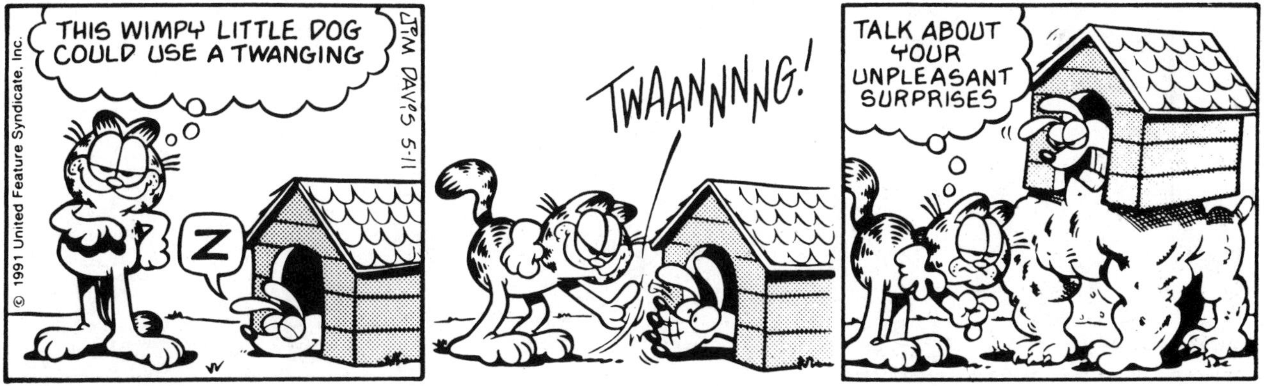
© 1991 United Feature Syndicate, Inc.
THIS WIMPY LITTLE DOG COULD USE A TWANGING
JIM DAVIS 5-11
Z
TWAANNNNG!
TALK ABOUT YOUR UNPLEASANT SURPRISES

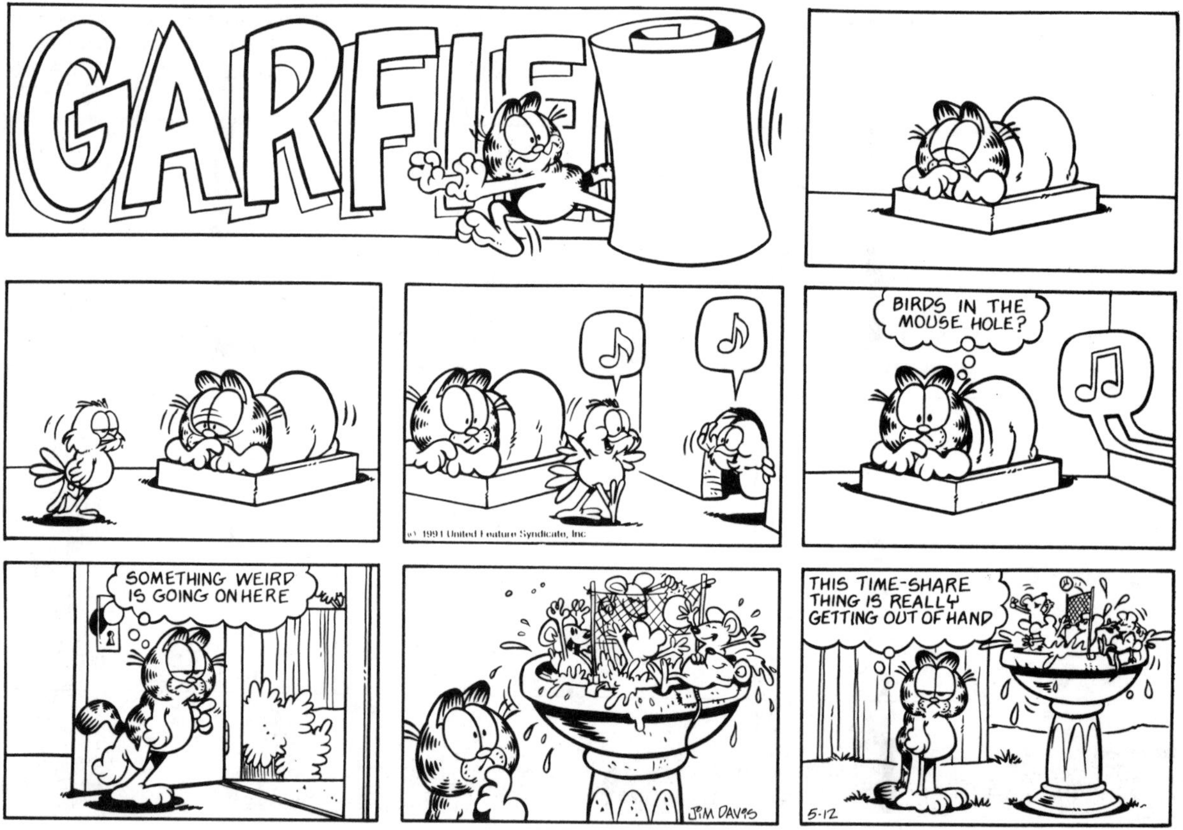
GARFIE
BIRDS IN THE MOUSE HOLE?
© 1991 United Feature Syndicate, Inc.
SOMETHING WEIRD IS GOING ON HERE
JIM DAVIS
THIS TIME-SHARE THING IS REALLY GETTING OUT OF HAND
5-12

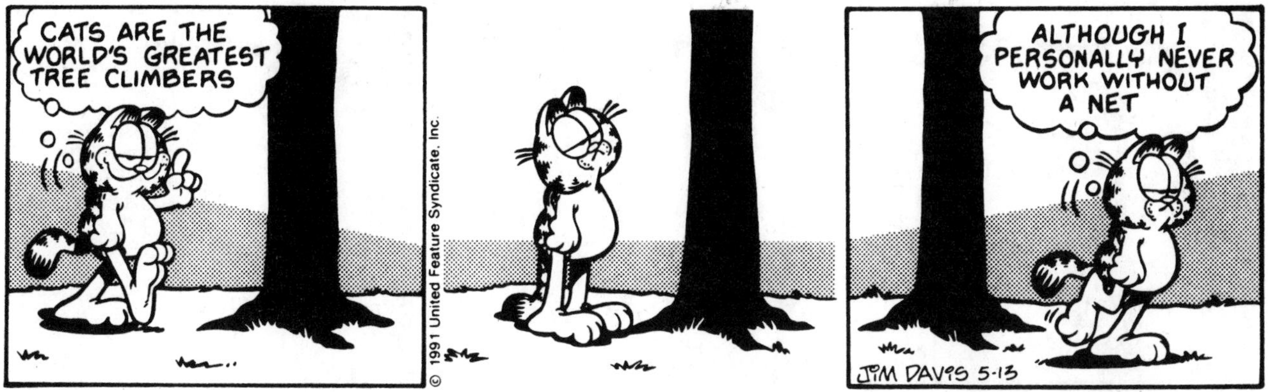
CATS ARE THE WORLD'S GREATEST TREE CLIMBERS
ALTHOUGH I PERSONALLY NEVER WORK WITHOUT A NET
© 1991 United Feature Syndicate, Inc.
JIM DAVIS 5-13

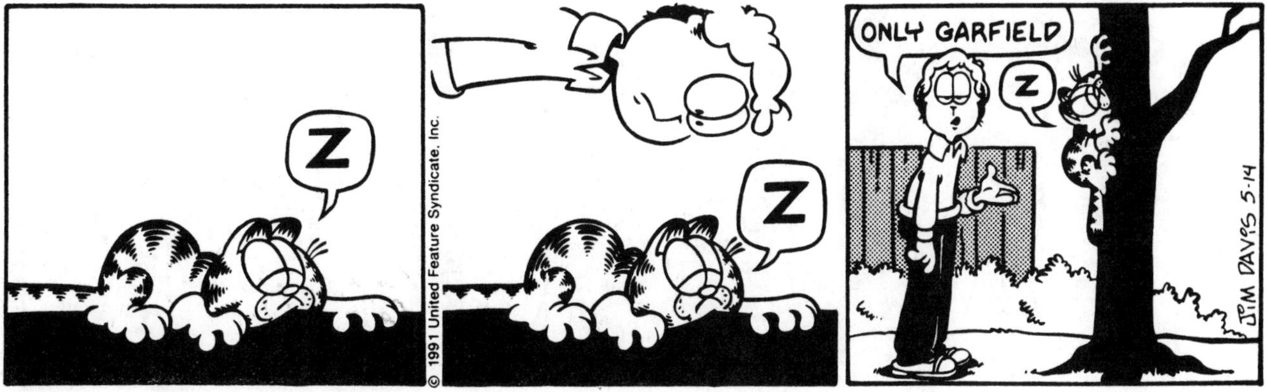
Z
Z
ONLY GARFIELD
Z
© 1991 United Feature Syndicate, Inc.
JIM DAVIS 5-14

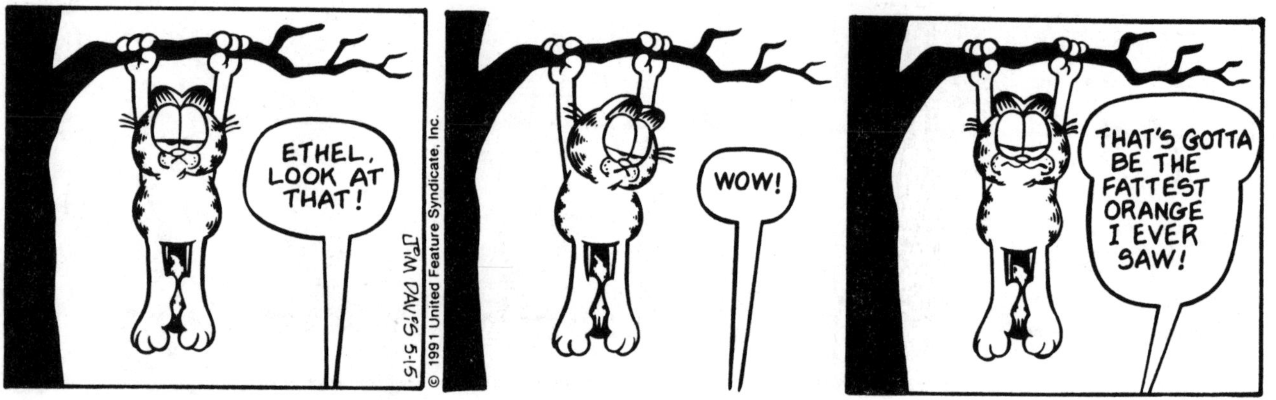
ETHEL, LOOK AT THAT!
JIM DAVIS 5-15
WOW!
THAT'S GOTTA BE THE FATTEST ORANGE I EVER SAW!

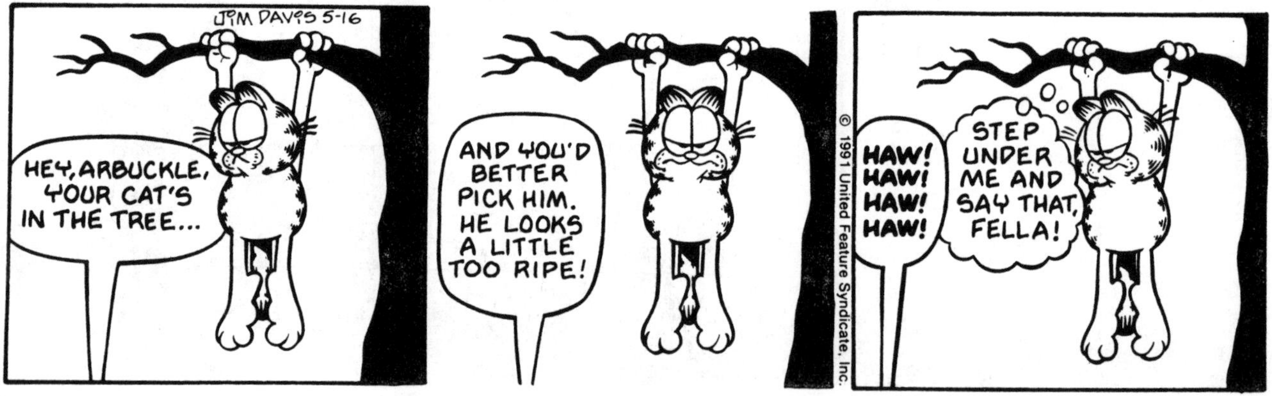
JIM DAVIS 5-16
HEY, ARBUCKLE, YOUR CAT'S IN THE TREE...
AND YOU'D BETTER PICK HIM. HE LOOKS A LITTLE TOO RIPE!
HAW! HAW! HAW! HAW!
STEP UNDER ME AND SAY THAT, FELLA!

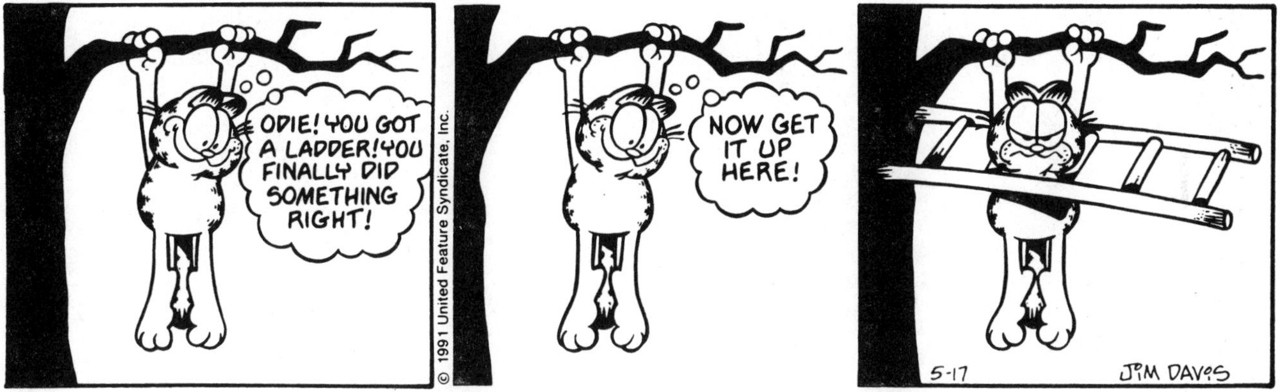
ODIE! YOU GOT A LADDER! YOU FINALLY DID SOMETHING RIGHT!
NOW GET IT UP HERE!
5-17
JIM DAVIS

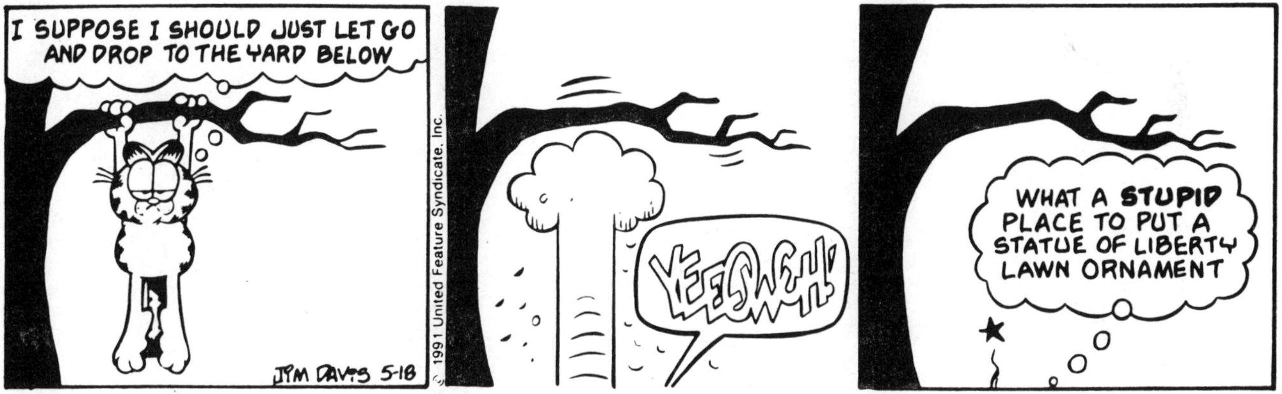
I SUPPOSE I SHOULD JUST LET GO AND DROP TO THE YARD BELOW
JIM DAVIS 5-18
YEEOWCH!
WHAT A **STUPID** PLACE TO PUT A STATUE OF LIBERTY LAWN ORNAMENT

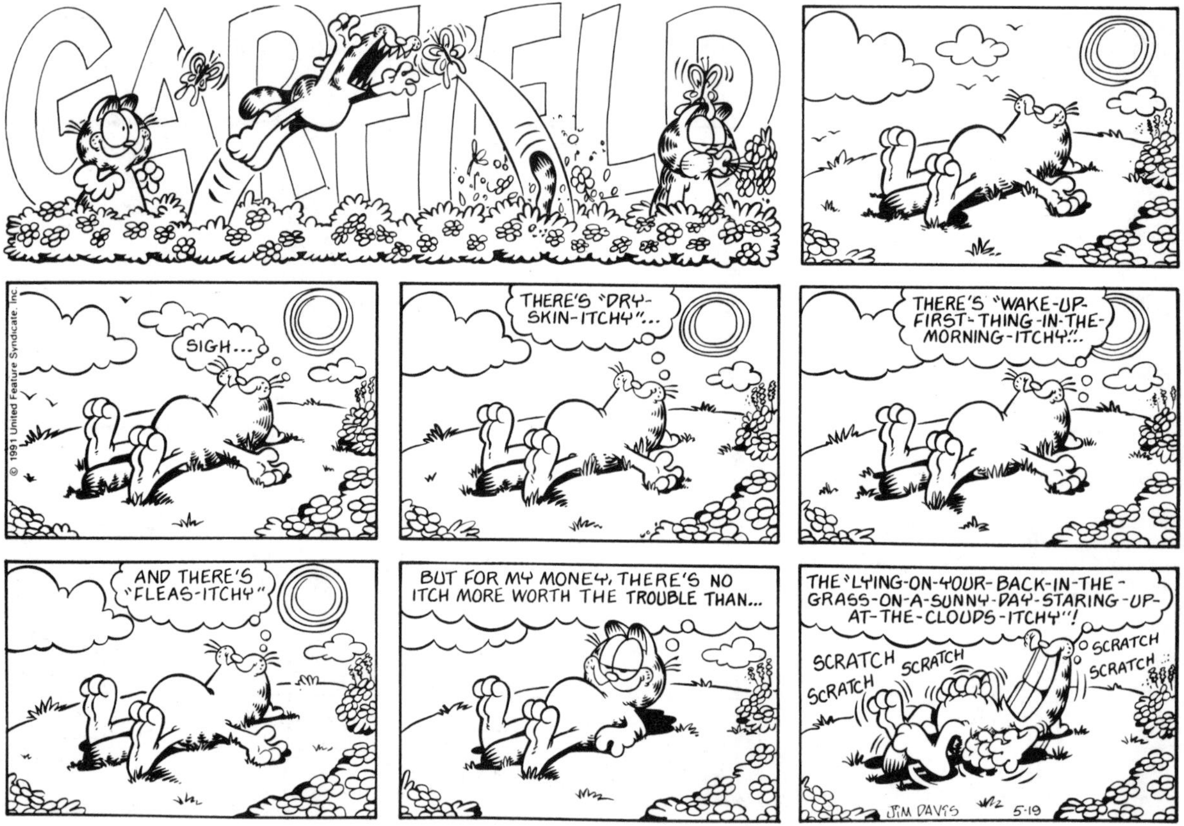
GARFIELD
© 1991 United Feature Syndicate, Inc.
SIGH...
THERE'S "DRY-SKIN-ITCHY"...
THERE'S "WAKE-UP-FIRST-THING-IN-THE-MORNING-ITCHY"...
AND THERE'S "FLEAS-ITCHY"
BUT FOR MY MONEY, THERE'S NO ITCH MORE WORTH THE TROUBLE THAN...
THE "LYING-ON-YOUR-BACK-IN-THE-GRASS-ON-A-SUNNY-DAY-STARING-UP-AT-THE-CLOUDS-ITCHY"!
SCRATCH
SCRATCH
SCRATCH
SCRATCH
SCRATCH
JIM DAVIS 5-19

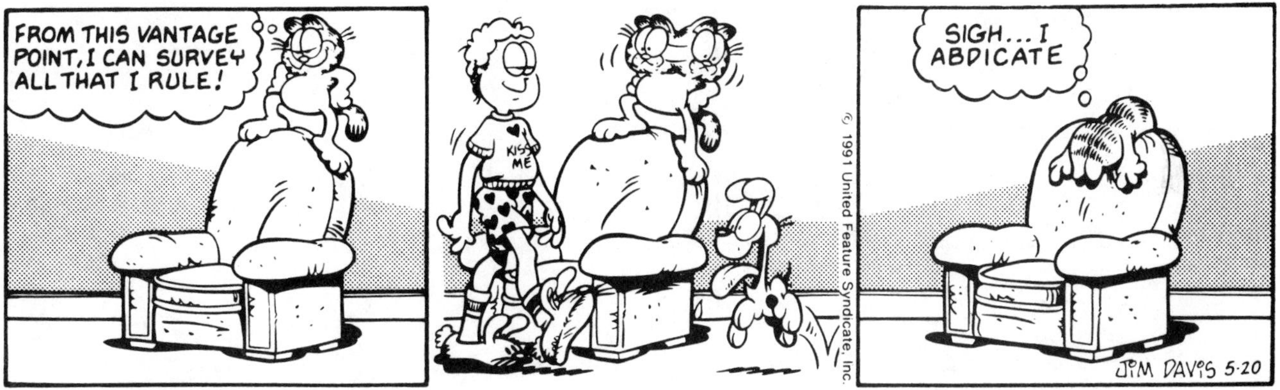
FROM THIS VANTAGE POINT, I CAN SURVEY ALL THAT I RULE!
KISS ME
© 1991 United Feature Syndicate, Inc.
SIGH... I ABDICATE
JIM DAVIS 5-20

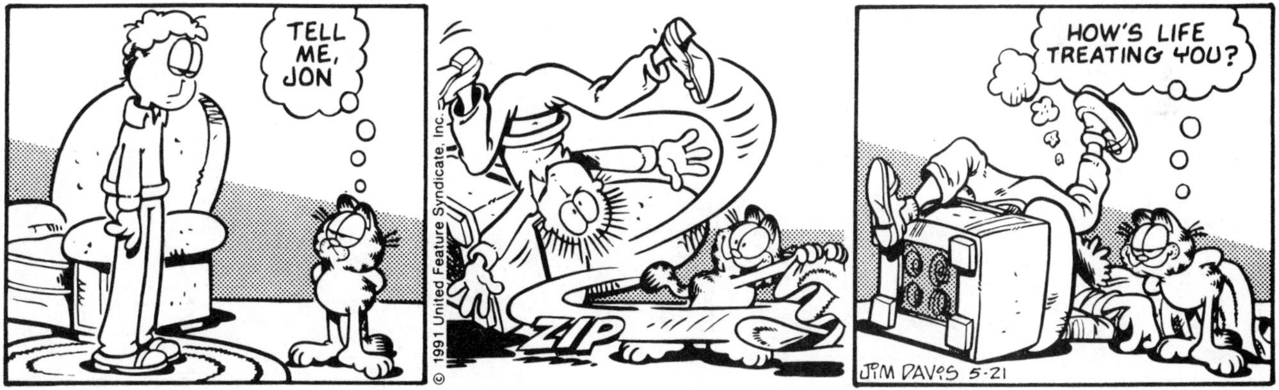
TELL ME, JON
© 1991 United Feature Syndicate, Inc.
ZIP
HOW'S LIFE TREATING YOU?
JIM DAVIS 5-21

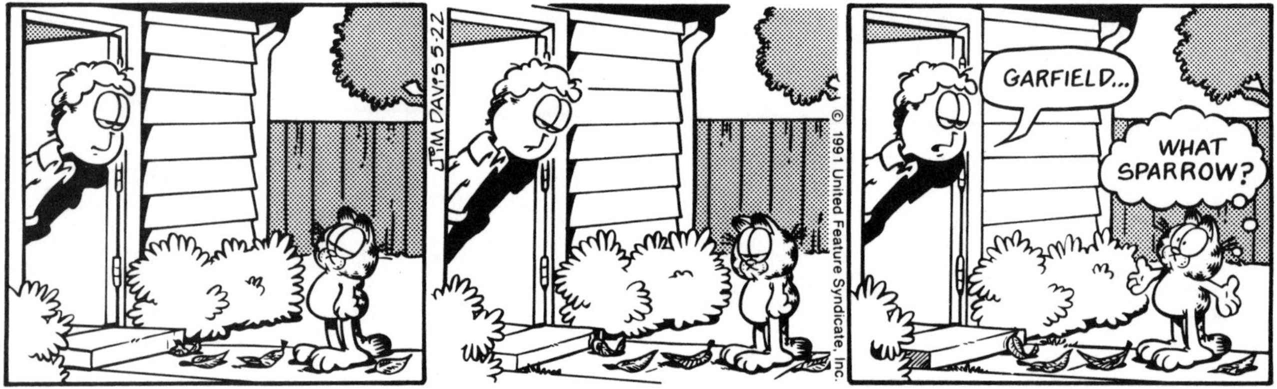
JIM DAVIS 5·22
© 1991 United Feature Syndicate, Inc.
GARFIELD...
WHAT SPARROW?

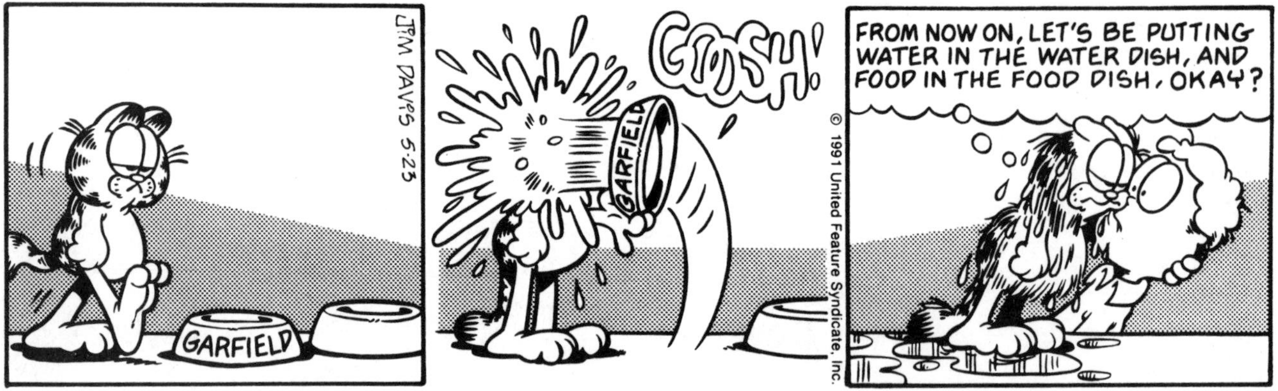
JIM DAVIS 5·23
GARFIELD
GOOSH!
GARFIELD
© 1991 United Feature Syndicate, Inc.
FROM NOW ON, LET'S BE PUTTING WATER IN THE WATER DISH, AND FOOD IN THE FOOD DISH, OKAY?

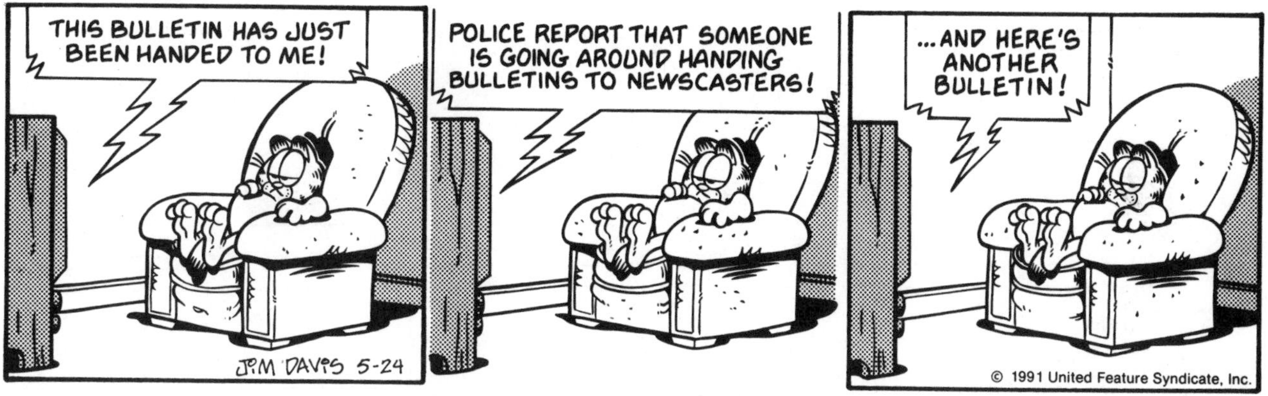
THIS BULLETIN HAS JUST BEEN HANDED TO ME!
POLICE REPORT THAT SOMEONE IS GOING AROUND HANDING BULLETINS TO NEWSCASTERS!
...AND HERE'S ANOTHER BULLETIN!
JIM DAVIS 5-24
© 1991 United Feature Syndicate, Inc.

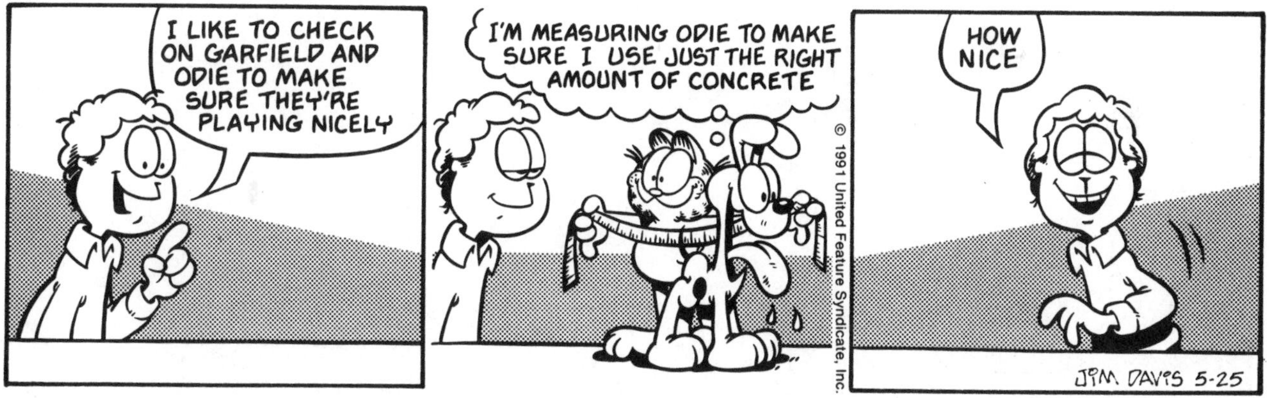
I LIKE TO CHECK ON GARFIELD AND ODIE TO MAKE SURE THEY'RE PLAYING NICELY
I'M MEASURING ODIE TO MAKE SURE I USE JUST THE RIGHT AMOUNT OF CONCRETE
HOW NICE
JIM DAVIS 5-25
© 1991 United Feature Syndicate, Inc.

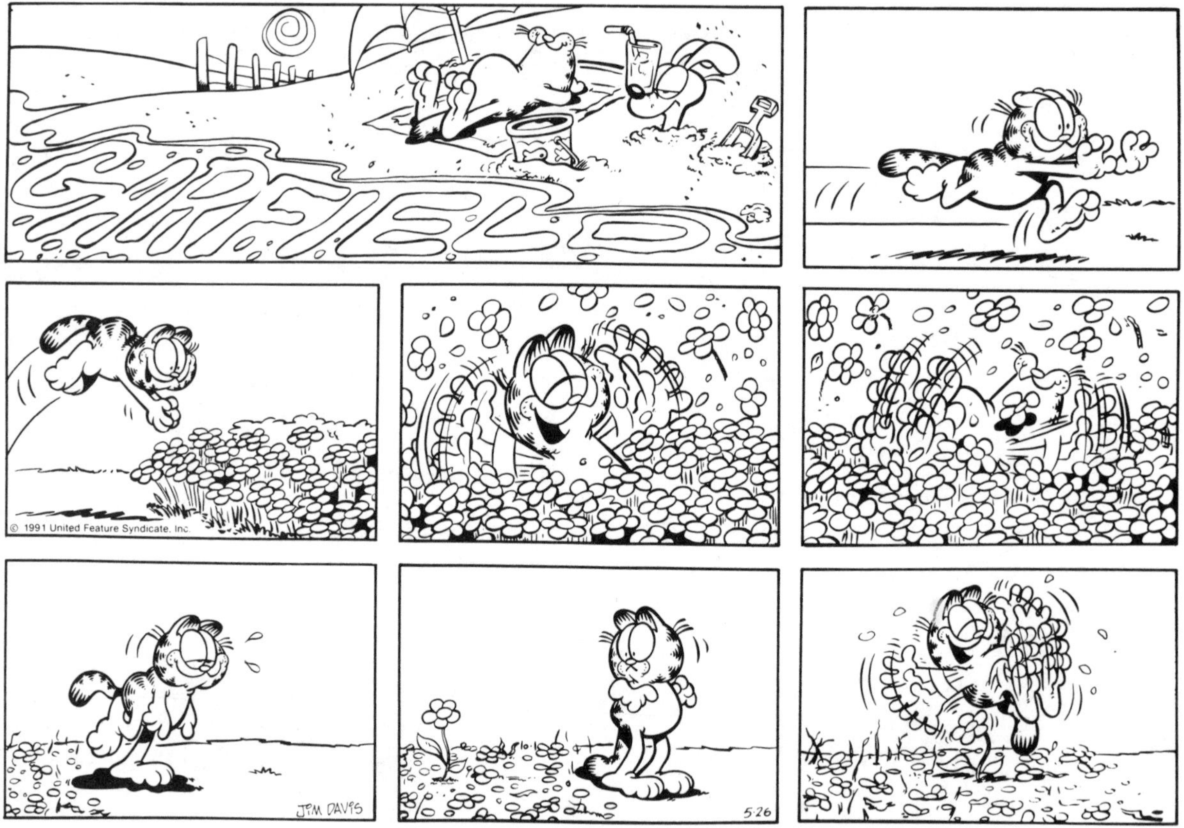
GARFIELD
© 1991 United Feature Syndicate, Inc.
JIM DAVIS
5-26

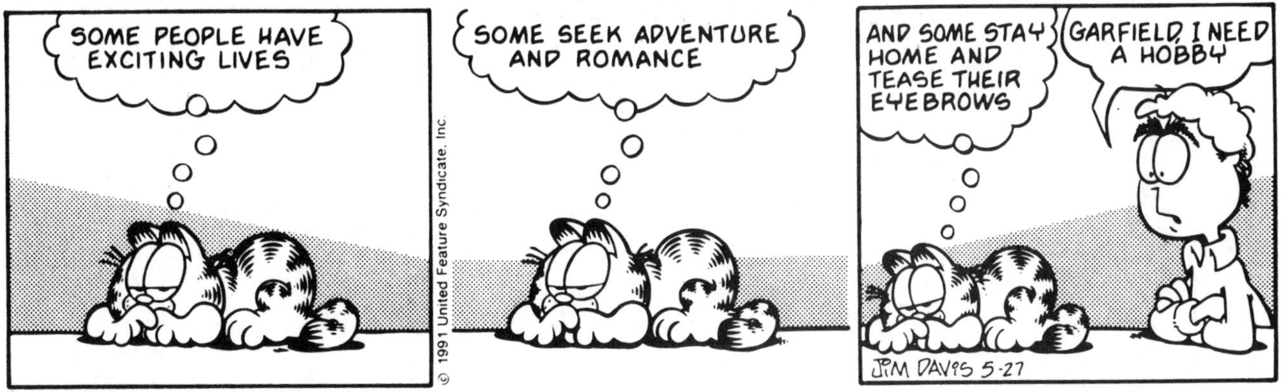
SOME PEOPLE HAVE EXCITING LIVES
SOME SEEK ADVENTURE AND ROMANCE
© 1991 United Feature Syndicate, Inc.
AND SOME STAY HOME AND TEASE THEIR EYEBROWS
GARFIELD, I NEED A HOBBY
JIM DAVIS 5-27

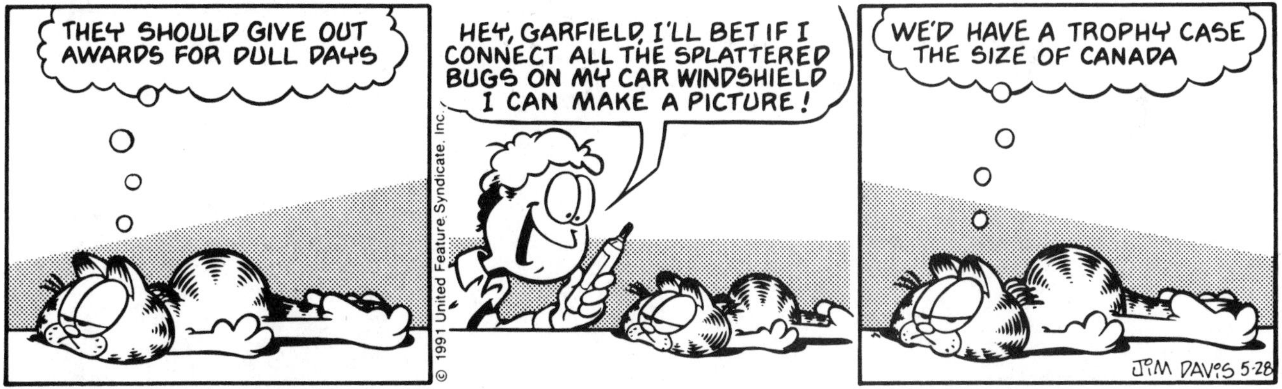
THEY SHOULD GIVE OUT AWARDS FOR DULL DAYS
HEY, GARFIELD, I'LL BET IF I CONNECT ALL THE SPLATTERED BUGS ON MY CAR WINDSHIELD I CAN MAKE A PICTURE!
© 1991 United Feature Syndicate, Inc.
WE'D HAVE A TROPHY CASE THE SIZE OF CANADA
JIM DAVIS 5-28

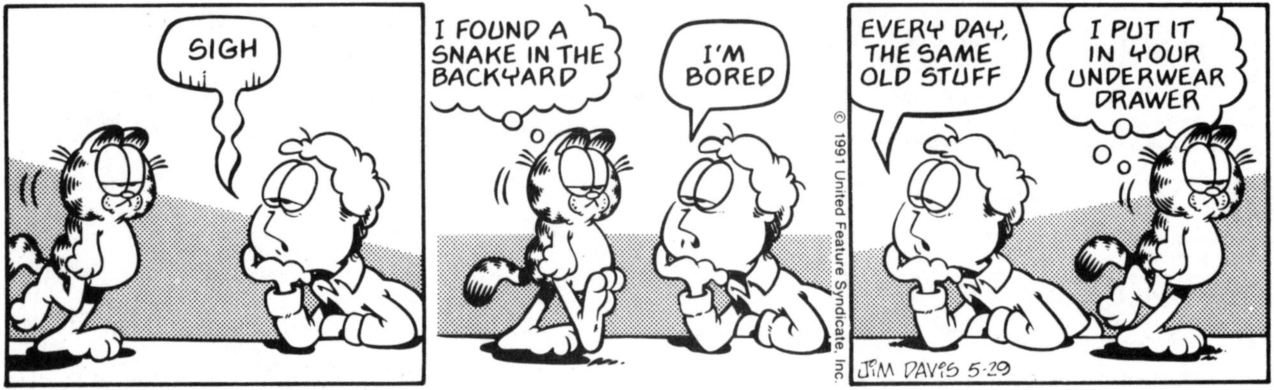
SIGH
I FOUND A SNAKE IN THE BACKYARD
I'M BORED
EVERY DAY, THE SAME OLD STUFF
I PUT IT IN YOUR UNDERWEAR DRAWER
JIM DAVIS 5-29

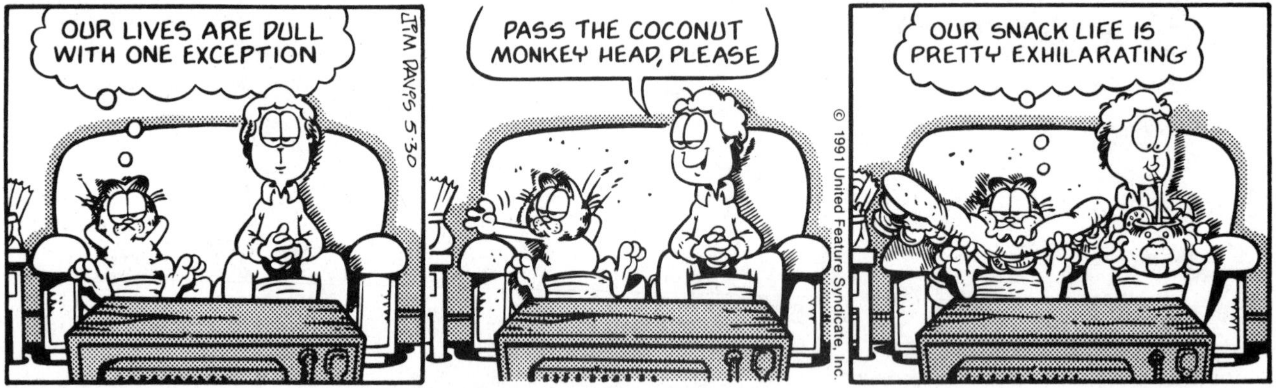
OUR LIVES ARE DULL WITH ONE EXCEPTION
JIM DAVIS 5-30
PASS THE COCONUT MONKEY HEAD, PLEASE
OUR SNACK LIFE IS PRETTY EXHILARATING

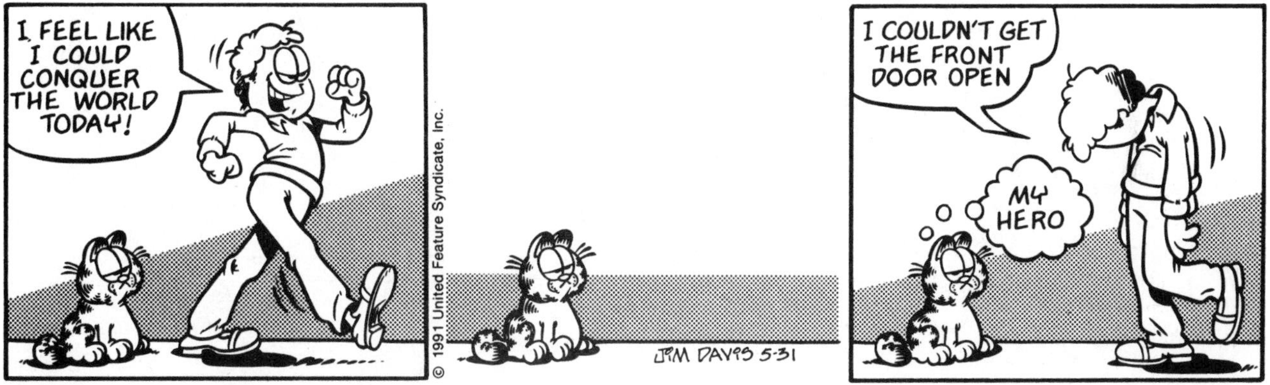
I FEEL LIKE I COULD CONQUER THE WORLD TODAY!
© 1991 United Feature Syndicate, Inc.
JIM DAVIS 5-31
I COULDN'T GET THE FRONT DOOR OPEN
MY HERO

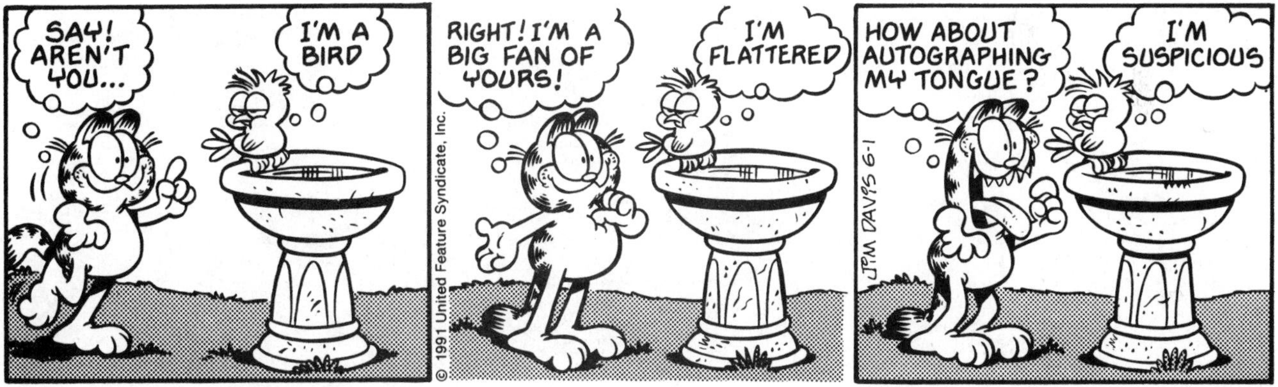
SAY! AREN'T YOU...
I'M A BIRD
© 1991 United Feature Syndicate, Inc.
RIGHT! I'M A BIG FAN OF YOURS!
I'M FLATTERED
JIM DAVIS 6-1
HOW ABOUT AUTOGRAPHING MY TONGUE?
I'M SUSPICIOUS

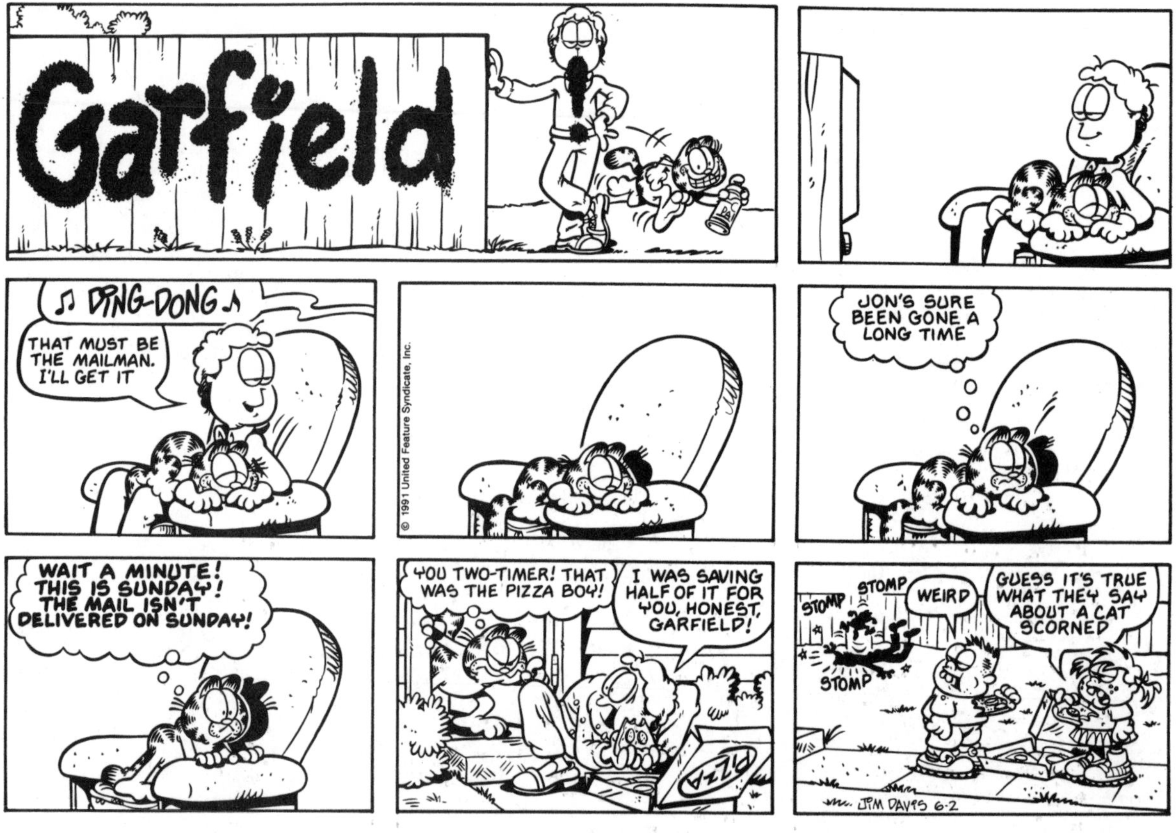
Garfield
♫ DING-DONG ♪
THAT MUST BE THE MAILMAN. I'LL GET IT
© 1991 United Feature Syndicate, Inc.
JON'S SURE BEEN GONE A LONG TIME
WAIT A MINUTE! THIS IS SUNDAY! THE MAIL ISN'T DELIVERED ON SUNDAY!
YOU TWO-TIMER! THAT WAS THE PIZZA BOY!
I WAS SAVING HALF OF IT FOR YOU, HONEST, GARFIELD!
PIZZA
STOMP
STOMP
STOMP
WEIRD
GUESS IT'S TRUE WHAT THEY SAY ABOUT A CAT SCORNED
JPM DAVIS 6-2

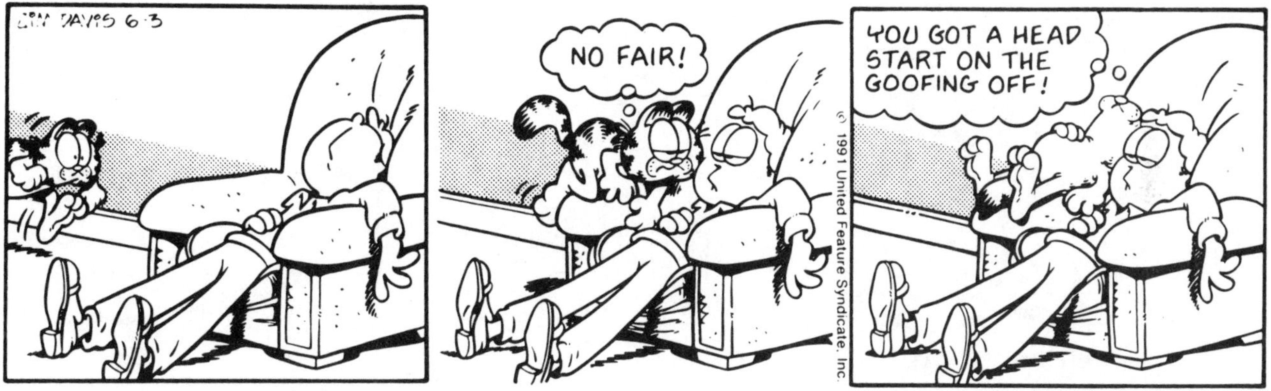
JIM DAVIS 6-3
NO FAIR!
YOU GOT A HEAD START ON THE GOOFING OFF!
© 1991 United Feature Syndicate, Inc.

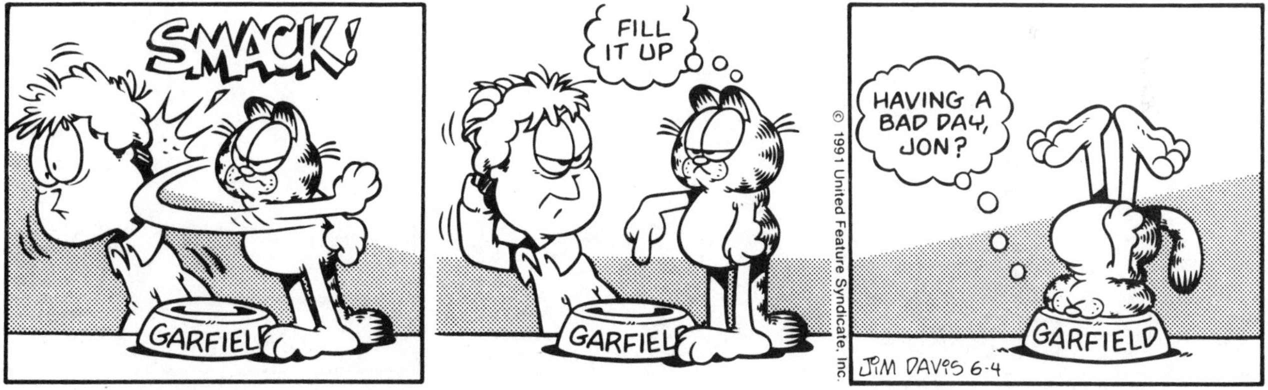
SMACK!
GARFIELD
FILL IT UP
GARFIELD
HAVING A BAD DAY, JON?
GARFIELD
JIM DAVIS 6-4
© 1991 United Feature Syndicate, Inc.

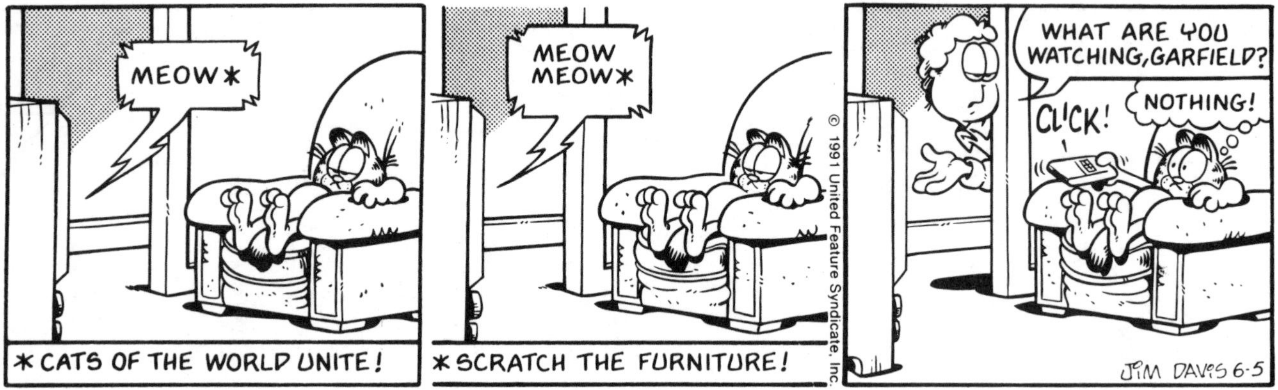
MEOW*
*CATS OF THE WORLD UNITE!
MEOW MEOW*
*SCRATCH THE FURNITURE!
© 1991 United Feature Syndicate, Inc.
WHAT ARE YOU WATCHING, GARFIELD?
CLICK!
NOTHING!
JIM DAVIS 6-5

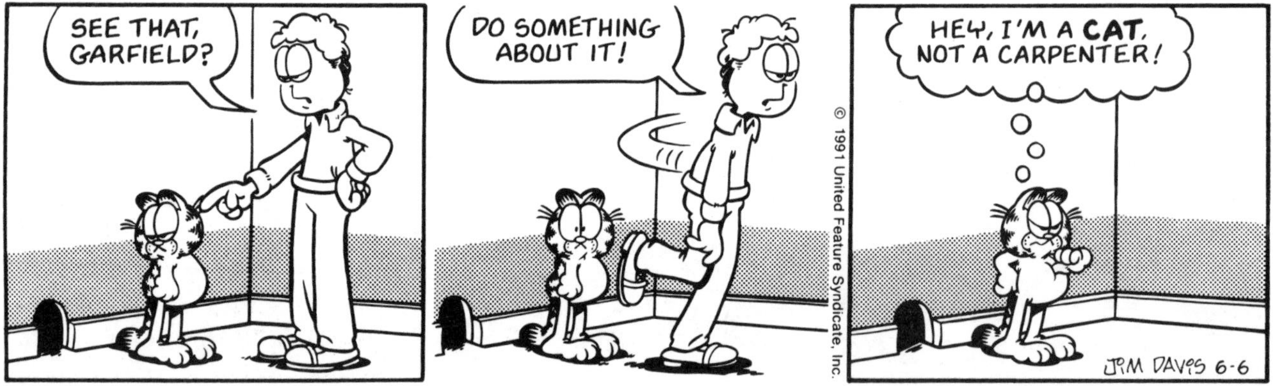
SEE THAT, GARFIELD?
DO SOMETHING ABOUT IT!
© 1991 United Feature Syndicate, Inc.
HEY, I'M A **CAT**, NOT A CARPENTER!
JIM DAVIS 6-6

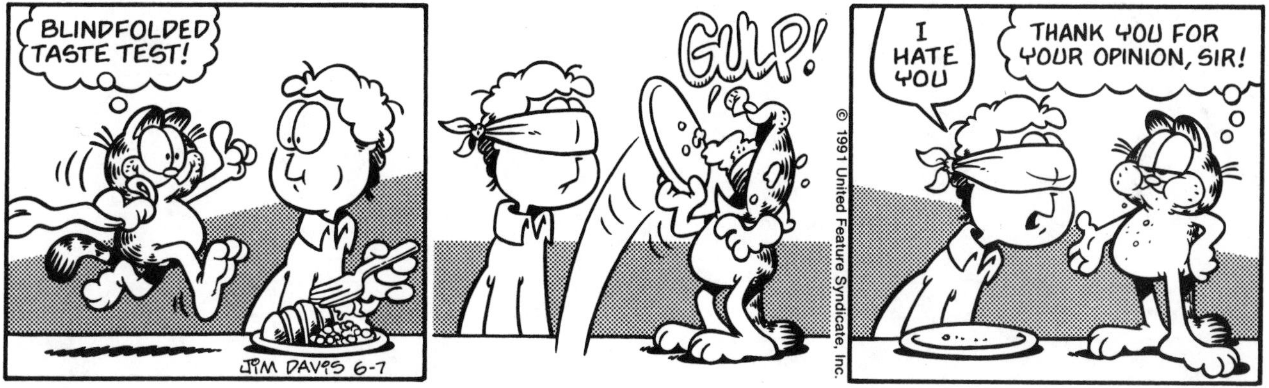
BLINDFOLDED TASTE TEST!
JIM DAVIS 6-7
GULP!
© 1991 United Feature Syndicate, Inc.
I HATE YOU
THANK YOU FOR YOUR OPINION, SIR!

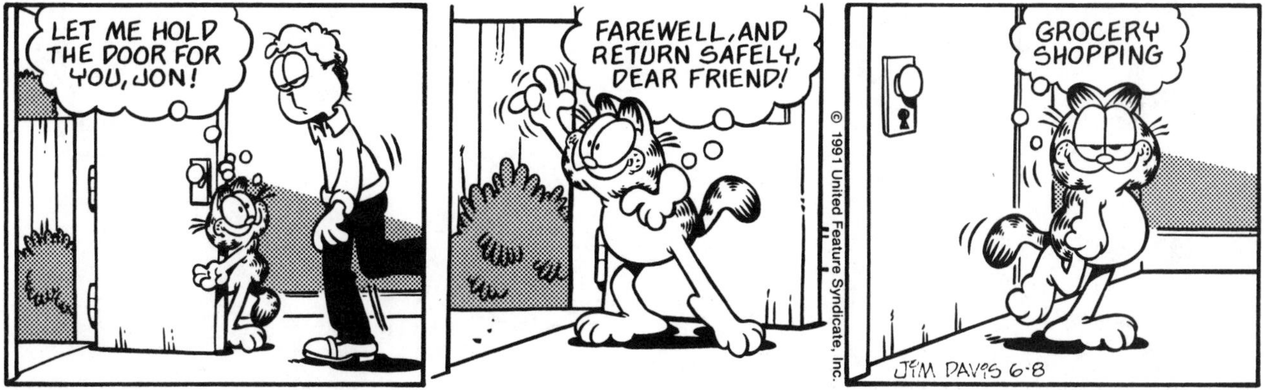
LET ME HOLD THE DOOR FOR YOU, JON!
FAREWELL, AND RETURN SAFELY, DEAR FRIEND!
© 1991 United Feature Syndicate, Inc.
GROCERY SHOPPING
JIM DAVIS 6-8

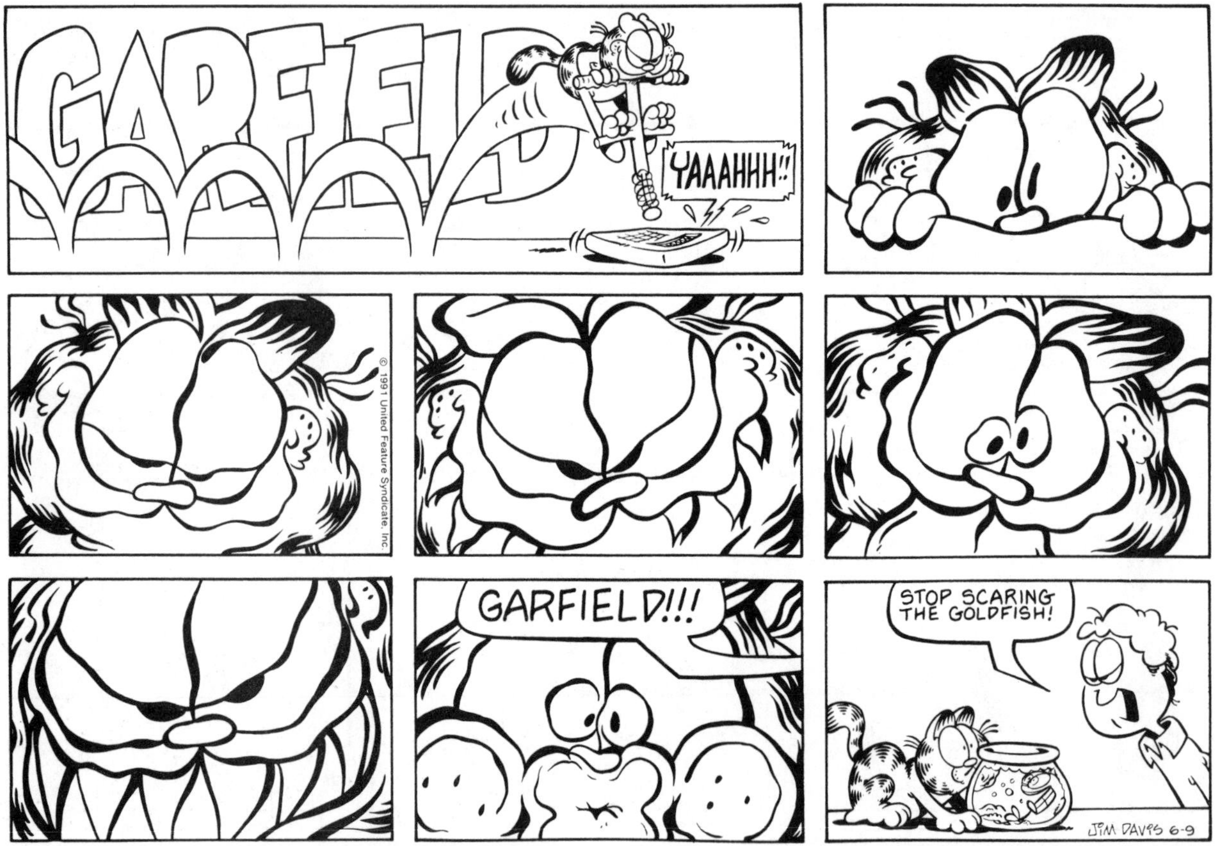
GARFIELD
YAAAHHH!!
© 1991 United Feature Syndicate, Inc.
GARFIELD!!!
STOP SCARING THE GOLDFISH!
JIM DAVIS 6-9

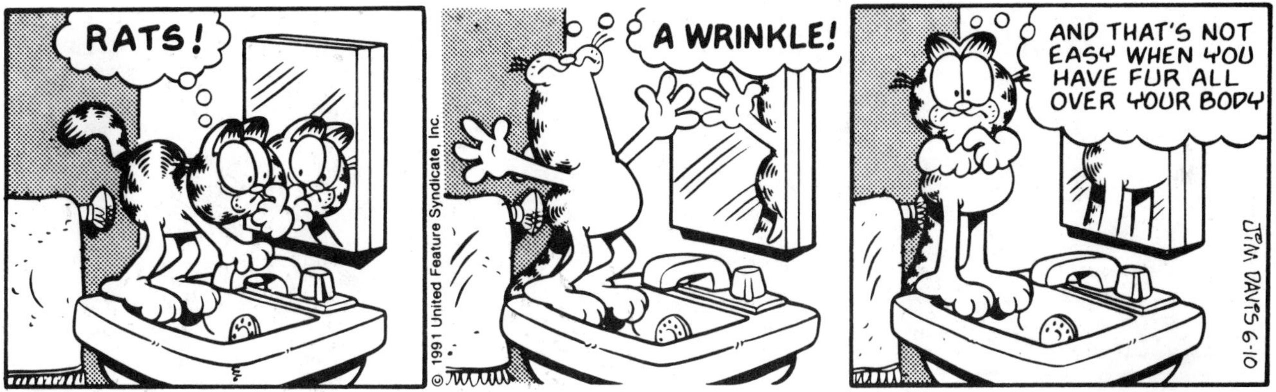
RATS!
A WRINKLE!
AND THAT'S NOT EASY WHEN YOU HAVE FUR ALL OVER YOUR BODY
© 1991 United Feature Syndicate, Inc.
JIM DAVIS 6-10

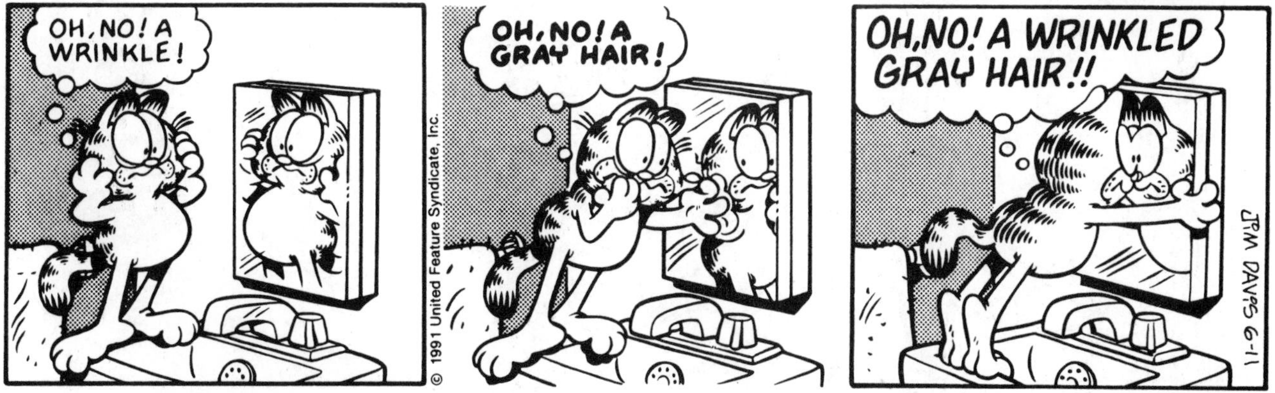
OH, NO! A WRINKLE!
OH, NO! A GRAY HAIR!
OH, NO! A WRINKLED GRAY HAIR!!
© 1991 United Feature Syndicate, Inc.
JIM DAVIS 6-11

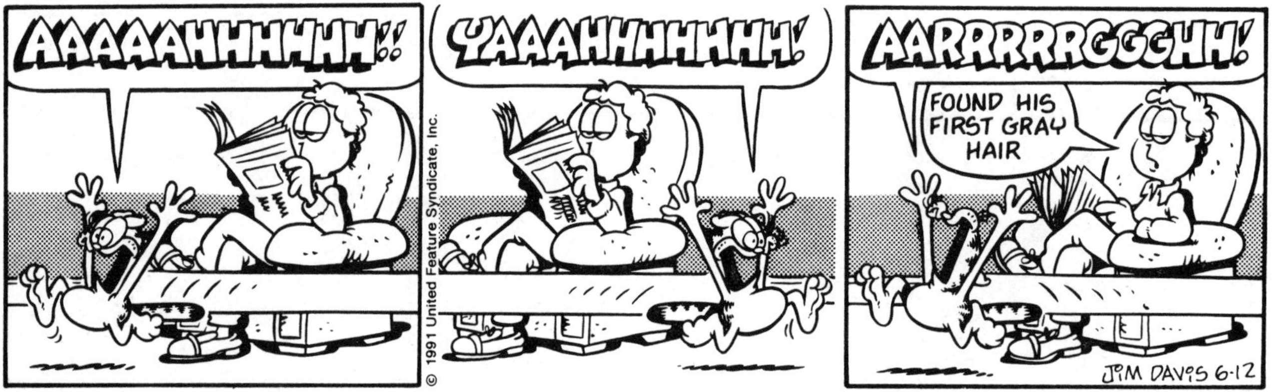
AAAAAHHHHHH!!
YAAAHHHHHHH!
AARRRRRGGGHH!
FOUND HIS FIRST GRAY HAIR
© 1991 United Feature Syndicate, Inc.
JIM DAVIS 6-12

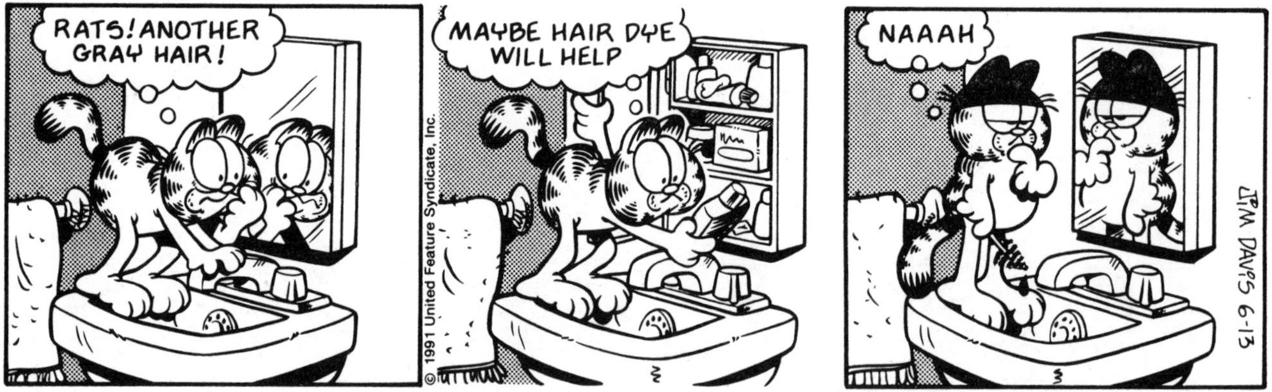
RATS! ANOTHER GRAY HAIR!
MAYBE HAIR DYE WILL HELP
NAAAH
© 1991 United Feature Syndicate, Inc.
JIM DAVIS 6-13

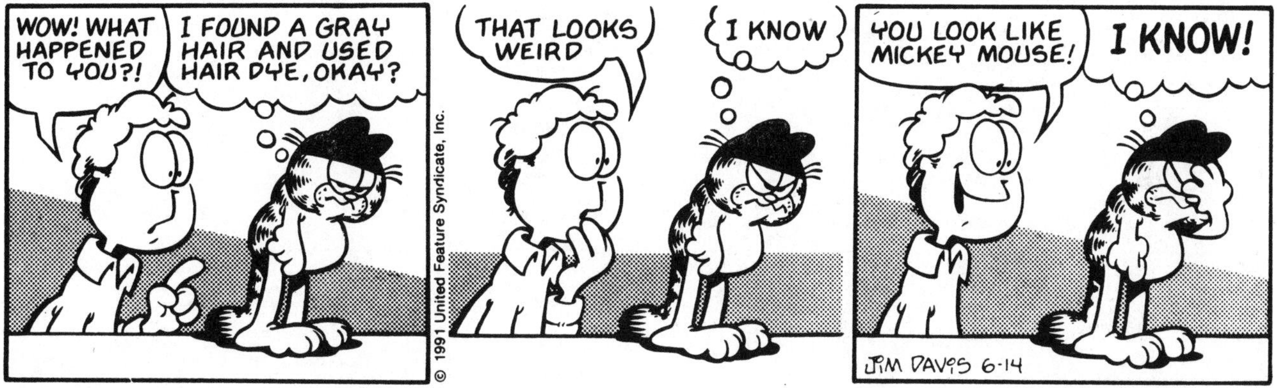
WOW! WHAT HAPPENED TO YOU?!
I FOUND A GRAY HAIR AND USED HAIR DYE, OKAY?
THAT LOOKS WEIRD
I KNOW
YOU LOOK LIKE MICKEY MOUSE!
I KNOW!
JIM DAVIS 6-14

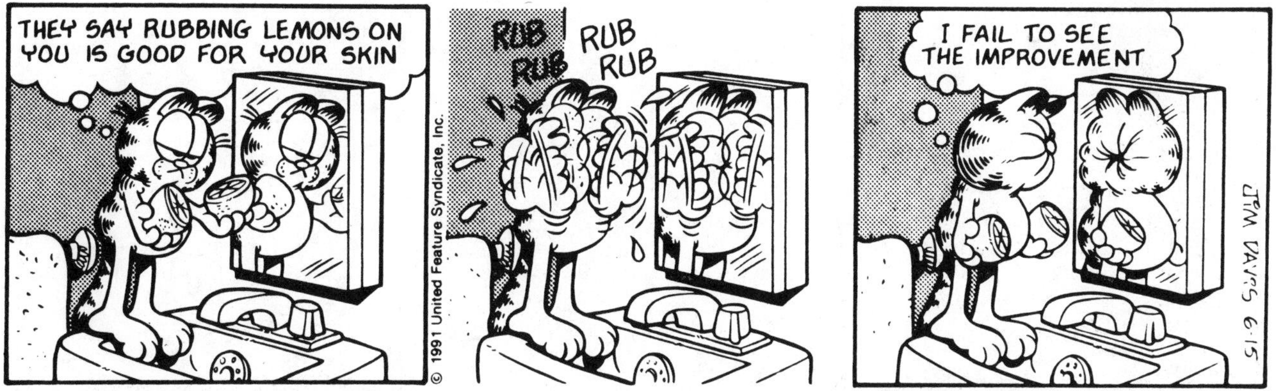
THEY SAY RUBBING LEMONS ON YOU IS GOOD FOR YOUR SKIN
RUB RUB
RUB RUB
I FAIL TO SEE THE IMPROVEMENT
JIM DAVIS 6-15

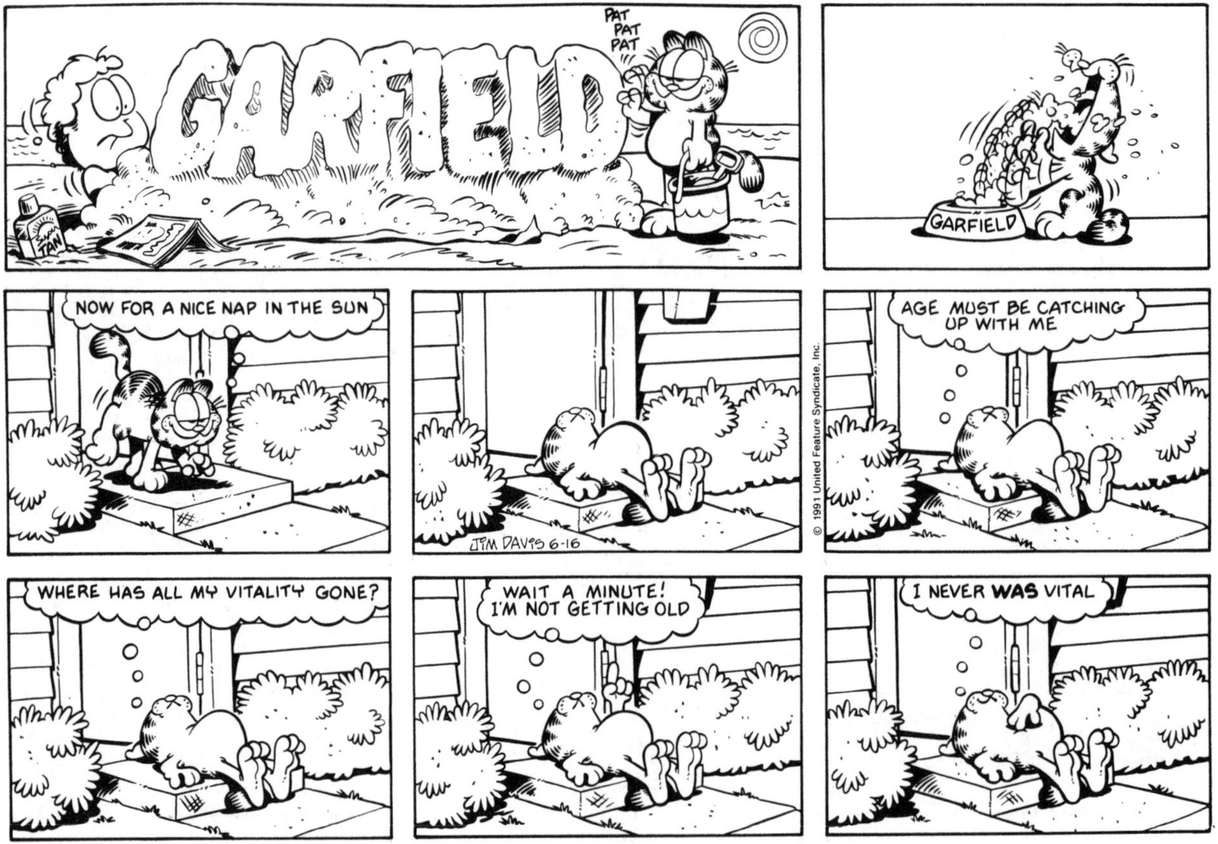
PAT
PAT
PAT
GARFIELD
SUPER TAN
GARFIELD
NOW FOR A NICE NAP IN THE SUN
JIM DAVIS 6-16
AGE MUST BE CATCHING UP WITH ME
© 1991 United Feature Syndicate, Inc.
WHERE HAS ALL MY VITALITY GONE?
WAIT A MINUTE! I'M NOT GETTING OLD
I NEVER **WAS** VITAL

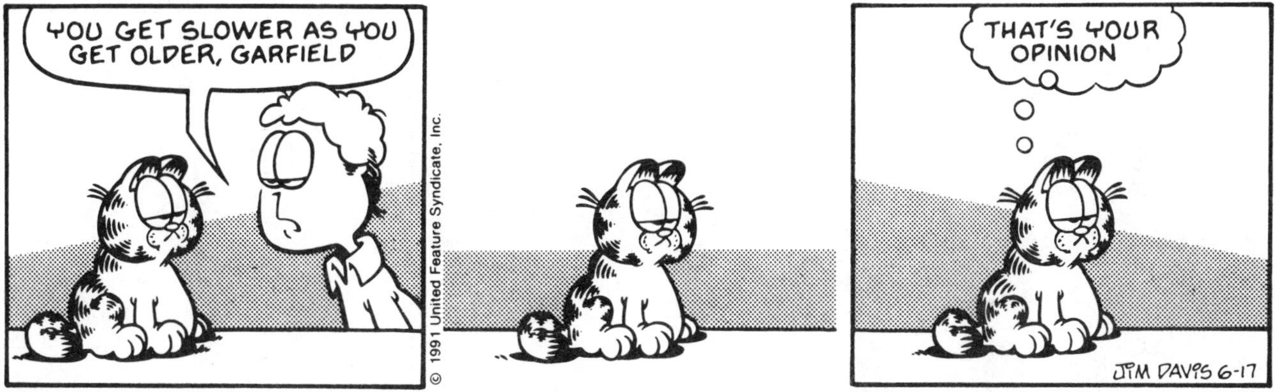
YOU GET SLOWER AS YOU GET OLDER, GARFIELD
THAT'S YOUR OPINION
© 1991 United Feature Syndicate, Inc.
JIM DAVIS 6-17

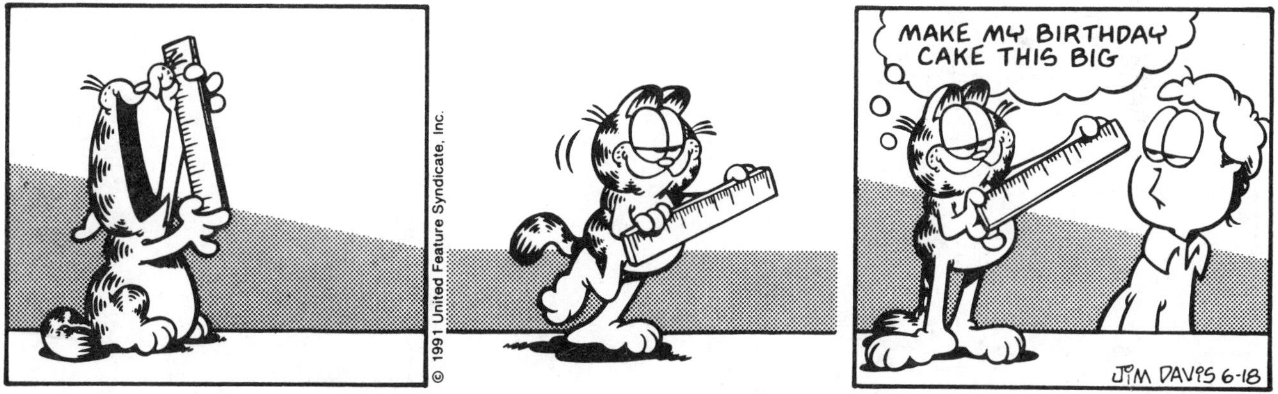
MAKE MY BIRTHDAY CAKE THIS BIG
© 1991 United Feature Syndicate, Inc.
JIM DAVIS 6-18

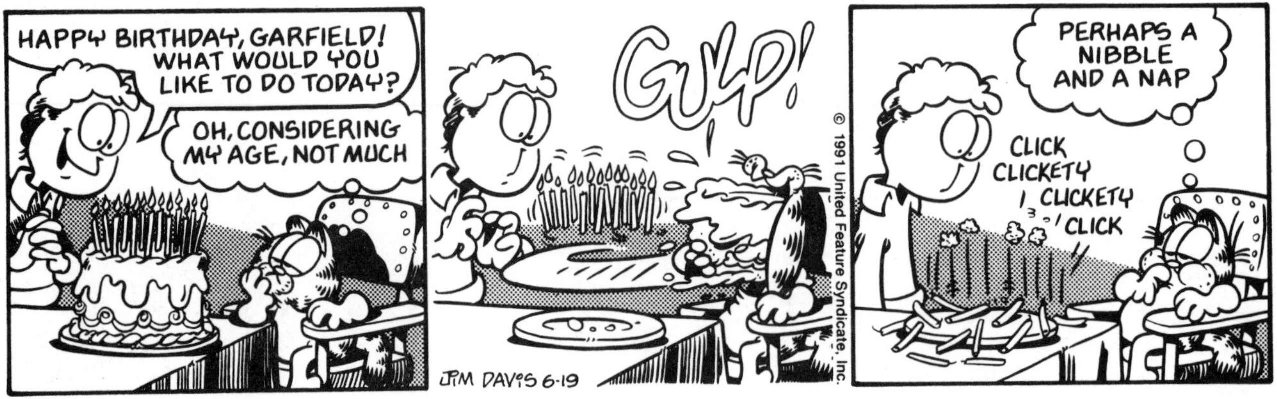
HAPPY BIRTHDAY, GARFIELD! WHAT WOULD YOU LIKE TO DO TODAY?
OH, CONSIDERING MY AGE, NOT MUCH
GULP!
JIM DAVIS 6-19
© 1991 United Feature Syndicate, Inc.
PERHAPS A NIBBLE AND A NAP
CLICK CLICKETY CLICKETY CLICK

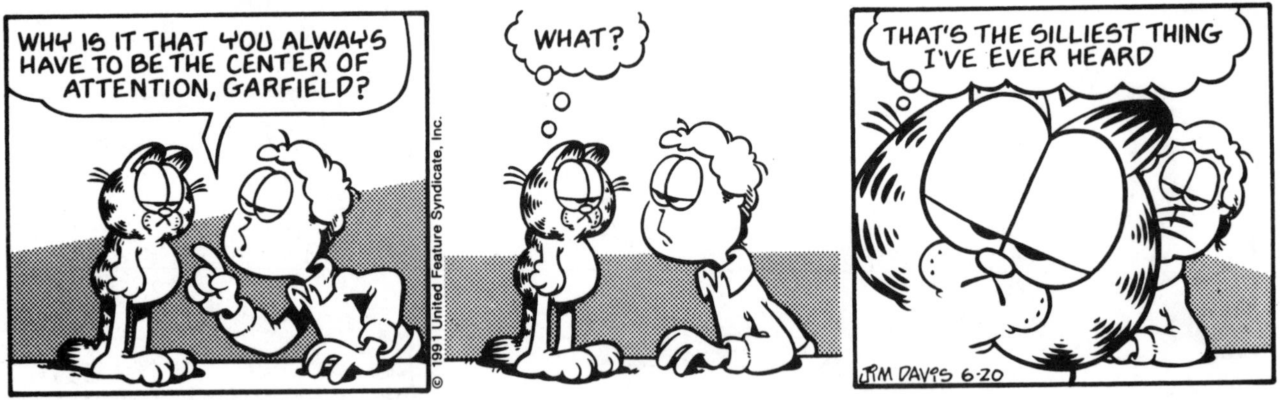
WHY IS IT THAT YOU ALWAYS HAVE TO BE THE CENTER OF ATTENTION, GARFIELD?
© 1991 United Feature Syndicate, Inc.
WHAT?
THAT'S THE SILLIEST THING I'VE EVER HEARD
JIM DAVIS 6-20

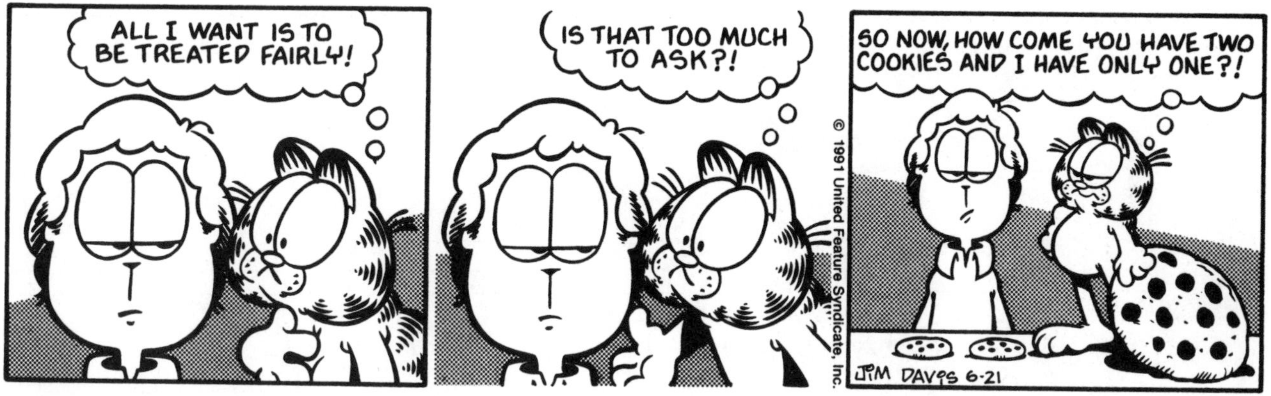
ALL I WANT IS TO BE TREATED FAIRLY!
IS THAT TOO MUCH TO ASK?!
SO NOW, HOW COME YOU HAVE TWO COOKIES AND I HAVE ONLY ONE?!
© 1991 United Feature Syndicate, Inc.
JIM DAVIS 6-21

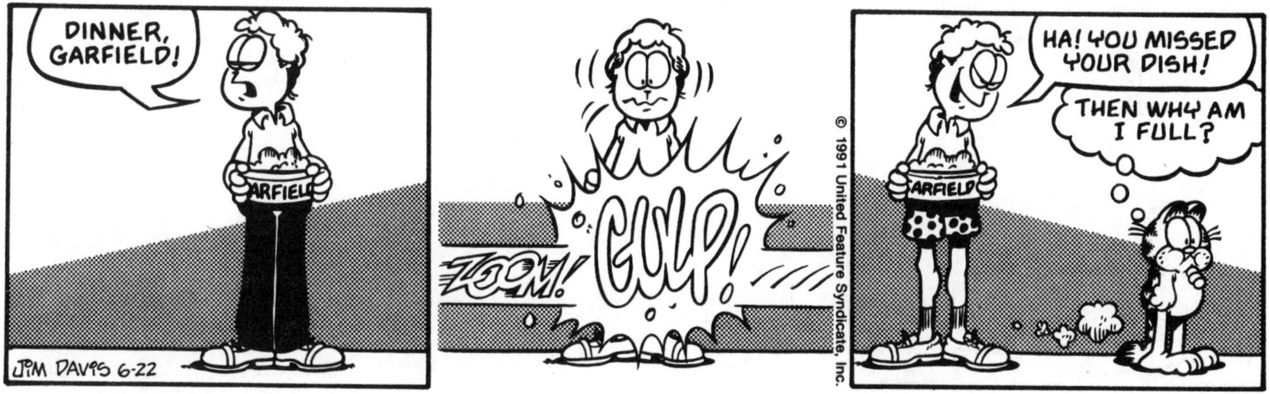
DINNER, GARFIELD!
GARFIELD
JIM DAVIS 6-22
ZOOM!
GULP!
© 1991 United Feature Syndicate, Inc.
HA! YOU MISSED YOUR DISH!
THEN WHY AM I FULL?

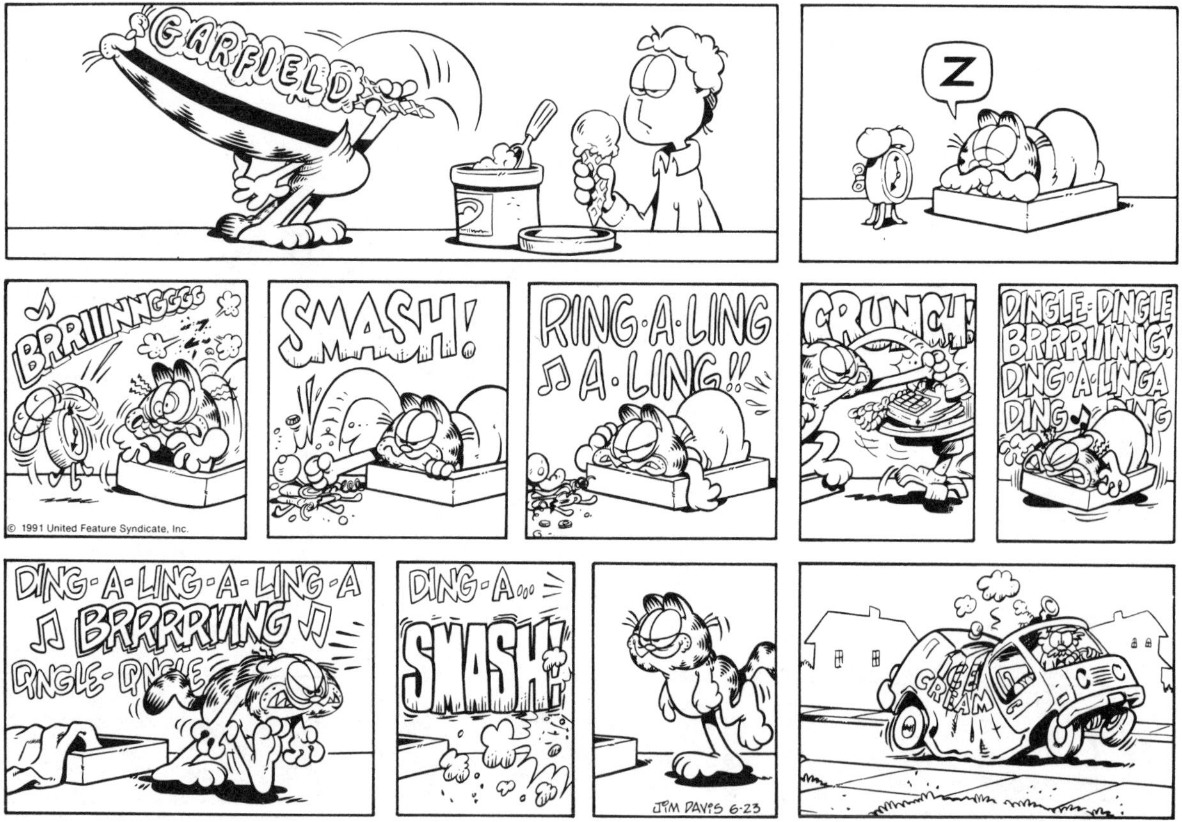

GARFIELD
Z
BRRIIINNGGGG
SMASH!
RING-A-LING A-LING!!
CRUNCH!
DINGLE-DINGLE
BRRRIIINNG!
DING-A-LINGA
DING
DING-A-LING-A-LING-A
BRRRRIIING
DINGLE-DINGLE
DING-A...
SMASH!
ICE CREAM
JIM DAVIS 6-23

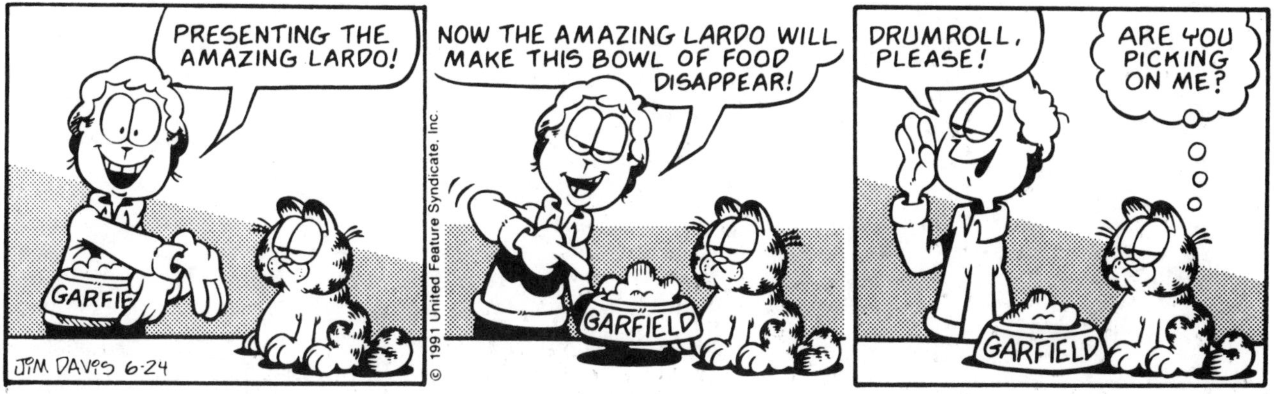
PRESENTING THE AMAZING LARDO!
JIM DAVIS 6-24
NOW THE AMAZING LARDO WILL MAKE THIS BOWL OF FOOD DISAPPEAR!
DRUMROLL, PLEASE!
ARE YOU PICKING ON ME?

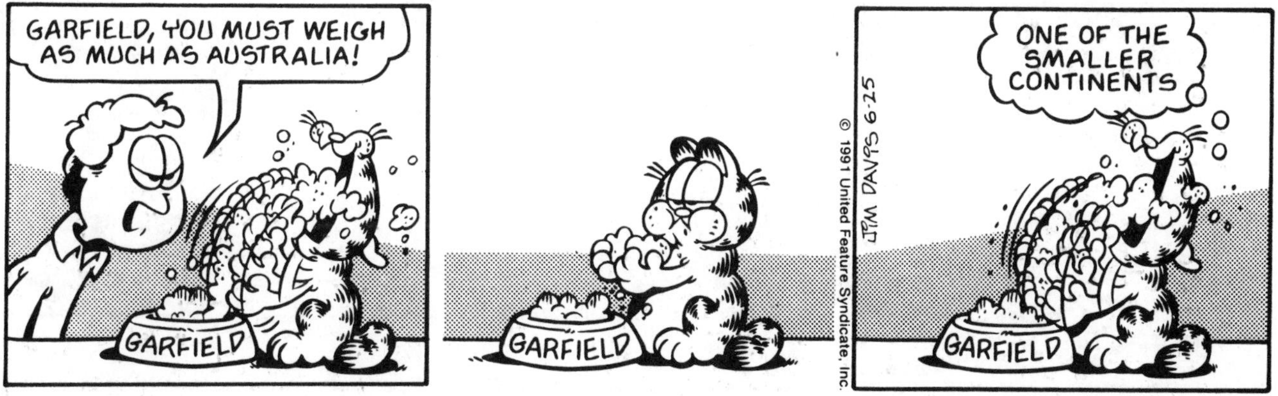
GARFIELD, YOU MUST WEIGH AS MUCH AS AUSTRALIA!
JIM DAVIS 6-25
ONE OF THE SMALLER CONTINENTS

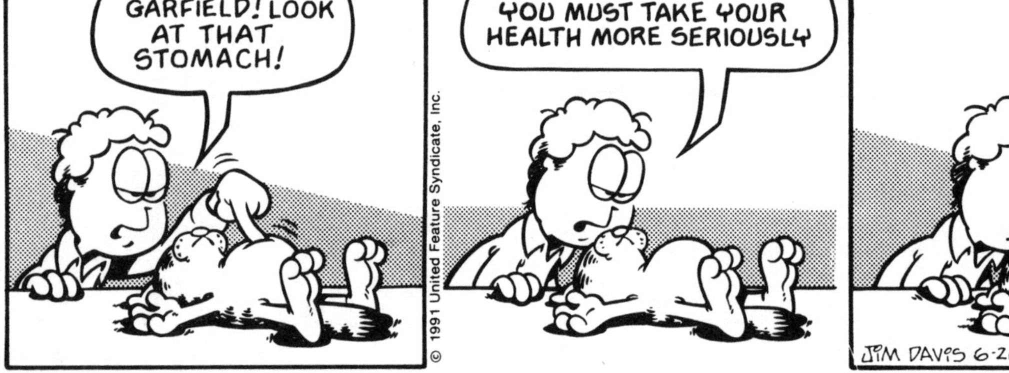
GARFIELD! LOOK AT THAT STOMACH!
© 1991 United Feature Syndicate, Inc.
YOU MUST TAKE YOUR HEALTH MORE SERIOUSLY
IT'S HARD TO BE SERIOUS WHILE STARING UP YOUR NOSE
JIM DAVIS 6-26

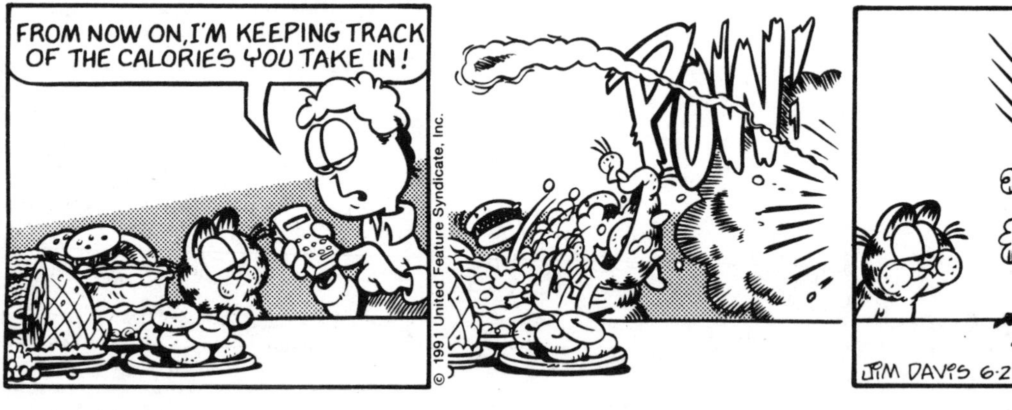
FROM NOW ON, I'M KEEPING TRACK OF THE CALORIES YOU TAKE IN!
© 1991 United Feature Syndicate, Inc.
MY CALCULATOR BLEW UP
JIM DAVIS 6-27

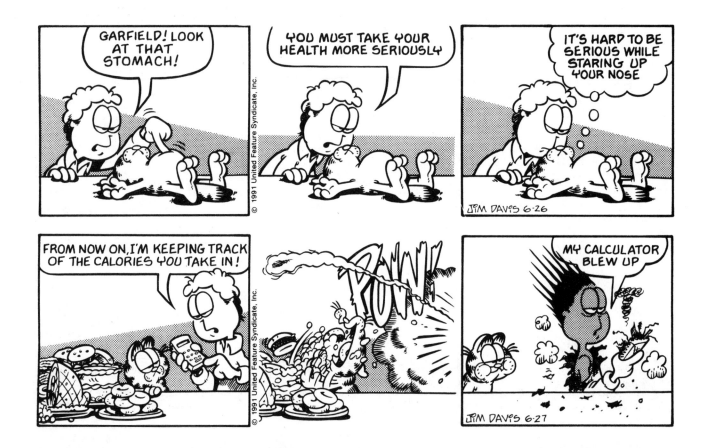

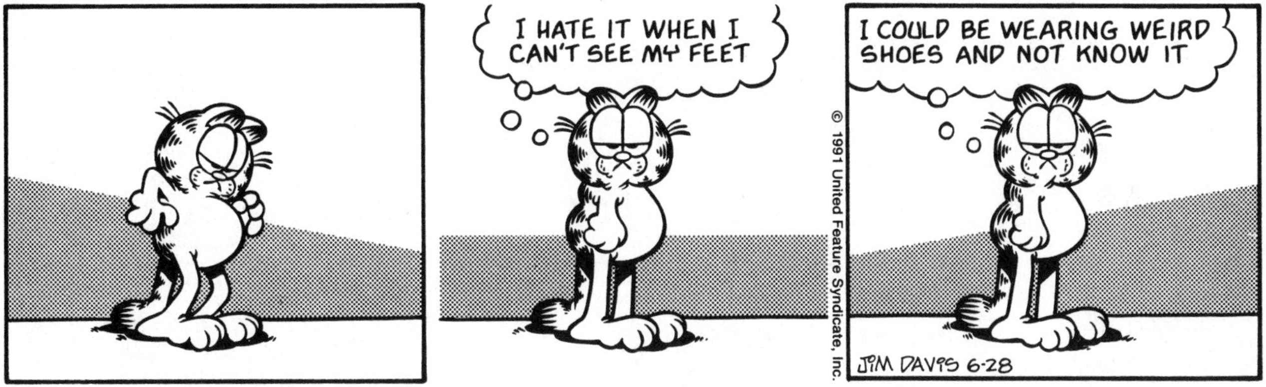
I HATE IT WHEN I CAN'T SEE MY FEET
I COULD BE WEARING WEIRD SHOES AND NOT KNOW IT
JIM DAVIS 6-28
© 1991 United Feature Syndicate, Inc.

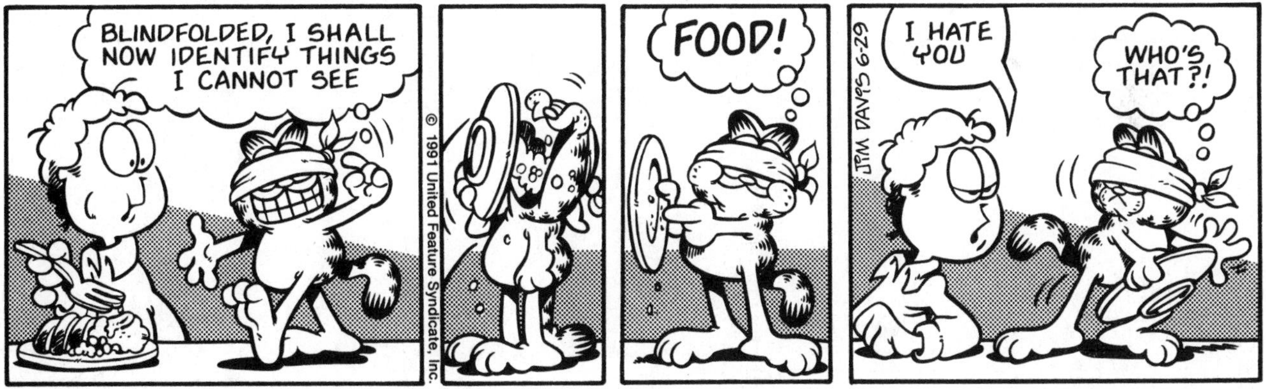
BLINDFOLDED, I SHALL NOW IDENTIFY THINGS I CANNOT SEE
© 1991 United Feature Syndicate, Inc.
FOOD!
JIM DAVIS 6-29
I HATE YOU
WHO'S THAT?!

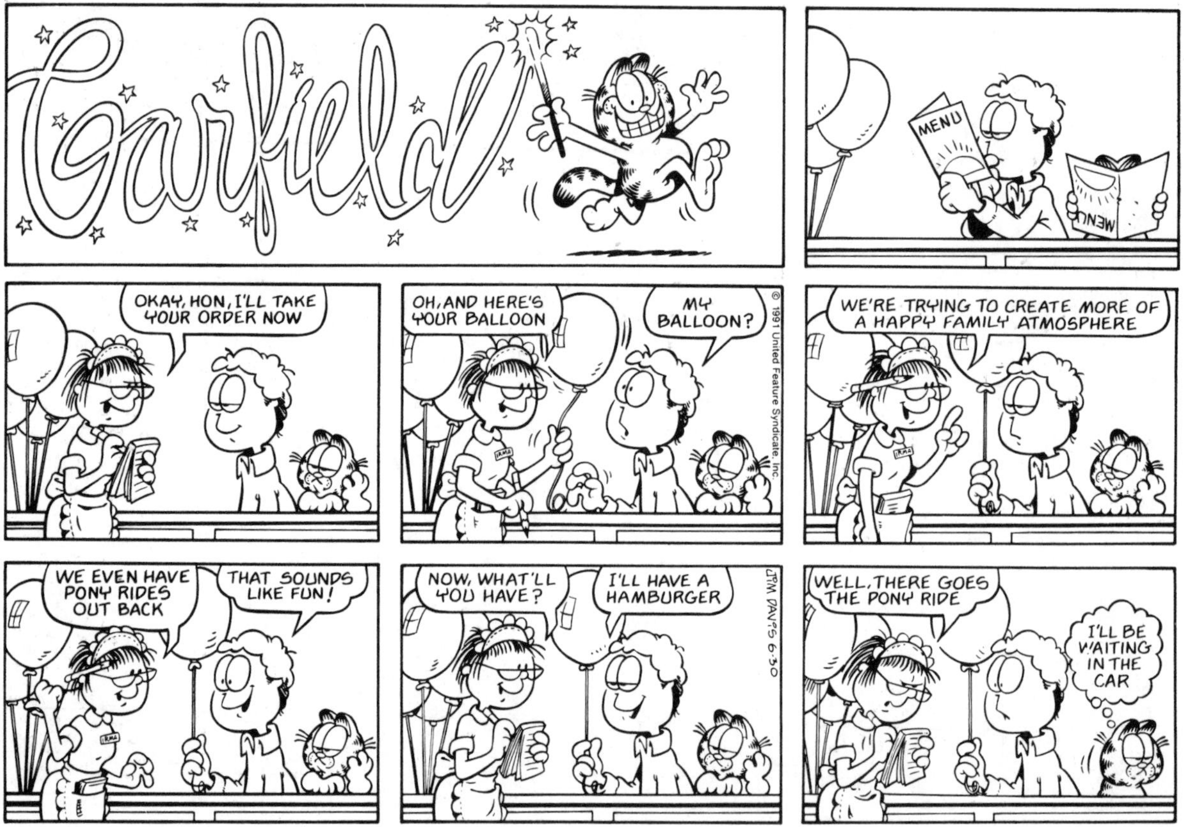
Garfield
MENU
MENU
OKAY, HON, I'LL TAKE YOUR ORDER NOW
OH, AND HERE'S YOUR BALLOON
MY BALLOON?
© 1991 United Feature Syndicate, Inc.
WE'RE TRYING TO CREATE MORE OF A HAPPY FAMILY ATMOSPHERE
WE EVEN HAVE PONY RIDES OUT BACK
THAT SOUNDS LIKE FUN!
NOW, WHAT'LL YOU HAVE?
I'LL HAVE A HAMBURGER
JIM DAVIS 6-30
WELL, THERE GOES THE PONY RIDE
I'LL BE WAITING IN THE CAR

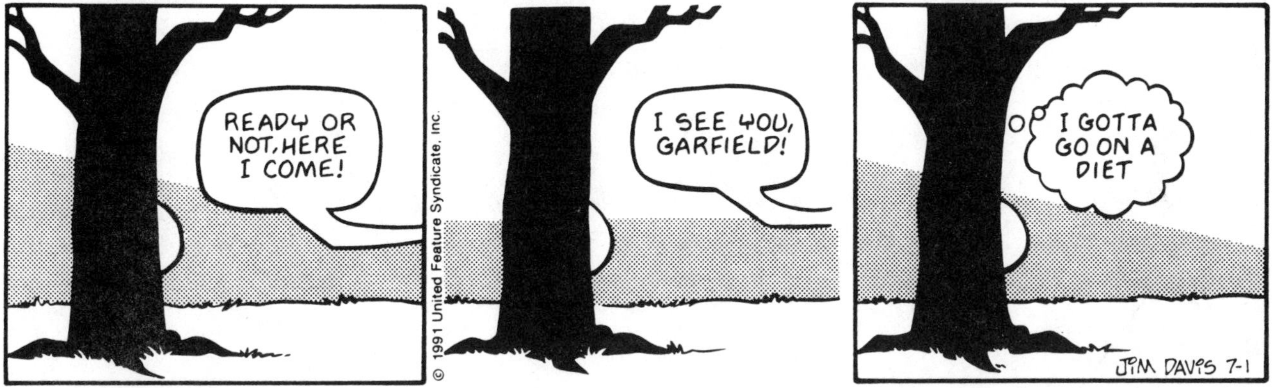
READY OR NOT, HERE I COME!
I SEE YOU, GARFIELD!
I GOTTA GO ON A DIET
JIM DAVIS 7-1
© 1991 United Feature Syndicate, Inc.

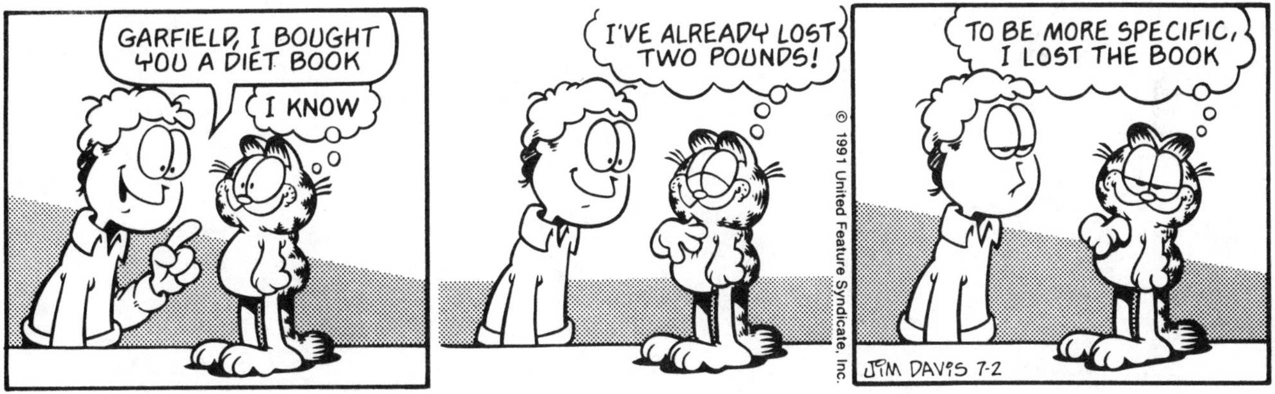
GARFIELD, I BOUGHT YOU A DIET BOOK
I KNOW
I'VE ALREADY LOST TWO POUNDS!
TO BE MORE SPECIFIC, I LOST THE BOOK
JIM DAVIS 7-2
© 1991 United Feature Syndicate, Inc.

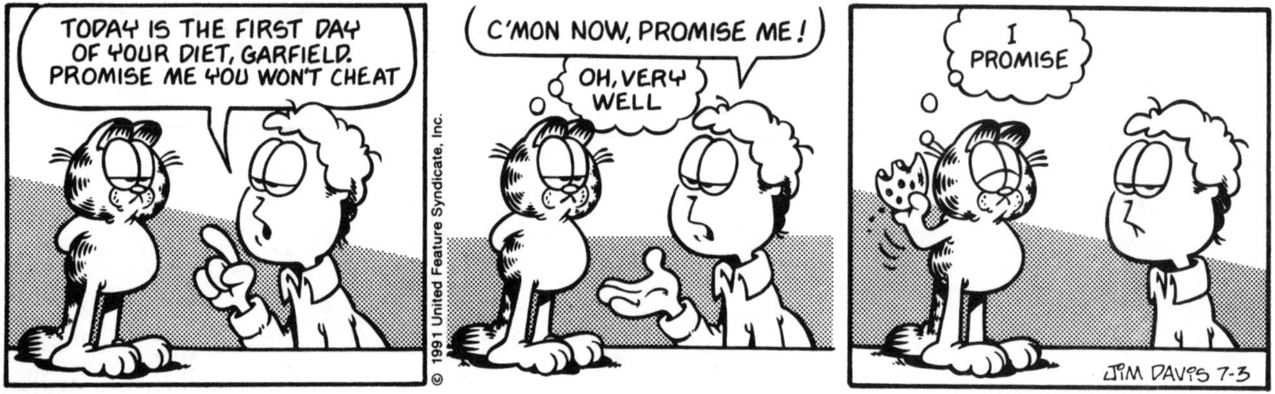
TODAY IS THE FIRST DAY OF YOUR DIET, GARFIELD. PROMISE ME YOU WON'T CHEAT
C'MON NOW, PROMISE ME!
OH, VERY WELL
I PROMISE
© 1991 United Feature Syndicate, Inc.
JIM DAVIS 7-3

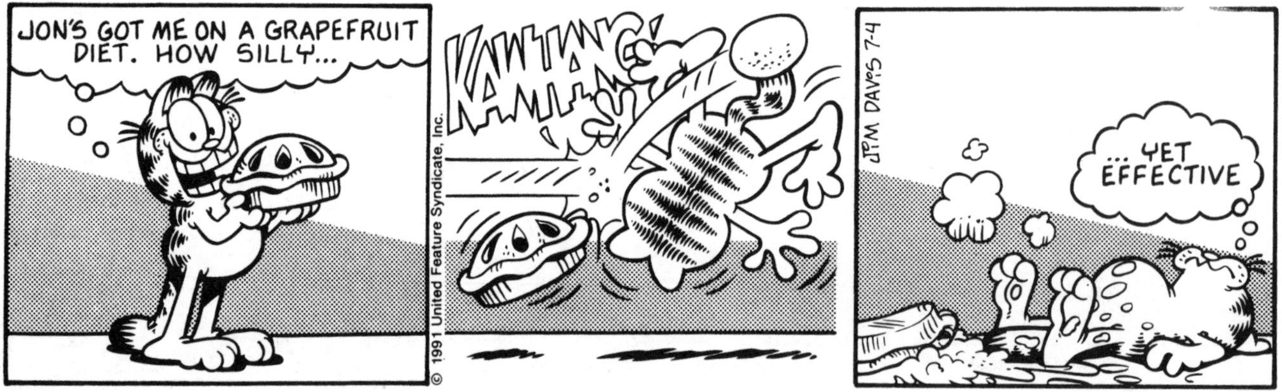
JON'S GOT ME ON A GRAPEFRUIT DIET. HOW SILLY...
KAWHANG!
... YET EFFECTIVE
© 1991 United Feature Syndicate, Inc.
JIM DAVIS 7-4

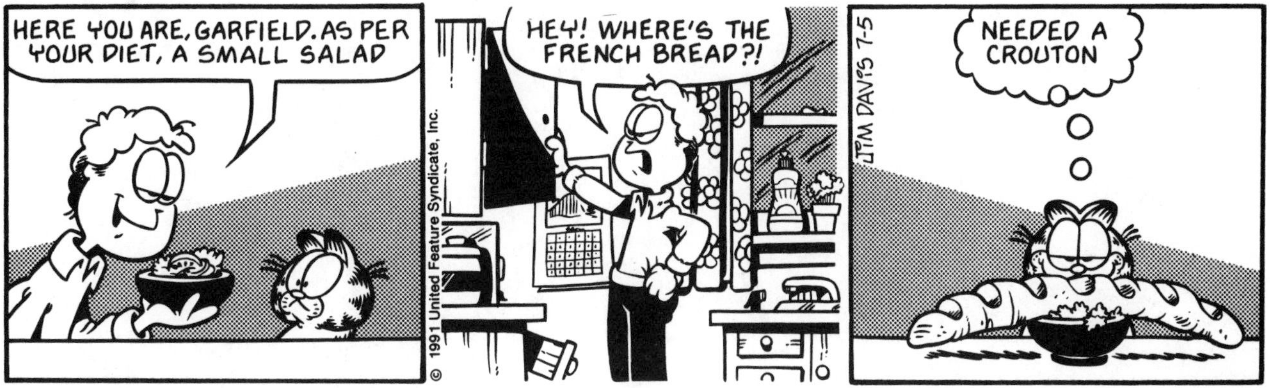
HERE YOU ARE, GARFIELD. AS PER YOUR DIET, A SMALL SALAD
© 1991 United Feature Syndicate, Inc.
HEY! WHERE'S THE FRENCH BREAD?!
JIM DAVIS 7-5
NEEDED A CROUTON

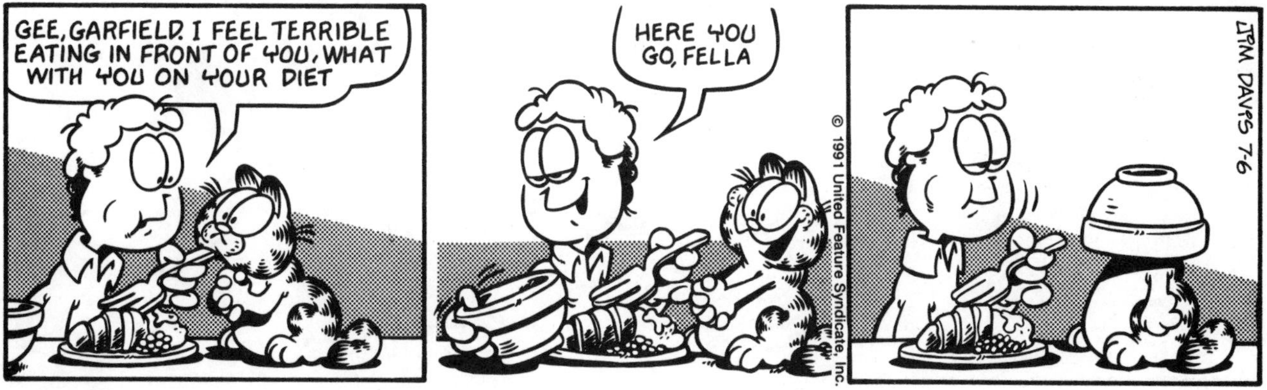
GEE, GARFIELD. I FEEL TERRIBLE EATING IN FRONT OF YOU, WHAT WITH YOU ON YOUR DIET
HERE YOU GO, FELLA
© 1991 United Feature Syndicate, Inc.
JIM DAVIS 7-6

Sometime in the 21st century...

GARFIELD PREDICTS

Days will be made longer so cats can get more sleep

France will officially change its name to "The Francster"

Scientists will develop a disposable dog

A large burp will devastate parts of Siberia

Astronomers will discover a huge flea collar encircling Pluto

Jon will be inducted into the "Geek Hall of Fame"

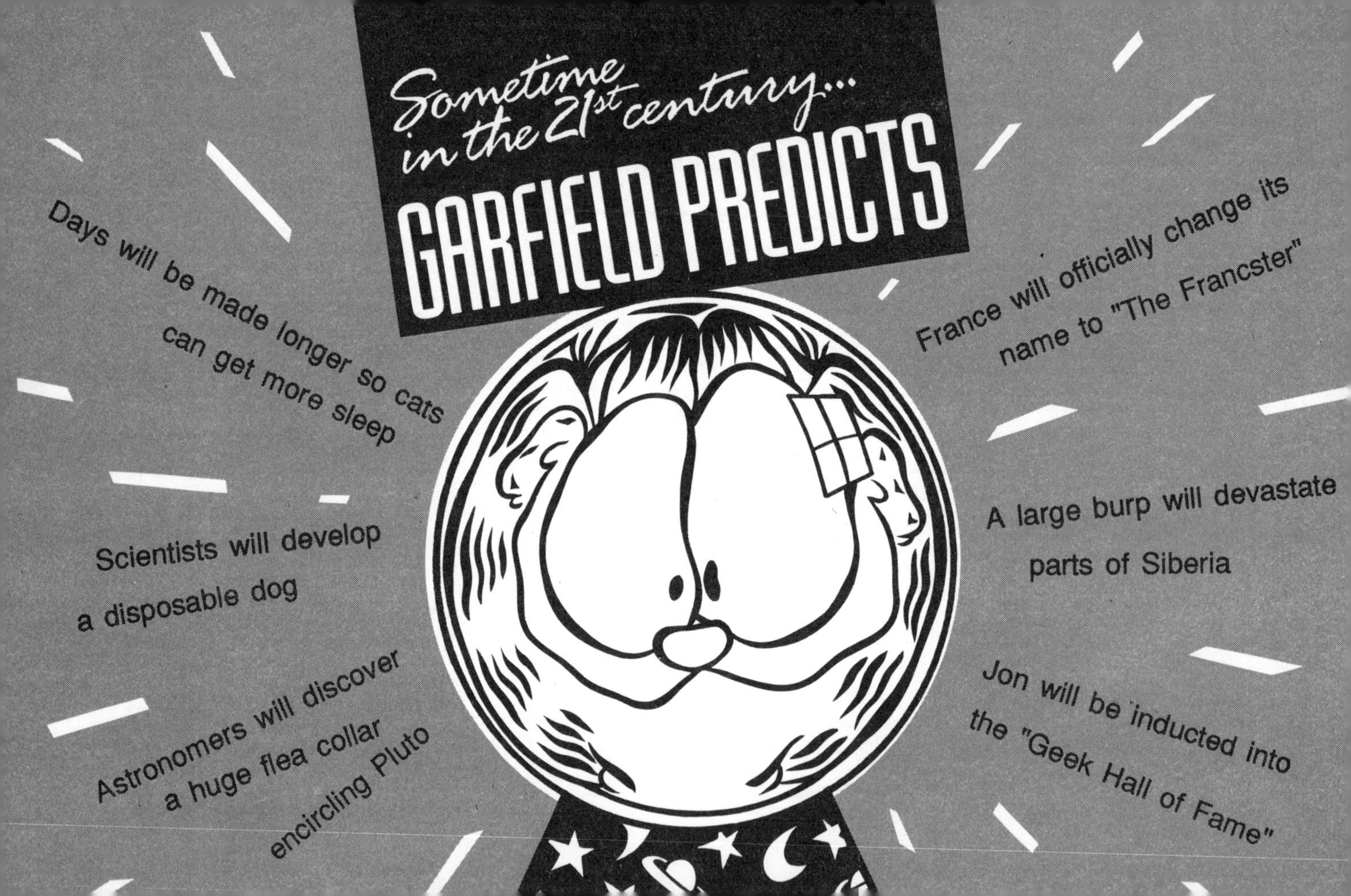

STRIPS, SPECIALS OR BESTSELLING BOOKS...
GARFIELD'S ON EVERYONE'S MENU

Don't miss even one episode in the Tubby Tabby's hilarious series!

BIRTHDAYS, HOLIDAYS, OR ANY DAY...
Keep GARFIELD on your calendar all year 'round!